NATURAL PROSTATE HEALERS

Mike Fillon
Foreword by Israel Barken, M.D.

PRENTICE HALL PRESS

DEDICATION

In memory of my father, George F. Fillon

Library of Congress Cataloging-in-Publication Data

Fillon, Michael.
    Natural prostate healers. / by Michael Fillon.
       p. cm.
    ISBN 0-13-011394-8. — ISBN 0-7352-0086-6 (pbk.)
      1. Prostate—Diseases—Alternative treatment. 2. Prostate—Diseases—Prevention.
    3. Naturopathy. I. Title.
    RC899.F526   1999
    616.6' 5—dc21   99-32992
                                                 CIP

Acquisitions Editor: *Doug Corcoran*
Production Editor: *Jacqueline Roulette*
Formatting/Interior Design: *Robyn Beckerman*

© *1999 by Prentice Hall*

Printed in the United States of America

10 9 8 7 6 5 4 3 2 1

ISBN 0-7352-0086-6(p)

This book is a reference manual based on research by the authors. All techniques and suggestions are
to be used at the reader's sole discretion. The opinions expressed herein are not necessarily those of,
or endorsed by, the publisher. Information is to be used as a guide to help restore balance within the
body, so it can heal itself. The directions stated in this book do not constitute the practice of medicine. Nor are they intended as claims for curing a serious disease and are in no way to be considered
as a substitute for consultation with a duly licensed doctor.

ATTENTION: CORPORATIONS AND SCHOOLS

Prentice Hall books are available at quantity discounts with bulk purchase for educa-
tional, business, or sales promotional use. For information, please write to: Prentice Hall
Special Sales, 240 Frisch Court, Paramus, New Jersey 07652. Please supply: title of book,
ISBN, quantity, how the book will be used, date needed.

PRENTICE HALL PRESS
Paramus, NJ 07652

On the World Wide Web at http://www.phdirect.com

CONTENTS

CHAPTER ONE
KNOW YOUR PROSTATE   1

CHAPTER TWO
EAT YOUR WAY TO PROSTATE HEALTH   25

CHAPTER THREE

NATURE'S REMEDIES FOR A HEALTHY PROSTATE   65

CHAPTER FOUR

EXERCISE YOUR WAY TO PROSTATE HEALTH   99

CHAPTER FIVE

SPICE UP YOUR SEX LIFE   137

CHAPTER SIX

HOW TO DEFEAT PROSTATITIS   167

CHAPTER SEVEN

TAKING THE WORRY OUT OF AN ENLARGED PROSTATE 185

CHAPTER EIGHT

HOW TO DEAL WITH PROSTATE CANCER 209

FOREWORD

In recent years, many books have been written about prostate disease and prostate cancer for the lay public. For the benefit and enlightenment of patients, well-known physicians have published their version of the "correct" way to diagnose and the "proper" way to treat prostate disease. These books invariably have photographs of long, sharp instruments, certain tools of the trade which make the reader cringe and of which the author is very proud. Or the author may include a picture of a wonderful machine—a state-of-the-art box guaranteed to freeze, cut or over-heat your prostate using microwaves, electricity, nitrogen gas, or who knows, maybe nuclear power. Perhaps the physician thinks that showing you a picture of the machine will make you rush to throw yourself on its lap. I doubt it.

Following a slew of books by physicians there came a slew of books by prostate patients. Whatever worked for one particular patient was touted as the route everyone else should therefore follow. It became a parade of blind men touching an elephant, each describing whatever he touched as if it were the whole elephant. Did he touch the tusk? Ah, therefore an elephant is a tusk. Did he touch a tail? Ah, then an elephant is a tail.

In that fashion, one book glorified the patient's fantastic experience with radiation seed implants and yet another extolled the benefits of cryosurgery. Similarly, some of the blind men smelled the elephant's breath and described all the wonderful plants and herbs that the elephant was chewing and therefore espoused only alternative medicine, banning all technology.

Mike Fillon has carved out new ground for those interested in a healthy prostate. Finally, we have a book which is readable, interesting, thorough, complete and based on reliable data. He takes from the world of science, quoting known authorities from academia and blends this with the less scientific, yet centuries old knowldege of natural medicine. Add a hefty dose of common sense, and we have a unique new book, *Natural Prostate Healers.* Where previous books tried to help the patient suffering from enlarged prostate, prostatitis, or prostate cancer, Mike Fillon's book explores every possible avenue to prevent these diseases. This is where his book is so different and yet so in tune with the direction researchers are taking nowadays—trying to prevent disease.

In my lectures, I often tell patients, "Ask not, 'Doctor, can you heal me?' Rather ask, 'Doctor, what can I do to heal myself?'"—*Natural Prostate Healers* is a perfect guide to what you can do for yourself. You will not need to reinvent youself as an amateur medical student, pouring over medical journals every night if you are willing to apply the basic information in this book to your own situation. What patients have in abundance is common sense, an intuitive understanding of their own body and a desire to heal. They need information, but they also need a professional guide to help them sort out, understand and apply this information to the unique biology which is theirs alone. What they need in the equation is a physician and here too, Mike Fillon has a refreshing understanding of the new role physicians can play.

Most books about the prostate written by patients tend to throw the baby out with the bathwater; these patients try to dump the doctor and become their own physicians. What do lawyers call defendants who insist on acting as their own attorneys—having a fool for a client? You get pretty much the same results when you try to be your own physician. As an educated, informed patient, you need the advice of an educated, informed physician to complete the team. As a science writer, Mike Fillon, brings us a unique viewpoint; he is not a prostate cancer patient nor a physician. He gives the reader a wealth of information and then gently nudges him in the right direction—toward professional help for guidance.

What Mike Fillon advocates is educate yourself and "find a nutritionally based physician" or a physician who is oriented to integrative medicine and work with him. Where once you had to go to either an M.D. or an N.D., nowadays, there are many traditional physicians practicing integrative medicine. We come from western medical schools but use principles of eastern medicine as well. We combine alternative, complementary and integrative approaches with technology and science. Most of all, we listen to our patients just as much as they listen to us. There are many of us out there nowadays and more coming from traditional schools of western medicine. It is a blend of the best of both worlds.

Patients once thought of their doctors as gods. Then insurance companies knocked them off their pedestals and made them mere "providers" of a service. A blizzard of insurance regulations and auditors created a climate where doctors had to take care of how the chart looked, not how the patient looked. Paperwork, not patient care, became the rule of the day.

We're not gods and we're not providers. Neither definition fits our new role. If you will allow us, we are physicians who took the Hippocratic oath, "First Do No Harm."

So, how can you best use your doctor? Use him as a Coach. First, get off the bench and become a player in your own healthcare. Get educated—just reading this book will give you some major league skills—and then let your doctor guide you in making those decisions. Behind every winning athlete is a great coach and behind every successful patient is a great doctor. Share with your doctor what diet you are following, what lifestyle changes you have made, what herbs and supplements you take. Tell him what works for you and what doesn't. A good coach will motivate you, focus your mental, emotional and physical abilities, and teach you how to play smart. A good coach will keep you from getting injured, hold you back when you need to sit out a game, put you in there when you're ready to play hard. Use his knowledge and advice to make yourself a winner in your healthcare. I applaud Mike Fillon on his book *Natural Prostate Healers* and am proud to be asked to write the foreword to his book.

Israel Barken, M.D., F.A.C.S.
Prostate Cancer Research & Education Foundation
San Diego, California

AUTHOR'S NOTE

Over the last decade and a half, I've researched and reported on countless new medical technologies on behalf of "Popular Mechanics" magazine and other publications. Although all of these techniques and devices—such as those featured in the January 1999 cover story, "The Bionic Man," and the January 1997 feature, "Bloodless Surgery,"—are ingenious, there is one indisputable fact: they're all last ditch efforts to relieve human suffering.

During my medical writing career, one question always nagged at me. Could anything be done in the first place to prevent the medical conditions requiring expensive technology? What better place to begin answering that question than with the prostate gland. Many thousands of lives are adversely affected every year by prostate disease. Prostate medical procedures, including surgery, alter the lives of men and their loved ones—often with dire consequences.

I knew there had to be a better way. There MUST be a better way. There is. That's the reason for this book.

HOW TO USE THIS BOOK

Most men have some vague notion that their prostate is "down there"—someplace above our testicles and below our navel. That is, unless it's caused you problems. Then you know EXACTLY where it is.

Even if you haven't had a problem, I'm sure you know someone who has, don't you? Perhaps a co-worker, a neighbor, maybe a relative. You might even worry that you're next—especially if you've experienced:

BATHROOM TROUBLES, SUCH AS:

- The need to urinate frequently at night
- A weak or interrupted urine flow

BEDROOM TROUBLES, SUCH AS:

- Reduced sexual ability
- Discomfort during intercourse

Basically, there are three diseases that can strike the prostate:

- Benign Prostatic Hyperplasia (BPH)
- Cancer of the prostate
- Prostatitis

BPH, which is an enlarged prostate, is the most common condition seen by urologists. The fact is, half of all men in their 50s and 70 percent of men in their 60s have some degree of prostate enlargement.

Conventional treatments include "watchful waiting" to see how bad symptoms become, followed by drug therapy and then surgery. Drugs and surgery treatment of BPH cost Americans $2 billion annually, and both can cause side effects including impotence. It's no wonder, then, that more and more men are turning to natural (and cheaper) therapies for relief.

Research also shows that even by the age of 30 up to 25 percent of men have some prostate CANCER cells present. In 1997, new prostate cancer cases totaled around 210,000—one new case every two-and-a-half minutes. Prostate cancer continues to be the most common malignancy (aside from skin cancers), representing 25 percent of all new cancer cases in the United States.

The number of deaths attributable to prostate cancer has climbed steadily since the beginning of the 1990s. Approximately 42,000 men died of prostate cancer in 1997, up from 30,000 in 1990. It's the second biggest cancer killer of men after lung cancer. Well-known men stricken with prostate cancer is a veritable "Who's Who" in the worlds of business, politics and sports. (See the list at the end of this section.)

Then there's Prostatitis, an infection in the gland. It can strike any male, any time.

* * *

Prostate diseases don't just strike and—"Ba-boom!"—you're flat on your back writhing in pain. No, prostate problems are much more subtle than that. They creep up on you; THEN maybe they'll be some pain. Then again, maybe not.

Take the case of former baseball slugger and New York Yankee General Manager, Bob Watson. When Watson took his annual physical on his 47th birthday he was feeling fine, and nothing seemed amiss. At the end of the physical, as the doctor asked him to get dressed, Watson requested a PSA test which is used to tell if a man has BPH or prostate cancer. (More on PSAs in Chapter One). Having already performed a digital exam, his doctor tried to talk him out of it. Watson, aware that a couple of Yankee scouts around his age had recently come down with prostate cancer, insisted.

Good thing he did. His score was very high. Watson immediately started cancer treatments.

Remember this: Bob Watson felt fine. His doctor even said he was fine. What saved Bob Watson? His knowledge.

Most men feel uncomfortable talking about the prostate, since the gland plays a role in both sex and urination. We turn a blind eye towards it. We say, "why fix what ain't hurtin'?" This shouldn't be.

And it doesn't have to be.

In fact, if you think about it, it's kind of childish.

In *Natural Prostate Healers,* we will provide all the information men need to deal with this manly problem. Through information gleaned from the leading research institutions and fortified with anecdotal evidence, we will arm you with the facts and scope of the problem. We will give you all the information you need about prostatitis, BPH and prostate cancer. We will explain the various treatments available, providing the pros and cons of each.

Although the actual "here it is" cause of prostate cancer is unknown, it is well accepted that dietary, lifestyle, environmental and emotional factors can harm the prostate. In particular, bad habits—a sedentary lifestyle, improper diet, venereal diseases, smoking, alcohol, stress and obesity—can increase your risk of prostate problems, particularly cancer.

While pharmaceutical and surgical treatments are more or less effective in relieving symptoms, they in no way address the underlying factors leading to prostate disease. That's why we're here.

With this book as a guide, you'll be surprised how easy it is to protect your prostate. In *Natural Prostate Healers*, we will provide a "game plan" to avoid, delay or recover from prostate problems.

We'll show you how to:

- Eliminate middle-of-the-night trips to the bathroom
- Ward off bedroom problems caused by your prostate gland
- Say "no" to unnecessary surgery and potentially harmful drugs
- Minimize your prostate cancer risk

I know, I know. Everyone thinks, "No pain, no gain." I certainly don't. Why suffer pain if you don't have to? Everything we suggest to you is simple and easy to achieve.

We're not going to ask you to dangle by your foot from a bridge and count from one to 1,000 backwards. Instead we will tell you the food needed to galvanize your prostate, what exercises to do to keep your love life on the fast track and your sleep long and pleasant.

You can adapt all of the principles here, or some of them. Even a few changes will help protect your prostate. It all depends what degree of safety YOU want.

Natural Prostate Healers is not intended as a replacement for professional medical advice and treatment. Rather, this book is intended to deepen your understanding of prostate problems so you can prevent them in the first place. Should you not be so lucky, this book, along with your doctor, will help you make informed decisions on treatment and prevention strategies.

Here is our first piece of advice. If you suspect you have BPH or prostate cancer, see your doctor. Self-diagnosing or hoping your problems will disappear is a poor plan.

By reading this book you've already embarked on a good plan for minimizing and possibly eliminating prostate problems. Good for you.

Here are a few of the well-known men who have suffered from prostate cancer, and their age (if known) when stricken. ((D) denotes deceased):

WORLD OF BUSINESS

Wayne Calloway—Pepsico Chairman—60

Jon M. Huntsman—billionaire industrialist and philanthropist, Utah, 60

J. R. Hyde III, Chair & CEO, Autozone, Inc.

Irving Kahn—Cable Television pioneer—76 (D)

Dr. Timothy Leary—75 (D)

Michael Milken—investment advisor—49

Dr. Linus Pauling—two-time Nobel prize winner—(D)

Steve Ross, CEO, Time-Warner—65 (D)

Thomas Witter—Dean Witter Reynolds, Inc.—63 (D)

Rev. Louis Farrakahn—Minister

Bishop Desmond Tutu—South Africa

CELEBRITIES

Dirk Benedict—actor, The A Team

Don Ameche—actor—85 (D)

Ed Asner—actor

Harry Belafonte—singer/actor

Bill Bixby—actor—59 (D)

Barry Bostwick—actor

Sean Connery—actor

Eddie Fisher—entertainer

John Gary—singer—65 (D)

Louis Gosset, Jr.—actor

Robert Goulet—singer—62

Merv Griffin—TV Producer—71

Jerry Lewis—actor/comedian—70

Victor Mature—actor—81

Roger Moore—actor

Fes Parker—actor

Sidney Poitier—actor—69

Dick Sargent—actor—64 (D)

Telly Savalas—actor—70 (D)

Frank Zappa—52 (D)

WORLD LEADERS

Moshe Arens—Israeli Defense Minister

King Baudouin—King of Belgium—(D)

General Charles de Gaulle, former President of France (D)

Ayutullah Khomeini—Iranian religious & political leader—89 (D)

King Hussein—King of Jordan—60 (D)

Francois Mitterand—President of France—79 (D)

Turgut Ozal—President of Turkey—66 (D)

King Norodom Sihanouk—King of Cambodia—72

GOVERNMENT OFFICIALS

Marion Barry—Mayor, District of Columbia—60

Herb Bateman—U.S. Representative (Virginia)—65

Harry Blackmun—U.S. Supreme Court Justice (D)

William Casey—Former CIA Director—(D)

Alan Cranston—Former U.S. Senator (California)—80

Bob Dole—U.S. Senator (Kansas), Presidential Candidate—72

Orval Faubus—Former Arkansas Governor—83 (D)

Hamilton Fish—U.S. Representative (R-New York)—(D)

Kirk Fordice—Mississippi Governor—59

Jesse Helms—U.S. Senator (North Carolina)—74

Henry J. Hyde—U.S. Representative (Illinois)

Hamilton Jordan—political strategist

Lester Maddox—Former Georgia Governor—80

J. J. Pickle—Former U.S. Representative (Texas)—80

Richard Riley—U.S. Education Secretary—61

Paul Sarbanes—U.S. Senator (Maryland)—62

John Paul Stevens—U.S. Supreme Court Justice—75

Kwame Toure (Stokeley Carmichael)—SNCC & Black Panther leader—54

John Tower—Former U.S. Senator (Texas)—(D)

MEDIA

Roone Arledge—President, ABC News

Jamie Bragg—all news radio, Washington, D.C.—68

David Brinkley—TV Journalist

David Broder—columnist, The Washington Post

James Herriott—author, *All Creatures Great and Small*—78 (D)

Michael Korda—Editor-In-Chief/Author, Simon & Schuster—62

Bob Maynard—Publisher, *The Oakland Tribune*—56—(D)

Bob Novak—TV Commentator, Novak & Dean; member, The Capitol Gang

Hobart Rowan—columnist, The Washington Post—76 (D)

Dr. George Sheehan—running guru, physician & author—74 (D)

Joseph Wortis, M.D.—editor, *Biological Psychiatry*—80 (D)

MILITARY LEADERS

Frank Borman—Astronaut (Commander, Apollo 8)

H. Norman Schwarzkopf—General, (USA Ret.)—61

Frederick Walker—Brigadier General—60

SPORTS

Eddie Arcaro—jockey—80

Bill Arnsparger—Defensive Coordinator, San Diego Chargers—68

Phil Barkdoll—Daytona 500 driver—57

Fred Biletnikoff—Los Angeles Raiders

Ray Dandridge—Hall of Fame third baseman—79 (D)

Len Dawson—former quarterback, Kansas City Chiefs

Lee Elia—hitting coach for the Seattle Mariners—59

Walter A. Haas, Jr.—Oakland Athletics owner—79 (D)

Vic Janowicz—Heisman Trophy Winner '55—66 (D)

Marv Levy—NFL coach, Buffalo Bills—67

Stan Musial—baseball Hall of Famer

Joe Nuxhall—Cincinnati Reds radio announcer—63

Gary Ormsby—race car driver—47 (D)

Arnold Palmer—Pro Golfer

Richard Petty—retired NASCAR driver—57

Tommy Prothro—NFL Hall of Famer—74 (D)

Tubby Raymond—football coach, University of Delaware—67

Bobby Riggs—tennis player—77 (D)

Norm Stewart—basketball coach

Joe Torre—New York Yankees' Manager—58

Johnny Unitas—former quarterback, Baltimore Colts

Bob Watson—New York Yankees' General Manager—47

CHAPTER ONE

KNOW
YOUR
PROSTATE

Most of us can recall the carefree, "steady-stream" days of our youth. It's no wonder we wanted to become firemen.

But as we age, we notice our streams weakening, and for some, slowing to a trickle. Or we wake up during the night ready to put out a four-alarmer, but when we get to the bathroom and yank up the seat, it's as if the Department of Public Works shut off the flow to our hydrant.

If this describes you, you're not alone. To some degree, this will happen to every man. It's all due to a small male-only gland known as the prostate.

How widespread are prostate problems? Extremely widespread—and what we just described is just one of them.

Nine out of ten men who live into their 70s (the average life span of a man in the United States is about 74) can expect some type of prostate problem before they die. Prostate problems usually start at a much younger age, commonly in the 40s.

Your best protection? A thorough understanding of prostate health issues, yearly examinations by a qualified physician, and changes in your lifestyle. With diligence it's possible to eliminate or at least minimize prostate woes.

For now it's important for you to know that prostate problems can adversely affect two of the things we men crave most:

- SLEEP
- SEX

And not necessarily in that order.

First, you need some basic information.

1

UNDERSTANDING THE ROLE OF YOUR PROSTATE

The prostate—also called "The Seat of Masculinity"—is a small gland located in front of the rectum and just below where urine is stored in the bladder. The prostate also surrounds the urethra, the canal through which urine passes out of the body from the bladder to the penis. The gland is composed of two lobes, or regions, enclosed by an outer layer or capsule of tissue. It is comprised of not just secreting glands, but a mass of muscle and connective tissue.

Scientists don't know all the prostate's functions. They do know it's vital for proper bladder operation and urine flow-rate control. They also know that one of its main roles is to make, then squeeze, the milky seminal fluid into the urethra as sperm moves through and out of the urethra. The prostate also furnishes the power to expel this fluid through your penis during sexual climax. (If you remember schoolboy biology, your testes manufacture spermatozoa which is then stored in the epididymis.

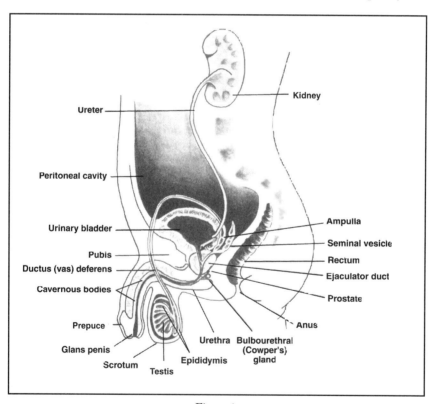

Figure 1

During orgasm, the vas deferens pushes the sperm into the urethra.) The prostate makes about 90 percent of the semen in which spermatozoa travel outside the body during orgasm and ejaculation.

The prostatic fluid produced by the prostate does two other things: it makes the woman's vaginal canal less acidic and also guards a man's urinary system and genitals from infection.

If this all sounds too clinical, suffice it to say, no prostate, no orgasm. And who knows what that can mean for you and yours.

But this leads to one of the biggest misconceptions about the gland—that prostate problems automatically mean no erections. Not true. In fact, the majority of men who are treated for prostate problems report no loss in at least that part of their sexual ability.

However, don't click your heels just yet. Because the urethra runs right through the middle of it, a growth spurt of the prostate will squeeze the urethra and begin to choke off its ability to move things through. This can affect both your ability to urinate and perform sexually.

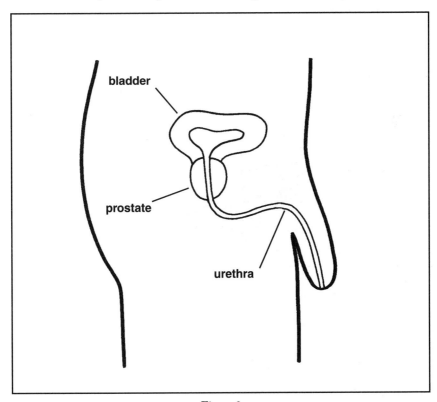

Figure 2

Most men feel uncomfortable talking about the prostate, since the gland plays a role in both sex and urination. That's unfortunate. A great deal of unnecessary pain and suffering can be avoided with some basic knowledge about the gland, and a healthy dietary and exercise regimen.

The gland has become the focus of great controversy since surgical and pharmaceutical treatments of prostate enlargement, inflammation and cancer carry many of their own risks, depending on the individual. The treatment of problems related to the prostate, perhaps more than those related to any other gland, organ or body part, cries out for patient education and full patient participation in medical decision making.

THE THREE MAJOR PROSTATE DISEASES

Basically, there are three diseases that can strike the prostate:

- Benign Prostatic Hyperplasia or Hypertrophy (BPH)
- Prostatitis
- Cancer of the prostate

While prostatitis—an infected prostate—can strike men at any age, it is at age 40-plus that most men will start to display symptoms relating to the other prostate problems. For high-risk males, symptoms can start much younger.

THE FIRST WARNING SIGNS OF PROSTATE TROUBLE

There are several symptoms of prostate trouble. Unfortunately, regardless of malady, they're often similar. For example;

You may urinate more frequently, especially in the middle of the night.

Urination may be more difficult, uneven or unintentional.

You may have blood in your urine.

Sometimes you'll feel burning when you "take a wizz" or ejaculate.

You also may feel pain in your upper thighs, lower back or pelvis.

These symptoms often indicate nothing more than normal enlargement as you age. Or they may be simply the result of other factors, for example, if you've been drinking more liquids, or have been under extra stress.

But be warned. While prostate cancer can cause these symptoms, it can also unfortunately be symptom-less. Prostatitis and BPH are benign diseases, but prostate cancer can and does kill. I repeat, prostate cancer is the second leading cause of cancer deaths among men, after lung cancer. The American Cancer Society estimates that more than 320,000 American men will be diagnosed with prostate cancer this year, and 42,000 will die.

Some good news. The appearance of BPH does NOT mean you're more likely to get cancer. This is important enough to repeat:

BPH and Prostatitis DO NOT cause cancer.

It's a popular myth that they do. Of course, having BPH doesn't mean you won't get cancer; it just doesn't cause it. Also, sometimes there's a misdiagnosis which adds to the confusion. But while neither disease is as life-threatening as cancer, they CAN cause serious problems if left untreated.

DO SOMETHING BEFORE IT IS TOO LATE

If you have any concern at all about your prostate, see a doctor. You may think your doctor is so far behind the times that he still has the stethoscope he received for a graduation present in 1910. Maybe you think the American Medical Association (AMA) is plotting to keep alternative treatments out of the hands of lay people so they'll keep getting sick and require medical services.

It's not true, at least not lately. The AMA says it recognizes the need for medical schools to respond to the growing interest in alternative health care practices. Doctors are well aware of the growing interest in alternative treatments. They say they recognize the dissatisfaction with conventional health care, which is often perceived as ineffectual, too expensive or too focused on curing disease rather than maintaining good health. Surprised?

Recently, Miriam S. Wetzel, Ph.D., of Harvard Medical School, Boston, and colleagues surveyed 125 US medical schools. The purpose was to document the prevalence, scope and diversity of medical school education in complementary and alternative medicine topics.

As reported in the *Journal of the American Medical Association* (JAMA) in September, 1998, researchers found that more than 60 percent of United States medical schools now offer courses that include alternative medical topics such as acupuncture, chiropractic and herbal therapies. And no wonder why. The authors found also that approximately one in three adults in the United States uses chiropractic, acupuncture, homeopathy or other alternative therapies.

So don't feel you're being a weirdo by exploring alternatives to toxic medicines and surgeries. If your doctor doesn't understand or approve, it should be easy enough for you to find a competent one who does.

Having said that, many doctors still consider only drugs and surgery as the "medically approved" treatments for prostate disorders. Most will not recommend a treatment program based on nutrition and/or supplements. Still, there are many enlightened physicians who understand how some simple-to-follow guidelines can decrease if not eliminate prostate problems.

So now you've found a doctor you like and trust. Several tests will help your doctor identify your problem and decide what treatment to recommend. The tests your doctor gives vary from patient to patient, but the most common is also the most dreaded.

The Digital Rectal Exam

In this exam the doctor inserts a gloved finger into the rectum and feels the part of the prostate next to the rectum. This exam gives the doctor a general idea of the size and condition of the gland. While a normal prostate feels smooth and elastic, the presence of lumps or other abnormal texture, or rock-hard consistency may point to disease.

Although the test sounds demeaning, it's not. A good doctor can feel the prostate in a few seconds and be done before you have time to blush.

Urine Flow Study

It is also advisable to have your urine flow rate tested. Sometimes the doctor will ask a patient to urinate into a special device which measures how quickly the urine is flowing. A reduced flow often suggests BPH.

You can also purchase your own urine flow meter from a pharmacist. Testing the flow rate yourself provides a valuable monitor of your progress during treatment.

Other tests which can uncover prostate problems include:

- Prostate Specific Antigen (PSA) Test
- Transrectal Ultrasound
- Intravenous Pyelogram (IVP)
- Cystoscopy

We'll discuss these later in the chapter.

YOU CAN PROTECT YOUR PROSTATE

Most men suffering from prostate cancer are undergoing unnecessary operations and being treated with outdated toxic drugs. Most of the drugs prescribed for BPH have been shown to be only marginally effective. Many also have quite debilitating side effects. Although doctors will readily prescribe them, you may not be made aware of the drawbacks associated with their use:

Most are slow to take effect and relieve symptoms, if they do at all.

Many have significant side effects, including reduced sexual desire and performance.

As for surgery for prostate cancer, 70 percent of patients become impotent after surgery, and 40 percent become incontinent (cannot control urination).

For those with a positive diagnosis, many experts now recommend the Swedish approach to treatment, "watchful waiting." This approach, as the name would suggest, means keeping a close eye on any signs of the disease progressing, but holding off on extreme treatments, such as drugs, surgery and chemotherapy, unless absolutely necessary.

Here's why: Statistics show that a healthy 60-year-old man has an average life expectancy of another 18 years. A 60-year-old man with prostate cancer, who does NOT have prostate surgery, has a life expectancy of another 16 years, while a 60-year-old man with prostate cancer who DOES have surgery has a life expectancy of another 17 years. Not much of a difference, don't you think?

So your best course of action may very well be no action at all. There probably is no need for you to rush off to the surgeon, at least not until you carefully weigh your alternatives.

More and more doctors are coming to believe that an enlarged prostate can be treated or deterred by feeding the body the nutrients it lacks. They understand that some nutrients, foods and herbs influence prostate enlargement and some of them may also influence cancer spread or development.

Remember while pharmaceutical and surgical treatments are more or less effective in relieving symptoms, they in no way address the underlying causes of prostate disease. There are dietary, lifestyle, environmental and emotional factors known for stressing the prostate.

So, over and above factors out of your control, doesn't it make sense to take advantage of safe nutritional guidelines which very well may deter prostate enlargement or prostate cancer?

For example, high fat diets (and high cholesterol) have been directly linked to prostate cancer. It makes sense, therefore, that reducing the fats in your diet will help ward it off.

Some men are more at risk for developing prostate cancer than others. Some factors are hereditary while others are environmental.

For example, you may be more at risk for prostate cancer if a female relative has had a brush with breast cancer. According to the September, 1998 issue of *Epidemiology*, researchers at the American Cancer Society looked at 480,000 men and found that the risk of fatal prostate cancer for men over 65 increased 65 percent if their mother or sister had been diagnosed with breast cancer before age 50.

You are at higher risk for prostate cancer than other men if you are over 55, African-American, or married (which may reflect on your sex life, diet or both). Also a study of Swedish men who had a diagnosis of prostate cancer between 1959 and 1963 traced the records of 5,496 of their sons and confirmed that there is a higher risk of developing prostate cancer among men whose fathers had the disease. All the more reason for you to change your living habits.

As for environmental factors, you are also at greater risk if you are a welder, rubber worker, electroplater, alkaline-battery worker or are otherwise exposed to cadmium. Farmers are also more vulnerable.

For you non-welding city dwellers, there are some simple changes you can make to, at least, minimize prostate problems. For tried-and-true treatments—besides lowering fat in the diet—experts recommend:

Give Up Tobacco

Prostate cancer is not usually seen as one of the malignancies related to smoking. But two recent studies have resulted in controversial findings attributing increased risk to smokers. To find out if those were simply freak results, or if they really represented a trend, this group of American researchers went to one of the largest databanks of men's smoking habits available: the Multiple Risk Factor Intervention Trial (MRFIT). Examining the records of 348,874 men both black and white, researchers found evidence that a connection does exist, and that it may be stronger in men who smoke more heavily. By the way, cigarette smoke contains traces of cadmium. (See previous page).

Cut the Caffeine

Caffeine in any form—coffee, tea, chocolate or soft drinks—tends to tighten the bladder neck and make it more difficult to urinate. Since part of the prostate is made up of smooth muscle, anything that causes that muscle to constrict will make urination more difficult. Caffeine does this quite a bit.

Sometimes little changes in eating—or drinking habits—can make a big difference. When Glenn, a 63-year-old real estate agent in the Midwest, complained to his doctor about prostate pain from his BPH, she asked him a few simple questions about his daily habits. It turned out Glenn was a chronic coffee drinker, and rarely drank water.

When she suggested Glenn drink four large glasses of water a day, and decrease his coffee drinking to a bare minimum, he noticed his BPH symptoms improved 50 percent within one week.

Cut Back Your Booze

Alcohol also tightens the bladder neck to hamper urination. Since it is a diuretic, it increases the amount of urine that builds up inside the bladder. Drinking alcohol also makes the bladder operate a lot less efficiently, and the more you drink the more problems you'll likely have.

Watch the Cold Medicines

Antihistamines and decongestants can harm some men. In fact, taking large doses of cold medications occasionally leads to urinary retention, a potentially life-threatening condition in which you completely stop urinating. Decongestants—known as a sympathomimetic—cause the muscle at the bladder neck to constrict, restricting the flow of urine. Antihistamines can actually paralyze the bladder.

So if you have allergies as well as prostate problems ask your doctor about prescribing astemizole (Hismanal) or terfenadine (Seldane), two medications that have no antihistamines. If you must buy over-the-counter medication, take half of the suggested dose. If no problem ensues, move to the full recommended dosage. Needless to say, more is not always better. Follow the directions on the label and don't take more than is recommended. Common sense should tell you not to take any medicine beyond the expiration date, right? Right.

Cut Back on Spicy Foods

Spicy and acidic foods bother some men with enlarged prostates. If you notice more problems after eating salsa, chili or other spicy or acidic foods, avoid them.

Other nutritional tips for BPH include reducing sugar in your diet, which improves the body's ability to heal. Also, keeping pesticides out of your diet by eating as many organic foods as possible also benefits the prostate.

Manage Your Stress

Perhaps the most underrated trigger is unmanaged stress. Stress plays a major role in prostate-related discomfort, because the bladder neck and prostate are both very rich with nerves that respond to adrenal hormones. When you're under stress there are more of those hormones floating around which cause more difficulty in urinating.

Stress also triggers the release of adrenaline in your body, prompting a fight-or-flight response. Just as it is difficult to get an erection during the fight-or-flight response (why you would want one then is beyond me!), it can make urination difficult, too.

Good Lovin'

One way urologists help ease urination problems is to massage the prostate. For men with mild to moderate voiding difficulties, an alternative may simply be to have more sex. Many men notice that the more they ejaculate, the easier it is to urinate. That's because the ejaculation helps empty the prostate of secretions that may hamper urination. Should your partner balk, show em' the book!

Hit the Head Before Hitting the Hay

Many men get the urge to urinate in the middle of the night, and that can be a real nuisance. But if you limit your intake of beverages after 6 P.M., and make sure you urinate before going to sleep, you can eliminate much of this problem.

Flee South in the Winter

For some unknown reason, people in the South have fewer prostate problems. (Surprising, since so many retirees head south.) It would seem to make sense, therefore, that, if at all possible, you should spend winters somewhere in the Sunbelt.

HOW TO TELL IF YOU HAVE BPH

The most common prostate problem is Benign Prostatic Hyperplasia (BPH), the noncancerous enlargement of the prostate. BPH is as common a part of aging as gray hair or losing your hair, for that matter. As life expectancy rises, so does the occurrence of BPH. In the United States alone, 350,000 operations take place each year for this malady. Doctors suspect hundreds of thousands of other cases go untreated.

It is not clear whether certain groups face a greater risk of getting BPH. Studies done over the years suggest that it occurs more often among married men than single men, and is more common in the United States and Europe than in other parts of the world. However, these findings have been disputed, and no definite information on risk factors exists.

It is common for the prostate gland to become enlarged as a man ages. A normal prostate in a man under age 45 is about the size of a walnut. Again, the urethra runs right through the center of the gland.

As a male matures, the prostate goes through two main periods of growth. The first occurs early in puberty, when the prostate doubles in size. At around age 25, the gland begins to grow again. It is this second growth phase that often results, years later, in BPH.

Its cause is not well understood. For centuries, it has been known that BPH occurs mainly in older men and that it doesn't develop in males whose testes were removed before puberty. For this reason, some researchers believe that factors related to aging and the testes may spur its development.

Here's one theory. Throughout their lives, men produce both testosterone, an important male hormone, and small amounts of estrogen, a female hormone. Testosterone—besides being the topic of male jokes—is responsible for many of the traits that make us guys, well, guys; such as our muscle mass and sexual appetites and drive. It's believed testosterone may help control the prostate's growth.

As men age, the amount of active testosterone in the blood decreases, leaving a higher proportion of estrogen. Studies done with animals have suggested that BPH may occur because the higher amount of estrogen within the gland increases the activity of substances that promote cell growth.

Another theory focuses on dihydrotestosterone (DHT), a substance derived from testosterone in the prostate. It's known that the enzyme, 5-alpha-reductase, is used to turn testosterone to dihydrotestosterone, or DHT. DHT plays a key role in the development of a normal male fetus and the development of normal male sexual characteristics during puberty.

However, around the age of 40, 5-alpha-reductase kicks into "overdrive," converting our declining levels of testosterone into excessive amounts of DHT. Although this is great when we're teenagers, it's bad for a man in his forties; it can make your hair fall out and your prostate enlarge.

Most animals lose their ability to produce DHT as they age. Male Homo Sapiens do not. Research indicates that even with a drop in the blood's testosterone level, older men continue to produce and accumulate high levels of DHT in the prostate. This accumulation may encourage the growth of cells. Scientists have also noted that men who do not produce DHT do not develop BPH.

Some researchers suggest that BPH may develop as a result of "instructions" given to cells early in life. According to this theory, BPH occurs because cells in one section of the gland follow these instructions and "reawaken" later in life. These "reawakened" cells then deliver signals to other cells in the gland, instructing them to grow or making them more sensitive to hormones that influence growth.

Though the prostate continues to grow during most of a man's life, the enlargement doesn't usually cause problems until late in life. BPH rarely causes symptoms before age 40, but more than half of men in their sixties and as many as 90 percent in their seventies and eighties have some symptoms of BPH.

One thing researchers note is that the onset of BPH parallels the typical age when exercise or physical activity levels start to decrease. This sedentary behavior, they also note, causes testosterone levels in the blood to increase.

Unless the man suddenly becomes a Don Juanish sex machine, there's no place for the elevated testosterone to go. His body converts the male hormone to dihydrotestosterone (DHT), which causes prostate cells to multiply quickly and excessively, making the prostate grow. It is this enlarged prostate, which constricts the urethra, that gives men their problems.

Although BPH is usually not a health-threatening condition in and of itself, it can lead to other potentially serious conditions over time. For example, BPH can prevent the bladder from being completely emptied, which allows bacteria to collect, and can cause an infection in the urinary canal or bladder. Besides urine retention, strain on the bladder can lead to urinary tract infections, bladder or kidney damage, bladder stones, and incontinence (involuntary leaking).

Left untreated, an infection can progress to the urethra and kidneys. If the bladder is permanently damaged, treatment for BPH may be ineffective. In a worse case scenario urine can show up in your blood, and that can be deadly.

No doubt, severe BPH can cause serious problems. But don't freak out with worry. When BPH is found in its earlier stages, there is a lower risk of developing such complications.

The symptoms of BPH vary, but the most common ones involve changes or problems with urination such as:

- A hesitant, interrupted, weak stream.
- Urgency and leaking or dribbling.
- More frequent urination, especially at night.

IF YOU'RE AROUND AGE 45 EXPECT AN ENLARGED PROSTATE.

As the prostate enlarges, the surrounding capsule stops it from expanding, causing the gland to expand in the other direction, pressing against the urethra like a clamp on a garden hose. The bladder wall compensates by pressing harder. This causes it to become more muscular, thicker and smaller causing the urge "to go" more frequently even when it contains only small amounts of urine. Also, BPH can prevent the bladder from emptying itself completely, thus leaving urine behind. The narrowing of the urethra and partial emptying of the bladder cause many of the problems associated with BPH including "urge incontinence." This means your bladder is irritated by retained urine which causes it to spasm.

The result? You don't make it to the bathroom in time. It can also cause bladder infections, stones and even kidney damage. The size of the prostate does not always determine how severe the obstruction or the symptoms will be. Some men with greatly enlarged glands have little obstruction and few symptoms, while others, whose glands are less enlarged, have more blockage and greater problems.

Sometimes a man may not know he has any obstruction until he suddenly finds himself unable to urinate at all. This condition, called acute urinary retention, may be triggered by, again, taking over-the-counter cold or allergy medicines. When partial obstruction is present, urinary retention also can be brought on by alcohol, cold temperatures, or a long period of immobility.

It is important to tell your doctor about urinary problems such as those described above. In eight out of ten cases, these symptoms suggest BPH, but they also can signal other, more serious conditions requiring prompt treatment which can be ruled out only by a doctor's exam.

You may first notice symptoms of BPH yourself, or your doctor may find during a routine checkup that your prostate is enlarged. When BPH is suspected, you may be referred to a urologist, a doctor who specializes in problems of the urinary tract and the male reproductive system.

Men who have BPH with symptoms usually need some kind of treatment. However, several recent studies have questioned the need for early treatment when the gland is just mildly enlarged. These studies report that early treatment may not be needed because the symptoms of BPH clear up without treatment in as many as one-third of all mild cases. Instead of immediate therapy, they suggest regular checkups to watch for early problems. If the condition begins to pose a danger to the patient's health or causes a major inconvenience to him, treatment is usually recommended.

Since BPH may cause urinary tract infections, a doctor will usually clear up any infection with antibiotics before treating the BPH itself. Although the need for treatment is not usually urgent, doctors generally advise going ahead with treatment once the problems become bothersome or present a health risk.

Today, conventional treatments include watchful waiting to see how bad symptoms become, followed by drug therapy and then surgery. Again, these last two treatments cost Americans $2 billion annually, and both can cause side effects including impotence.

There's got to be a better way, and there is. Educating yourself is a giant leap in understanding what you're facing, and how to eliminate unnecessary suffering and expense.

HOW TO TELL IF YOU HAVE PROSTATITIS

Any man at any age can develop prostatitis, an infection or inflammation of the prostate gland. Unlike BPH, prostatitis can affect young men in their prime of life. Though non-fatal, it is still often a disabling disease, causing intense pain, urinary complications, sexual dysfunction, infertility, and a drastic reduction in the quality of life. It's not a fun thing to have.

Prostatitis is a common, yet confusing ailment, often used to describe a variety of inflammatory conditions of the prostate gland. It is also used as a "catch-all" phrase for a number of different urinary-tract infections and conditions. Granted, with the prostate's proximity to the urethra and bladder, conditions affecting one or the other often have similar or overlapping symptoms.

This infection can be a one-time occurrence, or it can be chronic, persistent or recurrent. Bacteria or some other microorganism can cause the disease, or it can result from factors other than bacteria.

Basically there are two kinds of prostatitis:

- Non-bacterial (or non-infectious) prostatitis.
- Bacterial (or infectious) prostatitis.

Non-bacterial prostatitis isn't a disease, it's a condition. Doctors usually divide it into two categories:

- Congestive prostatitis (sometimes called prostatostasis).
- Prostatodynia.

Congestive prostatitis occurs when too much prostatic fluid, the milky fluid in semen, accumulates within the prostate gland rather than being ejaculated out through the penis. The gland is said to be "congested" or "engorged."

Prostatodynia is a condition in which pain "seems" to originate in the prostate but is much more likely to be coming from the muscles of the pelvic floor, from an inflammation in one or more of the pelvic bones, or from a disease in the rectum. Despite its name, prostatodynia really has nothing to do with the prostate.

In addition to being a tough disease to diagnose, effective treatment of prostatitis is sometimes difficult. This combination often leads to frustration for both patients and doctors. The patient may show a variety of symptoms which often include:

- Low back pain.
- Burning upon urination.
- Frequent urination.
- Urgent urination.
- Pain deep in the rectum and scrotal areas.

At times the symptoms may also include:

- Generalized malaise.
- Joint aches.
- Muscle aches.
- Fever or pain almost anywhere within the pelvis and scrotum.

These symptoms may be mild or they may be overwhelming.

WHAT CAUSES PROSTATITIS

The causes of prostatitis are sometimes well understood but are more often obscure. As previously mentioned, it can be caused by bacteria similar to those which cause other types of urinary infections. Some patients, however, have no evidence of bacteria in their prostates, yet are thought to carry microorganisms such as Chlamydia or Ureaplasma, which are harder to identify by standard culture techniques. Still other patients have no evidence of any microorganisms at all. The reasons for their prostatitis symptoms are poorly understood and are possibly related to stress and/or congestion. As we discussed earlier, certain medications such as cold remedies with antihistamines and decongestants may be a cause of symptoms.

To further complicate things congestive prostatitis can be caused by:

- Too much sex.
- Not enough sex.

Confused? You should be. Every day a healthy prostate secretes between one-tenth and two-fifths of a teaspoon of fluid. When you're sexually aroused you produce four to ten times that amount. Normally (or at least ideally), you release it by ejaculating. If you don't your prostate becomes congested. Moreover, an abrupt fall-off in sexual climaxes—maybe your partner is mad at you—can engorge the prostate.

On the other hand, let's say you have a "wild weekend" after a long period of celibacy. Your prostate, which isn't used to your being so debonair, works overtime to produce secretions for several ejaculations. As a result it becomes inflamed, or "pissed off" if you prefer.

When your physician examines you, a digital rectal exam may reveal a very tender prostate gland. At times, however, your prostate may not be tender at all. Your physician may choose to examine either your urine or the prostatic secretions following a massage of the prostate. Since there is such a wide variety of symptoms and causes for prostatitis, many physicians approach it differently. All examinations for this infection, however, should include a digital rectal exam.

Prostatitis is most commonly treated with antibiotics that may be effective when there is actually an infecting agent (bacteria). Many times, however, they are not effective in these cases, either because they don't eradicate the infection or because there never was an actual infection. It is common for some patients to receive multiple courses of different antibiotics in an attempt to find one that works. Patients may respond to certain pharmacological agents (drugs) which have a tendency to relax the muscles of the bladder neck and prostate gland.

Anti-inflammatory therapy and sitz baths are often helpful regardless of the cause. We'll give you additional tips in later chapters.

Prostatitis, which is difficult to treat or stubbornly recurrent, can be treated with surgery. This procedure is done by removing part of the prostatic tissue through a scope placed in the urethra. This is only a last resort for a troublesome inflammation.

A recent report in the United States linked bike riding with impotence. There are those investigating whether it might also cause prostatitis. Whether it does or not, biking can make your prostatitis worse if you don't have your clothing and your seat configured properly.

It's highly unlikely a bike will give you a bacterial infection. If you have a diagnosis that shows you have bacteria in your prostate gland, no amount of biking or not biking will affect the fact that you have an infection. If you don't have a lab analysis showing an infection, and your bike is not configured properly, you may have nothing more than irritation to your prostate gland from this activity.

Your prostate is fairly close to the surface of the area that touches the seat of the average road bike. So every bump and pothole you go over is transmitted to that region.

You should find a seat that has a soft central area (midway between front and back). Several makers have holes cut in the underlying material at this part of the seat. Also your seat should always be pointed down in front as much as possible. If it is level it could mash your prostate gland too much. Put bar ends on to have two different hand heights on your handle bar, and constantly move your position (both seat and hands) so that you do not remain in any one posture for very long while riding. If you're using a road bike, put "Aero" bars on the front and use them. The "Aero" bar position raises your seat quite a bit and saves your prostate some wear and tear.

You should also always wear padded bike shorts. Two pairs are better than one. Also consider a gel pack seat.

Over the last ten years great strides have been made in the treatment of prostate cancer and BPH, diseases which affect mostly older men. For the most part, the non-fatal but often disabling prostatitis affecting men of all ages has been somewhat neglected. That doesn't mean it's any less painful or worrisome. Usually with patience and care, a treatment regimen can be found which will afford relief.

EVERY MAN'S GREAT FEAR: CANCER

Prostate cancer is almost always a "primary" cancer, meaning it originates in the gland, rather than traveling from another part of the body. Malignant prostate cancer is a serious disease since, if undiagnosed or neglected over time, the cancer cells multiply without control, forming too much tissue and invading healthy cells nearby. While it can occur at any age, 80 percent occurs in men 65 or older, and one in nine American men will develop it.

Remember, this year more than 320,000 men will be diagnosed with prostate cancer and more than 42,000 men previously diagnosed will die as a result. This makes prostate cancer the second leading killer of men in this country, behind lung cancer. As our male population ages, especially with baby-boomers crossing the 50-year-old threshold, the numbers of men facing this cancer will swell.

Although its actual cause is unknown, the major contributing factor is an increased level of testosterone. But just as important, bad habits—a sedentary lifestyle, improper diet, venereal diseases, smoking, alcohol, and obesity—can increase your risk of problems, particularly cancer.

In the United States, 50,000 men were treated for advanced metastatic prostate cancer in 1993. Castration is the usual treatment for advanced cancer, but in recent years, non-steroidal antiandrogens have become more commonly used, in addition to castration, to slow further the progression of the cancer and increase survival. Cost is a major issue with these drugs for two reasons:

Medicare does not reimburse oral anti-cancer medications, so their considerable cost must be assumed by the patient himself.

There is some doubt as to the cost-effectiveness of this therapy in terms of life-years saved.

This second issue is complicated by the fact that one major study found significantly better survival outcomes than another. As well, many physicians are concerned about the gastrointestinal side-effects that affect 10 to 15 percent of men taking these drugs.

There are no clear symptoms of prostate cancer which can be easily assessed by the patient himself. This differentiates it from breast cancer or testicular cancer in which regular self-examination is critical to early detection.

One big problem with prostate cancer is that many of the early signs of the disease can be caused by other disorders or, worse still, are just among the normal consequences of growing older. Another is the absence of signs or symptoms for many years after the disease starts to develop.

SYMPTOMS OF PROSTATE CANCER

Despite the fact that prostate cancer has no definitive set of symptoms, all of the following have been identified by the National Cancer Institute as possible indicators of prostate cancer and many other clinical problems:

- Frequent urination (especially at night).
- Inability to urinate.
- Trouble starting to urinate or trouble holding back urination.
- Pain during ejaculation.
- A weak or interrupted urine flow.
- Pain or a burning feeling during urination.
- Blood in the semen or in the urine.
- Frequent pain or stiffness in the lower back, hips or upper thighs.

See? Sounds like BPH or prostatitis, doesn't it?

Since all these symptoms may be caused not only by prostate cancer, but also by a number of other disorders (and not just other disorders of the prostate), it would be wise to talk to your family doctor if you or someone else in your family is having one or more of these problems on a regular basis. Only a properly trained, experienced physician will be able to tell whether these symptoms are, in fact, associated with the possibility of prostate cancer.

YOU ARE NOT ALONE

Prostate cancer research has been generally neglected until recently. Men's modesty (or embarrassment), the difficulty of detection, and under-reporting by doctors have relegated it to the back burner. Though it kills approximately the same number of people as AIDS and breast cancer, only

$59 million was spent in 1995 on prostate cancer research while $313 million was spent on breast cancer and $1.3 billion for AIDS.

If you recall, public awareness of breast cancer risks skyrocketed after former First Lady Betty Ford proclaimed she suffered from it, and we know all the publicity AIDS has received. Now the same thing is happening with prostate cancer.

As our population ages, more and more public figures have contracted the disease. It has already taken the lives of Frank Zappa (age 52), Bill Bixby (59), Telly Savales (70), Bobby Riggs (77), and Francois Mitterand (79).

When General Norman Schwarzkopf and former Presidential candidate Bob Dole contracted it, public awareness shot up. Then financial guru Michael Milken contracted it and declared a personal war on the disease, pledging $25 million for prostate cancer research. He also set up a public charity called CaP CURE not only for treatment but prevention. Additional money for research is pouring in. More on CaP CURE and how its findings can help you in later chapters.

REDUCE YOUR MEDICAL BILLS BY FOLLOWING THESE GUIDELINES

The National Cancer Institute's official dietary guideline, nationally promoted as the "5 a Day for Better Health" program, is a minimum of 5 servings of fruits and vegetables a day. (For men eating the median 2,270 calories a day, the minimum is seven servings.) Unfortunately, only one in four people really follows this advice.

THE FIRST STEPS TOWARD PEACE OF MIND

There are a number of tests you should take to discover whether you—or reassure yourself that you don't—have prostate cancer. If BPH or cancer are caught early enough, treatment will cost you less in money, time and stress than if you sit at home "hoping nothing is wrong."

These tests include:

- Transrectal Ultrasound.
- Intravenous Pyelogram (IVP).

- Cystoscopy.
- Prostate Specific Antigen (PSA) Test.
- Digital Rectal Exam (mentioned earlier.)
- Urine flow (also mentioned earlier.)

Transrectal Ultrasound

If there is a suspicion of prostate cancer, your doctor may recommend a test with rectal ultrasound. In this procedure, a probe inserted in the rectum directs sound waves at the prostate. The echo patterns of the sound waves form an image of the prostate gland on a display screen.

Intravenous Pyelogram (IVP)

IVP is an X-ray of the urinary tract. In this IVP test, a dye is injected into a vein, and the X-ray is taken. The dye makes the urine visible on the X-ray and shows any obstruction or blockage in the urinary tract.

Cystoscopy

In this exam, the doctor inserts a small tube through the opening of the urethra in the penis. (This procedure is done after a solution numbs the inside of the penis so all sensation is lost.) The tube, called a cystoscope, contains a lens and a light system, which help the doctor see the inside of the urethra and the bladder. The doctor can then determine the size of the gland and identify the location and degree of the obstruction.

PSA Test

Besides the Digital Rectal Exam, probably the best known test for prostate problems is the Prostate Specific Antigen, or PSA test. Almost all doctors recommend it depending on your age or concerns.

The PSA test is performed on a blood sample taken from the patient. It measures the blood level of a protein produced by all prostate cells. Although this test is limited in the information it can give, it does seem to be able to identify whether or not there is a problem. When the prostate begins enlarging the growing number of cells causes a slight rise in the PSA count. When prostate cells are cancerous and begin multiplying, the level jumps dramatically.

PSA testing is the most reliable test now available to screen for prostate cancer. PSA "velocity," or the increase in PSA from one year to the next, has been considered potentially more reliable than PSA alone in identifying prostate cancer. But high PSA velocity is only considered abnormal if it increases for two consecutive years. In other words, three tests would be needed.

Remember, though, conditions other than cancer, such as BPH or prostatitis, can also produce high PSA levels. Should you have a high PSA score, your doctor will take a biopsy—a tissue sample—to make sure.

PSA testing is not without controversy. When PSA testing for prostate cancer first became widespread in the United States, diagnosed cases of prostate cancer dramatically increased, with rates doubling between 1984 and 1991. Many were concerned about the burden this increase would place on the health care system. Also, it was feared that men were being diagnosed with insignificant tumors—and undergoing treatment—when the best course of action was no action. According to a study conducted by the Utah Cancer Registry, and confirmed by other health organizations, the increase in reported elevated PSA cases slowed after a peak in 1992. Today, well-informed doctors and patients are deciding together a course of action for high PSA levels.

It used to be that if you had a PSA score of "4.0" (commonly described as 4.0 ng/ml) you had a prostate problem. Doctors soon realized though that "one size didn't fit all," and so it's been revised.

Using 4.0 as a cutoff point does not take into account the increase in PSA production that occurs with age as the prostate gland enlarges. Studies suggested that modifying the PSA cutoff point according to a man's age would catch more cancers among younger men at a time when they were potentially curable. It would also detect fewer cancers in older men for whom insignificant tumors were unlikely to cause problems in the man's remaining lifetime. The revised cutoff points recommended in these studies and generally used today are:

- 2.5 for men 40 to 49 years old,
- 3.5 for men 50 to 59 years old,
- 4.5 for men 60 to 69 years old, and
- 6.5 for men 70 to 79 years old.

Blood tests that show PSA levels higher than these cutoff points should be followed up by biopsy to assess the need for treatment.

Remember, these are only guidelines. Sometimes a prostate biopsy or ultrasound can induce artificially elevated levels of PSA. Daily variations also occur. Granted they don't vary that much, but if you're straddling the top limit you may need a follow-up.

There has also been a belief (old wives' tale, perhaps?) that sex before a PSA test would skew the results. A recent study looked at PSA levels before and one and seven days after ejaculation in men 50 to 60 years old with BPH, and found that ejaculation prior to testing had no effect on the test's reliability.

So go ahead with your "normal" routine. You won't screw up your results.

Just because you get a low PSA score doesn't mean you're in the clear. The test is not foolproof. Take the case of General Norman Schwarzkopf. During a routine physical in 1994, he took a PSA test and scored a very low 1.8. When his doctor took an ultrasound he found a mass he suspected was a stone. To be on the safe side, he took a biopsy from the General's prostate. He had cancer. In this case, the PSA exam indicated nothing. As you can see, sometimes one test is not enough.

Rectal Exam (Redux)

The American Cancer Society (ACS) recommends a rectal exam each year for all men over the age of 40—or younger if they are in a high risk group like African-Americans. Once you hit 70, most doctors don't bother with the exam any more. Why? Because the cancer they're looking for begins growing so slowly it's just as likely the patient will die from other causes first.

Sadly, the ACS reports less than half of all American men who should have routine examinations do so. This means there are a lot of men who aren't taking care of themselves.

If that means you, at least you've made the first step by reading this book. Good for you. We're here to help.

Read on.

CHAPTER TWO

EAT YOUR WAY
TO
PROSTATE HEALTH

When our moms told us to eat our vegetables when we were boys, it's probably a safe bet none of us heard " . . . It'll improve your sex life later on, son!" They might have had better luck convincing us to scarf down our broccoli if they did.

But there's growing evidence that certain eating habits, especially eating more vegetables and fruits, will ward off prostate problems including cancer. And your rewards for working toward a healthy prostate can include better stamina, body weight, skin tone, perhaps an extra bounce in your step, all of which will increase your sex appeal. Both directly and indirectly, your efforts can lead to a better love life.

But Mom didn't—and so we haven't!

But even if for some reason you still shun what your mother tells you—(which is an entirely different issue and WAY beyond the scope of this book!)— you should at least heed the advice from Mother Nature.

There's no one magic bullet to prevent cancer, but there are dietary changes you can make that, when combined, will certainly reduce your risk of prostate problems. The sooner you make them, the better.

There are a number of dietary and nutritional steps any man can take today to either prevent or treat BPH or prostatitis. A diet high in fiber and complex carbohydrates, while low in fat and moderate in protein, can do the trick.

By the same token, avoid, when possible, sugar, alcohol, caffeine, tobacco, white flour products, hydrogenated fats, food additives and chemicals. (Other substances to shun when possible include fluoride, chlorine, aluminum and Teflon cookware, nonprescription recreational drugs, mercury amalgam fillings, electric blankets, and hair dyes.)

It's a fact that diets focused on red-orange fruits and vegetables (containing carotenes) are associated with decreased prostate cancer, as are diets higher in polyunsaturated fish and vegetable oils. Adequate fiber in the diet helps, by decreasing the pressure in the lower bowel area. Finally, some foods like sunflower and pumpkin seeds seem to have a positive effect on prostate symptoms.

Then there's soy. Diets containing a high amount of soy products have been recommended as preventing prostate enlargement and cancer. Why? Soy products contain isoflavones—natural substances which help minimize the effects of harmful DHT.

Do you doubt dietary changes can improve the health of your prostate? Consider the case of financier, Michael Milken, who in 1993, at age 46, discovered he had prostate cancer.

When Milkin decided to have his cancerous prostate removed it was too late. The cancer had spread to his lymph nodes and the removal of the gland wouldn't have helped. Instead, Milkin pored over every bit of research on prostate cancer he could find. He discovered:

- A higher rate of cancer in high-fat Western diets.
- Research at Sloan-Kettering showing rats fed a high-fat diet developed more rapidly growing tumors than rats on a low-fat diet. When the rats on a high-fat diet were switched to low-fat ones, their tumor growth slowed.
- Soy products reduced tumors in rats.

Along with hormone and supplemental radiation therapy, Milkin made drastic changes in his lifestyle, including a switch to a lowfat vegetarian diet heavy on soy. As a result, his swollen lymph nodes returned to normal size and his cancer did not spread to his bones. With his cancer in remission, he has returned to a full work schedule.

Did his new eating habits have an effect? Milken believes so, and there's mounting evidence he's right. In fact, he has set up a public charity called CaP CURE , to find a cure for prostate cancer. A large chunk of the research is dedicated to dietary studies.

Cancer usually develops slowly, over many years, and goes through a number of stages. Sound nutrition is most likely to impact on the early precancerous stages known as initiation and progression. These stages include potentially halting, even reversing, changes in a cell's genetic material, which are often the result of damage caused by chemical reactions in the body. Once the genetic changes are complete, however, and the now cancerous cell begins to multiply, nutrition's positive effect is diminished.

Researchers are still figuring out the exact details of a cancer-preventing diet, and they probably will be for a long time to come. Still, there are things you should eat—and not eat—that can ward off prostate cancer.

HOW TO CUT YOUR PROSTATE CANCER RISK BY 75 PERCENT

It has been estimated that 75 percent of all prostate cancer could be prevented with changes in diet and lifestyle. While it may be hard to believe that some simple changes can keep prostate problems, including cancer, at bay, scientific evidence shows they may account in large part for the variance of prostate cancer rates in different countries. For example, the rates of prostate cancer range from 3.5 per 100,000 in Singapore to 49.8 per 100,000 in Sweden. (The rate in the United States is 32.2 per 100,000.) Among all the risk factors for prostate cancer, only nutrition explains the differences between countries.

Beyond international comparisons of diet and lifestyle, there is even more compelling evidence that nutrition is important. It's been proven that when Japanese migrate to the United States, within one generation their rate of prostate cancer increases to levels found in Americans who have lived in the United States for many generations.

The same thing happens on their home turf. When United States companies introduce American fast foods to previously low-risk countries, their residents become more likely to develop prostate disease. For example, in Japan the rate of obesity has gone up from 5 percent to 20 percent over the last 20 years, at a time when the incidence of prostate cancer has also increased markedly.

This is not a sinister plot but simply the outcome of trying to provide good-tasting, low-cost foods economically. The reality is, in industrially developed countries, these foods promote the development of obesity and then chronic diseases such as diabetes, heart disease, hypertension and common forms of cancer, including prostate cancer. There really is nothing happy about these meals.

Compared with other cancers, prostate cancer can be relatively slow growing. It may take between five and ten years before it becomes aggressive. Also, unlike other cancers, prostate cancer can exist in some men for the duration of their lives without becoming life threatening. In fact, 30 percent of men worldwide have very small prostate tumors by the time they're 30 years old, but certainly not all die of prostate cancer.

This has prompted a radical new approach in cancer research. Perhaps the prostate cancer doesn't have to be eliminated completely. Maybe it's enough to control it or slow its growth rate to keep it from becoming life threatening. "The idea that you accomplish some of this with dietary intervention is tremendously exciting," says Dr. William Fair, a medical researcher studying dietary issues along with CaP CURE .

In laboratory studies, Dr. Fair has shown conclusively that animal tumors regressed or stayed the same with a diet consisting of less than 20 percent fat (most American diets are 40 percent fat or more). This means that with dietary intervention, tumor growth can be slowed to the point of not affecting life for 30 years or more. For a man in his sixties, this can almost be considered a cure.

"We can take a man with a high PSA, put him on a diet of 15 percent fat, and watch his PSA drop by 20 percent in three months," says Dr. Fair.

Dr. Fair bases his findings after extensive studies on the effects of low-fat diets—specifically, the elimination of red meat, whole milk, cheese and fried foods. This is with or without supplements of Vitamin E, selenium, and soy proteins to reduce the chances of developing prostate tumors.

His findings are consistent with those of other researchers. David Heber, M.D., Ph.D., Professor, Department of Medicine, UCLA School of Medicine offers the following guidelines for reducing the incidence of prostate cancer, or its recurrence following surgical or radiation treatment:

- Reduce dietary fat to 20 percent or less of total calories consumed.

- Increase the intake of fruits and vegetables to 5 to 9 servings per day, especially colorful fruits and vegetables rich in phytochemicals and natural antioxidants.

- Increase total fiber intake to greater than 25 grams per day, using high-fiber cereal and grain products as well as fruits and vegetables.

- Increase physical activity to reach and/or maintain a healthy body weight.

- Increase the intake of soy protein-containing foods or supplements containing soy protein isolate.

- Take a daily multivitamin/mineral supplement and 1000 mg of calcium per day.

Now, before we go any further I must tell you to expect to be hit with a bunch of high-falutin' sounding terms—like isoflavones, flavonoids and phytochemicals—that you may think are here just so I can dazzle you with my incredible intellect. I admit, this information won't help you much if you go into a restaurant and ask your waiter for an entre "heavy in phytochemicals, please." I doubt if he'll know what you're talking about.

If you're a baseball fan, it probably grates on you when a base runner scores and someone says, "Great! We got a point!" You wouldn't exactly count on that person to predict a pennant winner, would you?

Well, the same goes for nutrition. I have to use the right words. But when I do I'll try to explain what they mean. Then you can dazzle people with your own brilliance.

Here's one: FLAVONOIDS.

Flavonoids are part of a large class of chemicals that occur naturally in plants. Simply, they are substances found in fruits, vegetables and herbs essential for processing vitamin C. In fact, they give plants their vibrant color and protect them from harm. When consumed by humans, they can improve or maintain health.

There are 12 subcategories of flavonoids and approximately 4,000 different ones have been identified. They occur in high concentrations in the juice and peel of citrus fruits. They're also prevalent in onions, grapes and grape juice, papaya, broccoli, apricots, wine, greens, persimmons, green tea, soy products, cherries and grains, especially buckwheat.

You may have heard the term "bioflavonoids" used interchangeably with "flavonoids." All bioflavonoids are flavonoids; however, not all flavonoids are bioflavonoids.

Soy flavonoids genistein and daidzein are powerful antioxidants and cancer inhibitors which lower risks for prostate and breast cancer. So besides yourself, eating foods containing flavonoids will also be beneficial to females you know and love.

The best news about flavonoids is that they're found in many foods. If you eat a healthy diet, you probably get your quota. There are no set dosage or toxicity levels, and the average American diet contains about 1,000 mg a day.

Do you need to supplement? "Healthy people get the flavonoids they need in their diet," says Varro Tyler, Ph.D., of Purdue University. "But therapeutic amounts needed for antioxidant effect or capillary integrity may require supplementation. Grapeseed extracts and bilberry preparations are good flavonoid sources."

THE TEN NUTRIENTS YOUR PROSTATE CRAVES

Do you remember the Food Pyramid from Junior High? Believe it or not, the school nurse knew what she was talking about. In order to have a healthy prostate, it's important to choose a wide variety of foods from the five groups in the good ol' Food Pyramid.

Of the 40 known nutrients, ten are considered "leader nutrients." They are:

Protein

Carbohydrate

Fat

Vitamin A

Vitamin C

Thiamin

Riboflavin

Niacin

Calcium

Iron

The five food groups in the Pyramid are based on these leader nutrients. Here are some important facts:

- The foods in the "Grain" group are high in carbohydrate, thiamin, niacin and iron.
- The "Fruit" and "Vegetable" groups contain foods high in vitamins A and C.
- "Meat" group foods are high in protein, niacin, iron and thiamin.

- Foods in the "Milk" group are good sources of calcium, riboflavin and protein.

It may be an oversimplification, but generally any vitamin or mineral that's good for fighting one kind of cancer is good for fighting all kinds. For example, calcium is known as a nutrient especially effective in fighting colon cancer.

Although there is no known link between calcium and prostate cancer, it certainly can't hurt to make sure you consume adequate amounts of calcium.

There are a large number of foods that can specifically sack prostate problems. For example, a major new study confirms more dramatically than ever the power of produce. Researchers in the U.S. and Germany reviewed more than 200 human diet studies from around the world, and they found consistent evidence that people who are high up on the produce-consumption scale have about one-half the risk of developing a broad range of cancers, including prostate cancer. These people are compared with those who eat few fruits and vegetables.

Multiple studies find the strongest protection against cancer may come from:

Amino acids

Carrots

Citrus fruits

Cruciferous veggies (the broccoli family)

Garlic and onions

Green veggies

Legumes

Raw veggies

Soy beans

Tea

Tomatoes

Amino acids are often referred to as "the building blocks of life" because they are one of the fundamental requirements for life. They are the chemical units that make up protein, and it is protein that provides the structure for all living tissue.

Three amino acids in particular, glycine, alanine and glutamic acid, appear to have a direct link with prostate problems. In a "double-blind" study reported in the *Journal of the Maine Medical Association* to prove (or disprove) this link, a mixture of these 3 amino acids was given to half the men in a group of BPH sufferers. A placebo (an inert sugar pill) was given to the other half. Results showed that, within the group taking the amino acids:

- 92 percent experienced a reduction in prostate size
- 95 percent experienced less nocturia (need to urinate during the night)
- 81 percent found they had less urgency to urinate
- 73 percent needed to urinate less frequently
- 71 percent had reduced discomfort

Another study from the *Journal of the American Geriatrics Society* produced very similar results. Of the 45 men who took all three amino acids (as compared to a control group who did not receive the amino acids):

- 95 percent noted a reduction in nocturia
- 81 percent said they had a diminished sense of urgency to urinate
- 73 percent said they had to urinate less often
- 70 percent reported less "delay" in urination

None of the subjects reported any adverse side effects or reactions.

And how do you receive the benefits of these amino acids? Through protein. That could mean meat—preferably white meat or very lean cuts of other meat—fish, and a variety of beans.

NIBBLE AWAY YOUR CANCER FEARS

As mentioned in the previous chapter, the official dietary guideline of the National Cancer Institute, promoted as the "5 a Day for Better Health" program, includes a minimum of 5 servings of fruits and vegetables a day.

(For men eating the median 2,270 calories a day, the minimum is seven servings.) Unfortunately, only one in four people really follows this advice.

Dr. Susan M. Kregs-Smith, a research nutritionist with the National Cancer Institute, found that Americans are eating 20 percent more vegetables than they did a quarter-century ago. Guess what 25 percent of the vegetables eaten are?

French fries!

C'mon. What's the big deal? If you have a banana at breakfast, an orange during your mid-morning break, and an apple or pear at lunch, you are nearly half way there to your daily needs. And yes, if you do this on a daily basis you can, once in a while spoil yourself with some greasy fries.

CANCER CRUSHING NUTRIENTS

Fruits and vegetables deliver a legion of substances believed to fight cancer such as:

Vitamin C

Folic Acid

Beta-carotene

Vitamin C

Vitamin C helps prevent many internal cancers by neutralizing cancer-promoting nitrosamines. Nitrosamines are produced during the digestion of nitrites, the preservatives found in especially high concentration in meats such as hot dogs and ham. Vitamin C also helps maintain a healthy immune system, an additional cancer-fighting talent. Plus it may help build up vitamin E, another anti-cancer nutrient.

Folic Acid

The leafy greens—kale, spinach, and romaine lettuce—are loaded with a number of cancer-crushing nutrients. One in particular, folic acid—or folate—appears to help protect cells from cancer-inducing genetic damage caused by certain chemicals.

Folate deficiency can induce damage to the genetic material in a cell. This by itself can lead to cancer, making the cell even more vulnerable to cancer-causing chemicals. A folate deficiency also makes it harder for a cell to repair its genetic material, which also sets the stage for cancer.

In one study, researchers at the University of Alabama found that smokers treated with ten milligrams (10,000 micrograms) of folic acid and 500 micrograms of vitamin B12 each day had significantly fewer precancerous cells than an untreated group. (Vitamin B12 was added because smokers tend to be deficient in B12 and because folic acid needs B12 to be active.)

At Harvard Medical School researchers found that men consuming 847 micrograms and women getting 711 micrograms of folic acid daily had one-third less risk of precancerous colon polyps compared with men getting 241 micrograms and women getting 166 micrograms a day.

The amount of folic acid given in the University of Alabama study of smokers—10,000 micrograms—is far above the Daily Value of folic acid, which is 400 micrograms. To get that amount in your diet you'd have to fill up on dark green, leafy vegetables, oranges, beans, rice and brewer's yeast. (Some doctors believe people should be getting at least 400 to 800 micrograms of folic acid along with 1,000 micrograms of vitamin B12, every day to prevent cancer.)

Vitamin B12 is found in seafood and green, leafy vegetables. Obviously, supplements would probably be necessary to get this amount of folic acid and B12.

Because methotrexate, an early anti-cancer drug, worked by interfering with folate metabolism, there has been concern among cancer specialists that folic acid could fuel cancer growth. Not to worry. In animal studies, folic acid did not increase cancer growth. Rather, a folate deficiency increases the likelihood that a cancer will spread to other parts of the body. To this end, doctors at the Cancer Treatment Centers of America include 400 micrograms of folic acid in their treatment regimens.

You should be aware that high doses of folic acid can mask symptoms of pernicious anemia which is caused by vitamin B12 deficiency. So check with your doctor before you take more than the recommended daily value of folic acid.

BULK UP ON BETA-CAROTENE

When broken into individual nutrients, several components in fruits and vegetables appear particularly protective against cancer. One is beta-carotene, the yellow pigment found in a variety of fruits and vegetables. A recent study found that during the year prior to being diagnosed with cancer, men who got less than 1.7 milligrams (about 2,800 international units) of beta-carotene a day—the amount in about one inch of carrot—were twice as likely to develop the disease as those who got more than 2.7 milligrams (about 4,400 international units) per day.

In other cases, beta-carotene has slowed the progression of precancerous lesions and has even helped to reverse precancerous cell changes, possibly by promoting the cell's repair of genetic material.

An increasing number of nutritionally oriented doctors are recommending supplements of beta-carotene to help prevent cancer, usually 10,000 to 25,000 international units daily. Unfortunately, many people don't eat enough vegetables each day to consume even this relatively small amount. NOTE: One 7-1/2 inch carrot contains about 20,000 international units.) Of course you could use beta-carotene supplements. But even doctors who recommend them urge you to load up on orange, yellow and dark green, leafy vegetables which, besides carrots, include spinach, kale, sweet potatoes, winter squash and cantaloupe. Having even a single serving of any of these foods every day puts you ahead of the national average.

But beta-carotene is just one of the disease-fighting compounds known as carotenoids which are plentiful in fruits and vegetables and are potent antioxidants. They help thwart the harmful ways of those pesky free radicals as do vitamins C and E. In the body, some of the beta-carotene we eat is converted to vitamin A, an important regulator of cell growth.

But beta-carotene is not without controversy. One study conducted in Finland found it actually INCREASES the risk of cancer in some people. Longtime heavy smokers who took beta-carotene supplements of 20 milligrams (about 33,000 international units) a day were more, not less, likely to die from lung cancer. Although some doctors believe that this finding is purely chance, others think it warrants careful consideration.

Certainly, this study supports the argument that vitamin supplements alone cannot undo the damage wrought by years of bad habits or act as a substitute for eating well.

While beta-carotene has received most of the attention, evidence suggests that other components in vegetables may prove just as powerful in licking cancer. One of them, lutein, is found in broccoli, green peas, celery, kale and spinach.

There's also evidence that watercress may fight cancer. In one study, a compound in watercress called PEITC appeared to prevent lung cancer in experimental animals exposed to cigarette smoke.

There are dozens of other natural substances scientists are just beginning to uncover, like lycopene from tomatoes and ellagic acid from strawberries, that can soothe your prostate.

TOMATOES AND LYCOPENE: NATURE'S PROSTATE HEALER

The nutrient that gives the tomato its redness may also reduce, by up to 45 percent, a man's risk of developing prostate cancer. That's right—45 percent. The tomato's miracle nutrient is called lycopene, and it belongs to the carotenoid family of natural pigments we've already mentioned that are found in plants and animals.

In a recently completed six-year study at the Harvard School of Public Health on the dietary habits of 47,000 men, men who eat at least 10 servings a week of tomato-based foods are up to 45 percent less likely to develop prostate cancer. According to the study, tomato-based products and strawberries are the only foods of 46 fruits and vegetables they checked that seemed to have a protective effect.

Researchers also discovered that men of southern European descent, from regions where tomato-based foods are consumed more frequently (as part of the well-publicized Mediterranean diet), have a lower incidence of prostate cancer than American men who, typically, eat fewer tomato-based items. Even a pre-existing family history of prostate cancer did not change lycopene's protective effect, researchers report.

Of the 46 foods, tomato sauce, tomatoes, pizza, and strawberries were associated with a reduced risk of prostate cancer. The researchers learned that the first three of these foods were the primary dietary sources of lycopene, accounting for 82 percent of the lycopene intake for the men. (While strawberries were associated with a reduced prostate cancer risk, they are not a significant source of lycopene.)

"We found that more was better," said Dr. Edward Giovannucci, a researcher at the Harvard School of Public Health. Spaghetti sauce was the most common tomato-based food eaten by the men in the study group.

Your Best Sources Of Lycopene

Now, before you get grossed out, visualizing seeds and juice oozing down your chin as you bite into a Big Boy, the benefits of tomatoes can come from several forms of the food:

Tomato sauce

Tomato juice

Pizza (watch the fatty cheese, though)

Salsa (warning: spicy foods aggravate prostatitis)

Other good sources of lycopene include:

Ruby red grapefruit (and its juice)

Sweet red peppers

How Lycopene Protects Your Prostate

It's important to know that lycopene is the predominant carotenoid found in the blood, not only in the prostate, but in various tissues such as your liver, kidney, adrenal glands, and testes. Research suggests that lycopene is an essential part of the body's natural defense against harmful oxidizing agents such as free radicals. As such, it is now being touted as a highly capable antioxidant.

As the name implies, an antioxidant protects the body from the harmful effects of oxygen by intercepting free radicals before they can do any damage. (Free radicals are now considered to be one of the main causes of disease and aging. In a process known as oxidation, they accelerate the breakdown of our cells' structure, thereby damaging the DNA and weakening our immune systems.)

Damage to the body from oxidation has been associated with signs of aging and with degenerative diseases such as arthritis, heart disease and cancer.

Common antioxidants include vitamins C and E, selenium and beta carotene. They absorb or neutralize free radicals, eliminating damaging chemical reactions in your body. Presumably, lycopene, if present in adequate amounts, can help protect the body against free radical damage because studies show it to have roughly twice the power of beta-carotene and 10 times the strength of vitamin E.

One of the surprising recent discoveries is that processed rather than fresh tomatoes produce a greater protective effect. Lycopene from tomato juice is not easily absorbed, but when it's cooked with oil (as in making a sauce), this substantially increases intestinal absorption of its nutrients.

In other words, cooked tomato sauce is a more efficient way of delivering lycopene to the body than raw tomato juice, according to this study. Researchers declared that, based on a mini-study of blood samples and dietary patterns of 121 men, those who consumed the most tomato sauce were the most likely to have high blood levels of lycopene. Consuming tomato sauce cooked with oil raised the blood level of lycopene by a factor of 2 to 3 times, as measured 24 hours after consumption; in comparison, uncooked tomato juice produced no measurable increase.

Since tomatoes have emerged as a natural prostate protector, it's not surprising food scientists would seek a more lycopene-rich strain. They have. Scientists working for Lyco-Red Natural Products Industries in Israel used traditional cross-breeding methods to produce a tomato with up to four times more lycopene than normally found in tomatoes.

From these hybridized, organically grown tomatoes, they've produced an extract called Lyc-O-Mato. (It takes two metric tons of the lycopene-enriched tomatoes to produce one gram of the lycopene extract). Lyc-O-Mato is mixed with tomato oil, beta carotene, and vitamin E for better absorption and additional antioxidant benefits. The Lyc-O-Mato extract is already being used in over a dozen nutritional supplements.

Remember the strawberries in the Harvard study? How they didn't contain lycopene, but were the only other food associated with a low prostate cancer risk?

Well. if you like them, go ahead and enjoy. One serving (0.5 cup) of strawberries was associated with a significantly decreased risk of prostate cancer.

NATURE'S MIRACLE PROSTATE FOOD

There's been a great deal of cancer research focusing on foods common in Asia, where cancer rates are much lower than in Western countries like the

United States. One major difference between traditional Asian and American diets is the consumption of soy-based foods. Scientists believe the proteins found in soy slow the growth of tumors and may prevent recurrence. This may be because soy contains several naturally-occurring compounds, including phytochemicals—like isoflavones, protease inhibitors and saponins—which many believe (including researchers at the American Institute for Cancer Research) can protect us against the development of cancer. For instance, studies suggest that isoflavones may inhibit enzymes necessary for the growth and spread of many types of cancer.

Some other good news. Researchers also believe soy can slow down BPH.

Populations in Asia consume soybean protein in various traditional foods, including miso, tofu, tempeh and soy milk and cheese. The nine-fold decrease in prostate cancer mortality in Japanese men compared with those in the United States has been attributed, in part, to the high soy protein content of the Japanese diet. Likewise, in Taiwan, where prostate cancer rates are also low, the average consumption of soy protein is 35 grams-per-day per capita.

Animal and human cell studies have shown that soybeans contain several chemicals with proven anti-cancer activity. Specifically, the beneficial effects of soy have been attributed to genistein and daidzein, which are isoflavones. Isoflavones are known to inhibit the growth of prostatic cancer. Genistein, according to researchers at the University of Alabama in Birmingham, may be effective because it detoxifies the male hormones that promote prostate cancer growth and prostate growth in general (namely DHT).

Without getting into scientific gobbledegook, suffice it to say that there are compounds in soy that reduce the risk of cancer and prostate enlargement.

Why Tofu Is Important

Half a cup of this mild-tasting, cheese-like product (when it's been prepared with calcium sulfate) delivers nearly twice as much calcium (183 mg) as an equal amount of regular cottage cheese or as much as 1 oz. of part-skim mozzarella cheese. It serves up as much iron (1.6 mg) as a 3-oz. serving of roasted eye of round and twice as much protein as a hot dog. Plus, it yields a healthy boost of isoflavones (35 mg), those likely foes of prostate cancer. Best of all, 1/2 cup has just 106 calories.

(P.S. Check labels for calcium amounts; even products made with calcium sulfate have varying levels.)

How to Select and Store Tofu

Tofu is sold in four textures:

- Soft and silken both have a custard like texture, and they're a natural in dips, dressings, custard, cheesecake, and pudding. Soft tofu is easier to blend with other ingredients like stuffings for pasta, and silken tofu is creamy enough to be used in place of sour cream.

- Firm, with its medium-dense texture, holds its shape admirably when cut up for salads, casseroles, soup, and for barbecues.

- Extra-firm is just that—really firm. Use this style for stir-frying or crumbling, or just slice it for a sandwich in place of cheese.

You can use tofu straight from the box or package. No cooking is necessary. An unopened, aseptic box of tofu has a shelf-life of up to 10 months. Once opened, you need to refrigerate it and use within 2 days. Fresh tofu, packaged as cakes floating in water, should be refrigerated and water changed daily. You heard right. You need to change the water.

Other advice: Be sure to adhere to sell-by dates when purchasing. Don't buy a bloated container. Toss out tofu with a strong odor.

How to Enjoy Tofu

Now before you gag thinking you have to substitute a bland tofu burger for the greasy kinds you crave, maybe it's better if you don't think of it as a substitute, but as a unique eating experience.

The blandness of tofu is actually its strength—it has no conflicting taste. You can doctor it to taste nearly any way you want. Tofu has a memory like a super computer, soaking up and remembering all it comes in contact with. It can be cut into chunks and added to soups, stews, chili, marinara sauce.

Don't buy it? C'mon, be a man. Chances are you haven't given tofu a chance. Even though the Appendix is chock-full of prostate-friendly recipes, it might be a good idea for you to try these simple recipes right now.

So go ahead. I'll wait right here while you pull together the ingredients.

Tofu Burgers (Or call it something else if you like):
Combine and mash one pound extra-firm tofu with

> 1/2 cup cooked rice
> 1/2 cup dry bread crumbs
> 1/4 cup scallions
> 1 tbsp. chicken-flavor seasoning
> 1/4 cup grated carrots
> 1/4 cup grated low-fat Cheddar cheese
> 1 tbsp. low-sodium soy sauce
>
> Sauté in a skillet till golden.

Try this power-packed drink. You can also drink tofu. Here's a quick and easy recipe:

Raspberry RasCal:
Blend

> 1/2 cup fresh red raspberries
> 1/2 cup nonfat yogurt
> 1/2 cup soft or silken tofu
> 1/2 cup skim milk
> dash of vanilla extract
>
> Sweeten with honey to taste.

Not quite adventuresome just yet? You'd rather wait till later? No problem.

THE EASIEST WAYS TO BENEFIT FROM SOY

O.K., you're just not a tofu kind of guy. Well, there's good news. There are many other ways to benefit from soy beans.

In fact one of the good things about soybeans is that they are available in so many completely different forms and textures. They can be purchased fresh in the pods as edamame, sweet beans, at Asian and natural grocery stores in the summer, or they can be totally processed as soy milk. You should be able to find all these products in larger grocery stores, as well as in health or natural food stores.

Here's a bit more about soy:

Dried raw soybeans can be cooked in the same way as other dried beans and used in stews, soups and casseroles or mashed and added to meat loaf.

Miso is a salty condiment used in Japanese cooking to flavor soups, sauces, dressings, marinades and patés. Miso is made from soybeans and grains such as rice or barley, plus salt and a mold culture that have been processed into a smooth paste and aged in cedar vats for one to three years. Refrigerated, miso will keep for a long time and is handy when you want to make an "impromptu" soup.

Soy flour is ground from roasted soybeans and comes in two varieties. Natural or full-fat soy flour contains the natural oils from the soybean; the defatted variety has the oils removed during processing. Either can be added to bread and other baked goods or soups or used to make gravies and sauces. Defatted soy flour is the higher concentrated source of soy protein and both types should be stored in the refrigerator or freezer.

Soy milk, the liquid squeezed from soybeans that have been soaked and pureed, is available as regular, low-fat, non-fat and flavored. Low fat soy milk is one of the best sources of soy protein. Eight ounces of low fat soy milk contains three to four grams of soy protein, and two to three grams of fat.

Although you can buy non-fat soy milk, this is one case in which fat is not necessarily to be avoided. When soybeans are defatted, they lose some of their beneficial properties.

Luckily, soy milk is becoming easier to find in supermarkets around the country. Most come in plain and vanilla flavors. Westbrae®, Natural brand®, West Soy®, SoyUm®, Edensoy® and Vitasoy® are some of the top producers. Available brands will vary depending on where you live. Several companies produce soy milk with added soy protein and other nutrients, but they also contain additional calories and fat.

To develop a taste for soy milk, you may want to start out using it in cereal or oatmeal or in recipes calling for milk. Once you're used to the difference you can easily drink more.

Soy cheese and soy yogurt can be made from soy milk and substituted for sour cream or cream cheese in recipes.

Soy nuts are whole soybeans that have been soaked in water and roasted until brown. They come in a variety of flavors (even chocolate-covered), are high in protein, and taste something like peanuts.

Soy oil is composed of about 50 percent linoleic acid (LA) and 8 percent alphalinolenic acid (ALA), the essential ingredient in evening primrose, borage and black currant oils; it is used to make vitamin E supplements. The generic vegetable oil we buy in grocery stores is usually 100 percent soyoil and is high in polyunsaturated fat.

Soy Protein Powder mixes easily into any cold drink. Add soy powder to fruit juice every morning as an easy way to ingest your recommended daily intake of 45 grams. You can buy soy protein powder in most nutrition stores and whole food markets under the trade name "SuperPro®." This product contains Spirulina and other herbal products as well as soy protein. The soy protein contained in this powder is Supro 95, a product made by Protein Technologies, a subsidiary of Ralston-Purina®.

The same company also markets a powder called HP-20 that makes a flavored drink, and AB-20 that can be used as an additive in cooking. Two scoops of these taken twice daily will provide 40 grams of soy protein and 40 milligrams of isoflavones rich in genistein. An additional two-scoop serving can be used to bring the total to 60 grams of soy protein and 60 mg of isoflavones.

Soy sprouts are similar to mung bean sprouts and can be used in salads and sandwiches, but be aware that it takes five to ten days for soybeans to sprout.

Soy Sauces (Shoyu, Teriyaki, Tamari) are made from soybeans that have been fermented in various combinations with other grains.

Shoyu is a blend of soybeans and wheat.

Tamari is a byproduct of miso manufacture.

Textured Soy Protein (TSP or TVP) is made from defatted soy flour which is compressed and dehydrated into a ground meat-type product rich in protein and fiber, and low in fat and sodium. TSP is usually found with boxed dinner foods like macaroni and cheese. Just pour boiling water over the granules as instructed on the label, let sit five minutes and it's ready to use. Once rehydrated, you can add TSP to chili, spaghetti sauce, Sloppy Joes or to anything else in which you might use ground meat. Usually TSP-based products are labeled "meatless," "vegetable burger" or "chili mix."

Tempeh (TEM pay) is a chunky form of cooked soybeans formed into tender cakes and usually mixed with rice or millet and fermented. With its nutty or smoky flavor, tempeh is an excellent meat substitute when marinated and grilled and/or added to stir-fries, soups, casseroles, chili or spaghetti.

The amount of isoflavones in soy products varies depending on the type of soy protein used. Tofu, tempeh and soy milk are high in isoflavones. Isoflavone content in foods made from soy proteins—like soy burgers, hot dogs or sausage—depends on the way they are produced. Some are processed so that most of the isoflavones are removed, but there is no way of knowing this from the label.

Until research confirms the beneficial effects of isoflavones and producers make this information readily available, simply choose a variety of the soy foods you like without worrying about maximizing isoflavone content.

To Reap the Benefits of Soy Try These

In place of higher-fat peanut butter, spread soy nut butter on a sandwich.

Use soy milk in cooking or over cereal.

When baking, instead of using regular flour, substitute soy flour for as much as 25 percent of the total amount.

Try tofu and tempeh in stir-fries, soups and a variety of other dishes.

Still find tofu too exotic? Serve it with an old favorite: dice a block of firm tofu into half-inch squares, add to marinara sauce and pour over pasta.

It's easier to get some people used to soy when it's mixed into a dish—especially one where the soy product is crumbled and mixed into a sauce rather than standing alone, as with burgers.

If you're not ready to jump right into meatless spaghetti sauce or Sloppy Joes, start by using soy protein for only a quarter of the meat. The same goes for dishes like meat loaf.

When you make tacos or casseroles, try half meat and half soy protein. Rather than trying soy "sausage" on its own, you may be more comfortable mixing it into a soup or casserole.

Give TSP-based products a chance. Many people are adding soy into their diets through TSP-based meat substitutes like "hot dogs," "sausage," "bacon" and "ground beef."

Some people say these actually taste like beef, pork or chicken. Other soy products designed to replace meat taste and look nothing like it.

Frankly, I could never be a spokesman for the food companies making these "copycat" products. I've yet to eat any that even faintly taste like the meat products they're designed to replace. My mind expects one thing but my palate says another. (By the way, did you ever notice this is a one-way street? Have you ever seen ground beef shaped to resemble, say, a stalk of celery or a carrot stick? Just an observation.)

Soy products are unique and are quite tasty when prepared correctly. There's no need for them to mimic something else. Many of these foods are good in their own right, so give them a try.

With all these choices there's no reason why you can't easily benefit from the virtues of soy.

Does consuming soy products ward off cancer? Take the case of Michael Milken.

Soon after he had discovered at age 46 he had prostate cancer, Milken decided to have the gland removed. However, during a follow-up biopsy, his doctor discovered his cancer had metastasized and had spread to his lymph nodes. His doctor told him his scheduled prostatectomy—removal of the gland—would serve no purpose. It was too late. Once he got over his shock, Milken embarked on a personal crusade and started his CaP CURE foundation.

Personally, Milken has made major changes in his diet to fight off his cancer. In fact, everything served at his Santa Monica, California office is nonfat and vegetarian. Milken especially favors eating plenty of tofu after he learned soy reduced tumors in laboratory animals.

A typical Milken lunch consists of mushroom barley soup, a tofu mock egg salad sandwich made with tofu, carrots and lettuce, and a black bean and corn salad. He washes it down with a soy-based drink. Another Milken favorite is an Egg

McNothing—a fat-free crumpet, with soy cheese, vegetarian Canadian bacon and scrambled egg whites. At last report, Milken's cancer is at bay.

FEAST ON PHYTOCHEMICALS

You don't have to memorize a long list of phytochemicals to add more to your diet. These cancer-fighting substances are plentiful in foods, other than soy, that you already know are healthy—fruits, vegetables and grain products as well as herbs and spices like parsley, chives, garlic and ginger. Here are a few tips to get more phytochemicals into your diet without radically changing the way you eat.

Whoever mixed the first batch of blueberry pancakes may not have known they were fighting cancer but they were.

If you make your own cabbage-and-carrot coleslaw, or even if you buy it from the store, try adding shredded green, red or yellow peppers, radishes, onions or even the broccoli stems you might normally throw away.

Here are three snacks you may not have thought of:

1. Strawberries sprinkled with balsamic vinegar
2. Raspberry-yogurt pops
3. Chicken topped with blackberries and peach slices

If someone in your home likes to bake muffins (maybe you do), how about adding in a cup of grated carrots, apples or zucchini into the batter? By the same token, you could add corn kernels or finely chopped sweet or hot peppers to cornbread.

Power charge your pizza with novel combinations: artichokes, asparagus and onions; sliced yellow tomatoes with a little pesto; or spinach and slivered garlic with a bit of crumbled feta cheese.

Look in the supermarket for jars of chopped garlic, ginger and basil. You're more likely to add them to whatever you're cooking if you don't have to chop and peel.

Jazz up a Waldorf salad by using chopped fennel and dried fruit bits along with the apples and celery. Top it off with low fat raspberry dressing.

Get in the habit of keeping frozen vegetables in the house. You can throw together an instant meal by adding rice, pasta, couscous or other favorite grains.

Using fresh lemons, limes or oranges in a recipe? Don't toss out the peels without first grating a few slivers and throwing them into the dish for extra flavor—and phytochemicals.

DODGE CANCER BY BULKING UP ON FIBER

There's a common misconception that food fiber is a waste byproduct, and if it's processed out it's no big deal. Wrong!

Processing food such as wheat and rice often removes much of the natural fiber that has important health effects. Fiber binds to cholesterol and other unnecessary substances to remove them from the body before they can contribute to cancer and heart disease.

In the bowel, fiber bulks up the stool, increases acidity and reduces the concentration of potential cancer-causing bad guys. It also helps prevent constipation.

It's a fact: When fiber intake goes up, colon cancer rates go down. A high-fiber diet also seems to fight hormone-related cancers such as prostate cancer.

And there's another advantage. Fiber is filling and low in calories.

Not surprisingly, fruits, vegetables and cereals are high in fiber. There are commercially available fiber bars as well as psyllium seed products and bran wafers.

It's important for you to drink plenty of water when on a high fiber diet and to supplement your diet with calcium, zinc and iron. Substances called phytates in the fiber will bind with these elements and possibly create a deficiency unless supplements are taken. So be aware that besides some of the bad stuff fiber chases out of your system, it also drags along some good things, too.

Most Americans eat about 12 grams of fiber a day; experts suggest increasing that amount to 20 to 35 grams. You'll be well on your way if you eat a bowl of high-fiber cereal, a serving of beans, three slices of whole-grain bread, four servings of fresh vegetables and two pieces of fruit a day.

DRINK THIS AND REDUCE ALL
YOUR PROSTATE WORRIES

Tea has been a popular beverage for centuries in countries like China, Japan, India and England. In fact, tea consumption in the world ranks second only to water consumption.

Today, the United States is experiencing a surge in tea drinking. But its unique flavor is not the only reason for this increase.

For years, tea has been touted as a cure-all for many ailments. Recent research has confirmed that tea does indeed have many health benefits and may help fight prostate cancer.

The three basic tea types come from the evergreen shrub, *Camellia sinensis*. Black, green and oolong teas are produced from the tea plant by varying the processing conditions.

Black tea is produced by fermenting the leaves, while green tea leaves are not fermented. Oolong teas go through a shorter fermentation period than black teas and are regarded as semi-fermented. All three kinds go through a heating process to halt fermentation.

Although most people drink black tea (made from fermented leaves), about a quarter of all tea drunk is green (unfermented). All teas from *Camellia sinensis* contain compounds known as polyphenols—a class of bioflavonoids—which are found in all plants. Besides tea, these compounds are especially high in coffee, red grapes, kidney beans, raisins, prunes and red wine.

Polyphenols have anticarcinogenic, antioxidant, antibacterial and antiviral properties. Researchers found that the phenol epigallocatechin-3-gallate (EGCG) reduced rates of prostate cancers, as well as skin, lung and stomach cancers in mice exposed to carcinogens. In particular, researchers at the Case Western Reserve University School of Medicine reported that an ingredient in the polyphenols in green tea kills cancer cells while sparing healthy cells.

The researchers tested EGCG on cancerous human and mouse cells of the skin, lymph system and prostate, and on normal human skin cells. EGCG programmed cell death in cancer cells while leaving healthy cells unharmed. A summary of this study can be found in the *Journal of the National Cancer Institute*, December 17, 1997.

"It is likely that this compound conveys a message to cancer cells through a highly ordered and well-regulated signal transduction pathway . . ." says Hasan Mukhtar, the head researcher. "The chemical messenger tells the cells 'You must commit suicide (programmed cell death) or I am going to kill you.' The cells then decide that instead of being murdered, they will commit suicide."

Mukhtar believes study of green tea will lead to fuller understanding of the process of apoptosis. Researchers will try to understand green tea's protective effects at the molecular level. They will try to find out how it interferes with cancer development, said Mukhtar. The investigators expect to run clinical trials to see if green tea can indeed prevent cancer in humans.

No one is saying yet that drinking green tea cures prostate cancer. In fact, in tests researchers have used a strong concentration—about a hundred times what the Lipton company estimates is in one cup of tea. More lab work plus clinical studies on humans are needed to see if extracts of green tea can be effective as drugs for cancer prevention and to stop prostate and other tumors from growing.

"If you ask me if tea prevents cancer, I would say yes in animal models; no conclusions in humans." says Chung S. Yang, Ph.D., a researcher at Rutgers University, in New Jersey.

If it in fact does, you would need to slurp 3 to 10 cups a day to maximize your protection from common forms of cancer. I would guess after a few days you'd either be sick of tea, or you'll be running to the bathroom in the middle of the night—one of the things we're trying to avoid, right?

Suffice it to say, then, that drinking tea will help you. Even a minimal amount will provide some benefit. Still, much more research is needed in this area before making any whole-hearted recommendations for prostate cancer prevention.

With all the publicity about how tea can help your prostate, there are tea products appearing on the market fortified with prostate-healing ingredients. Celestial Seasons sells one.

As I'm sitting here, I'm examining a colorful box from Alvita called "Prosti-Brew," a green tea fortified with saw palmetto, pygeum, Korean ginseng, pumpkin seeds, soy extract and other ingredients. Nowhere on the package does it say how much of each ingredient is present. No doubt it contains everything it says, but how much? Be careful. You may be paying a premium for these "special blends" without getting a comparative benefit.

Can you hurt yourself drinking too much tea? Only if it's scalding hot and you burn yourself.

GOBBLE GARLIC

Garlic, (which in scientific jargon is officially named *allium sativum*) is probably the world's most popular herb, if we include its culinary uses along with its health-promoting benefits. This versatile herb is a common ingredient in soups and stews, and a key ingredient in Greek and Italian dishes like pesto. But for ages it has proven to be much more than just a seasoning since it contains more than 100 useful chemicals.

Garlic tablets and capsules are one of the top three drug products in Germany, outselling nearly all other medicines. They are taken daily by millions of Europeans and increasingly by Americans. As a food, drug or dietary supplement, garlic has proven health benefits with new discoveries each year. Hundreds of studies attest to the cardiovascular, antimicrobial, anticarcinogenic and immune-boosting effects of this medicinal plant.

For thousands of years, the "stinking rose," as garlic is sometimes called, has been praised for its ability to treat wounds, infections, tumors and intestinal parasites. There are even Sanskrit records dating back five thousand years citing its therapeutic use, and Greek physician Hippocrates documented numerous uses for it. In "modern times," the therapeutic roles of garlic have been described in more than 1,000 scientific studies.

The leaves on a garlic plant are long, narrow and flat like grass. The bulb—the only part eaten—consists of numerous cloves, encased in a whitish sac. Documents and stories boast of garlic's age-old usefulness as an antibacterial, antifungal and antiviral agent, used to treat everything from dandruff to diphtheria, fevers and swelling. But garlic also appears to be a potent anticarcinogen. Somehow—researchers aren't exactly sure why—it interferes with chemical reactions involved in the earliest stages of tumor promotion, stimulates immunity, and has direct effects against tumor cells.

Benjamin Lau, M.D., Ph.D., a researcher at the Loma Linda University School of Medicine, reported in *Molecular Biotherapy* in June 1997 that garlic "... is one of the most ancient of plants reputed to have an anti-cancer effect."

Dr. Lau identified three ways garlic protects against cancer: by directly inhibiting tumor cell metabolism, by preventing the development and reproduction of cancer cells, and by boosting a person's immune system—especially in the liver—to more efficiently fight cancer cells.

The National Cancer Institute has reported a 40 percent decline in stomach cancer in those who included garlic, onions and related plants in their diets. The more they used, the lower the risk of stomach cancer.

But Garlic? Yuck! you're thinking. Whole, the bulbs bear little odor. However, upon grinding or chopping, the enzyme allinase is released, activating the conversion of garlic's sulfur-containing amino acid alliin to the strong-smelling allicin. It's uncertain which of this hearty herb's array of naturally occurring chemicals are responsible for garlic's diverse medicinal effects, but allicin is believed responsible for the strongest impact on health.

Allicin also increases the levels of two naturally occurring antioxidant blood enzymes, catalase and glutathione peroxidase. These antioxidant enzymes form our front line of defense against damaging free radicals such as those found in cigarette smoke, car exhaust and other pollutants.

Garlic also contains detectable amounts of germanium and selenium, believed to play a role in garlic's antitumor effects.

Studies from around the world prove a relationship exists between cancer rates and garlic consumption: in areas where consumption of garlic, and onions for that matter, is high, cancer rates are generally lower. Likewise, in animals garlic extracts and allicin preparations have shown antitumor activity. In humans, garlic has been shown to inhibit the formation of cancer-causing nitrosamines, which are formed during digestion from the food preservatives nitrites and nitrates.

Besides cancer prevention, there are numerous other health benefits you can achieve from garlic. It is also believed to inhibit "blood platelet aggregation," (making the blood less sticky,) thereby reducing risk of blood clots and plaque formation in blood vessels. It has also been shown to reduce blood cholesterol levels, reduces the risk of atherosclerosis, and can reduce blood pressure.

Garlic has been recognized for centuries as an antiseptic and antibacterial agent. It's been proven to be an anti-inflammatory agent, a diuretic, an expectorant, an anti-nausea and digestive aid, and has been used to treat colic, indigestion and flatulence. New reports show that garlic may even exhibit an antioxidant effect on the brain, protecting neurons from oxidant destruction and guarding against senility.

Great! Sounds good, right? I know what you're thinking. "But it still makes your breath stink."

Even if you are turned off by garlic's distinct aroma there are many deodorized garlic products available on the market. While fresh garlic remains a shopper's bargain, garlic supplements contain most of the same beneficial chemical compounds, without the stink.

Besides garlic, onions, leeks, shallots and chives are members of the allium vegetable family—and contain the organo-sulfur compounds that reduce cancer risks.

PEEL AWAY PROSTATE FEARS

Lemon and orange oils contain limonene and geraniol, which have been shown to inhibit tumor growth. This ability is also found in cantaloupes, persimmons, strawberries and other yellow and orange fruits.

The oils are contained in the peels, not the pulp of the fruit. Ongoing research is examining filtered juices made to include the rinds.

The pulp does have pectin, and modified citrus pectin has been shown in one study to inhibit the spread of prostate tumors in mice. However, much more work is needed in humans before this is proven. When scientists measured total free-radical zapping power from the combined antioxidants in each of 12 common fruits, they found that, ounce for ounce, strawberries contain the most C and E vitamins, carotenoids (like beta-carotene), flavonoids and a slew of other compounds (*Journal of Agriculture and Food Chemistry*, March, 1996).

Remember, The National Cancer Institute recommends eating 5 servings of fruits and vegetables a day (ideally 2 fruits, 3 veggies). That sounds harder than it is. Have a banana on your cereal and an orange in the morning, and you've finished your fruits. (A serving is generally 1/2 cup of raw, cubed fruit, 1 medium-sized whole fruit or 2 tablespoons of dried fruit.)

OTHER HELPFUL FOODS

Add Spice to Your Life? Maybe, Maybe Not.

Do you like spicy foods? Do you want the good news first or the bad news? Let's start with the good news.

There are some ingredients in spices that, besides adding zip to your eating, may help you avoid prostate cancer, too. No doubt, the native foods and seasonings used in ethnic cooking give each cuisine its unique qualities. Could some of these ingredients also affect cancer risk in distinctive ways as well? The American Institute for Cancer Research has funded several research projects that examine eating patterns popular in other countries, studies which may provide important information for healthier American diets as well.

Turmeric, called "herbal aspirin" and "herbal cortisone" in some corners of the world, is used as medicine for stomach, liver and blood ailments. Turmeric has three phytochemical compounds called curcuminoids that give it a bright yellow-orange color.

Researchers believe curcuminoids—especially curcumin—protect the body from the degenerative processes which can lead to cancer. They discourage cancer by neutralizing free radicals and preventing the formation of new ones. Curcuminoids may also fight cancer by acting as a blocking agent, a substance that prevents toxic compounds from reaching or reacting with body tissues.

According to Dr. Porn-ngrm Limtrakul of Chiang Mai University in Thailand, Thai people have traditionally used curcumin to prevent and relieve rashes, itching, chafing and mosquito bites by applying it directly to the skin area. She also has noted a very low rate of skin cancer throughout the country. Besides skin cancer, and realizing that this chemical is a known antioxidant and has already been credited with lowering rates of colon cancer, Dr. Limtrakul decided to investigate additional cancer-protective roles for curcumin.

Although her study is in its early stages, Dr. Limtrakul hopes it will help confirm curcumin as a useful element against cancer. "Because of its possible use in everyday life as a spice and coloring agent in curry, mustard and other foods, eating curcumin could be encouraged to help offset agents thought to initiate or promote cancer in humans," she says.

Now the bad news, at least potentially bad news. It has been long believed that capsaicin, the compound in chili peppers that gives it its heat, might also have anti-cancer properties. One researcher believes otherwise.

At the Mexican Institute of Public Health in Mexico City, Dr. Lizbeth Lopez-Carrillo is investigating the chili pepper, a staple of Mexican food. Results from laboratory studies, however, indicate that capsaicin consumption may be linked to stomach cancer. Dr. Lopez-Carrillo's own research has found that stomach cancer risk is five times higher among people who eat large quantities of chili peppers than among those who don't.

Dr. Lopez-Carrillo is now conducting a second human study in three different areas of Mexico. It involves 300 stomach cancer patients and 600 other hospital patients who have no stomach illnesses. In addition to looking at chili pepper consumption, she will also test participants for a non-dietary risk factor—a bacterial infection common in Mexico that has also been associated with higher rates of stomach cancer.

While many Americans don't eat a fraction of the amount Mexicans do, Dr. Lopez-Carrillo notes that chili pepper consumption in the United States is rising. This may become a concern if her studies do uncover a strong link between capsaicin and stomach cancer.

Here's another warning. If you suffer from BPH or Prostatitis, spicy foods can aggravate your condition.

Get a Leg Up With Legumes

Legumes mean beans and peas, whether kidney beans in chili, chickpeas on your salad, or split pea soup. When you cut back on red meat, legumes provide a good source of plant protein and add fiber to the diet, which may decrease the risk of many kinds of cancer.

There are several beans to choose from: black-eyed peas, black beans, and so on. Be careful, though. Sometimes manufacturers add stuff to their products that you don't want, like fatty pork and thick syrup to enhance the taste. Your best bet is to get in the habit of checking the labels.

STARCHY STAPLE FOODS   Outside the United States, "minimally processed starchy staple foods" might mean a starchy tuber like cassava or a grain like millet. In the US, it usually means whole grains, such as whole wheat, or brown rice, instead of their white counterparts which lose fiber and valuable nutrients during processing.

You can also benefit from oatmeal or some of the more exotic grains available, like kasha, quinoa or amaranth. Shudder at the word exotic? Okay. You can gain just as much benefit by eating a baked potato or sweet potato including their skins.

THE BROCCOLI GANG   Broccoli and other cruciferous vegetables such as brussels sprouts, cabbage, kale and cauliflower contain sulfurophane, which increases the activity of enzymes that inactivate cancer-causing chemicals. These vegetables also contain 3-indole carbinol, which affects estrogen metabolism, and isothiocyanates, which interfere with cancer cell growth.

Since most research with this substance has been related to breast cancer and colon cancer, there is no specific evidence of its importance for prostate cancer. Nonetheless, these dark green vegetables contain many other antioxidants and phytochemicals. Therefore, they should also be included in any general dietary program for cancer prevention. Supplements made with dried broccoli and other vegetables have not been demonstrated to have the same effect as the whole vegetables.

As we said before, eating five servings or more per day of fruits and vegetables is thought to be beneficial in the prevention of many forms of cancer, including prostate cancer. As a result, the National Cancer Institute has developed a national program to encourage increased intake of fruits and vegetables because they provide dietary fiber and micronutrients which are substances found in small amounts that have nutritional effects. Among their functions is the ability to act as an antioxidant. The process of oxidation occurs when substances in living things are exposed to oxygen, ultraviolet light or heat.

Here's a simple example of oxidation: the browning of an apple when you slice it and expose it to air. This occurs in a short period because the inside of the apple does not contain adequate amounts of antioxidants at its surface to stop the oxidation process. The red-colored coating of the apple stops this process by neutralizing the oxygen that hits the outside of the apple.

Even the inside can stop the process at some point. If you slice away the brown surface of the cut apple, you will find more white apple underneath. This process of antioxidant defense is highly developed in man and is thought to be involved both in the process of aging and in its associated disorders such as prostate cancer.

Our bodies have both water-soluble and fat-soluble antioxidant systems. A well-known example of the water-soluble system is vitamin C. We do not make vitamin C in our bodies and have to obtain it from the fruits and vegetables we eat. The diet of ancient man had ample amounts of vitamin C, but today many Americans eat too few fruits and vegetables to get an adequate supply.

An example of a fat-soluble antioxidant is vitamin E. It is found in small amounts in oils, where it works to stop them from becoming rancid. Stale oils have a rancid taste due to oxidation damage of the oil.

In our bodies cell membranes are made of lipids (another term for fats) and can be protected by vitamin E and other fat-soluble antioxidants. (You may recall other well-known antioxidants include beta-carotene and other carotenoids such as lycopene, the red pigment found in tomatoes.)

SENSIBLE TACTICS FOR CHANGING
YOUR DIET AND LIFESTYLE

Here are some easy, practical hints for eating less fat and fewer calories according to CaP CURE , the prostate cancer foundation started by Michael Milkin. Granted, there is not direct cause-and-effect evidence that a particular food increases your chances of contracting prostate cancer.

For example, eating red meat may indicate a particular dietary pattern that may include other poor habits such as eating fewer fruits, vegetables, cereals and grains. Still, the following foods don't help . . .

FOODS YOU SHOULD LIMIT OR AVOID

Eschew the Fat

Fat has two functions, It increases the taste of foods and it provides increased calories. Increased calorie intake is very important in societies where people work hard, have a high incidence of infectious diseases and poor sanitation, and a low standard of living. In developed countries such as the United States, however, we have eliminated nutritional deficiency diseases such as rickets, beriberi, etc., by food fortification. Therefore, fat intake is not essential. Unfortunately, the intake of fat increased significantly between 1910 and 1980 in the United States. The increase occurred in hidden fats in foods such as vegetable oils, margarine, butter, processed baked goods (cakes, donuts, etc.), red meat, snack foods (nuts, chips, etc.)

The taste-enhancing properties of fat guarantee that higher-fat foods will always compete more successfully for consumer acceptance than lower-fat foods. It's odd. Compared to most of the world, our society has so minimized malnutrition that we have gone the other way and created an epidemic of "overnutrition." Lets face it, we are a nation of snackers and speed freaks. We crave fast foods that are high in fat and engineered to provide good taste at the lowest possible cost. But a high-fat diet ups your odds for most kinds of cancer. Experts say that an optimum cancer-preventive diet should contain no more than 20 to 25 percent of calories from fat—about half of what most Americans eat.

By cutting your intake of foods with hidden fats, you will also cut your total calorie intake. This will provide the necessary energy deficit to allow you to supplement your diet with two servings of soy protein per day without gaining weight. If you simply add the soy protein to your diet without making any other changes, you are likely to gain weight.

Before implementing these recommendations, you should check with your doctor and be sure you have some excess body fat to work with. If you are malnourished due to advanced prostate cancer, then this diet must be changed to work well.

No doubt some of these changes will be hard since food is sold on the basis of taste, cost and convenience. Plus, many foods have unnecessary fat added simply to enhance the taste. The goal is to change your taste buds permanently so you never go back to eating the foods that are probably harming your health.

The Best Ways to Reduce Fat In Your Diet

If you stick mostly with fruits and vegetables, whole grains and beans, fish and shellfish, lean meats and low-fat or non-fat dairy products, fat in your diet will automatically be reduced. Experts used to suggest that you get no more than one-third of your daily fat allotment from each of these sources:

- Saturated fats
- Polyunsaturated fats
- Monounsaturated fats

Saturated fats, which are hard at room temperature, include animal fats—lard and butter, for example—and hydrogenated vegetable oils, the white stuff that comes in a can. (Lots of processed foods are made with hydrogenated vegetable oils; make sure you read your labels carefully.)

Polyunsaturated fats include most vegetable oils, such as corn, safflower, sunflower and soy. Monounsaturated fats include olive oil, canola oil and the fat found in avocados.

There is growing evidence, however, that monounsaturated oils can help prevent certain kinds of cancer. That is why some researchers are beginning to suggest that the one-third rule be changed. They recommend that you get no more than ONE-FOURTH of your daily fat allotment from saturated fats, another one-fourth from polyunsaturates and the remaining half from the healthy monounsaturates.

You can increase your use of monounsaturates by switching to olive oil or canola oil or by mixing them equally with polyunsaturated oils when you cook.

Limit Red Meat

The most important thing you can do to lower your dietary fat and calories—and guard your prostate—is to cut back on red meat. This includes veal, beef, pork and lamb.

In a recent study, individuals eating the highest amount of meat had a risk of developing prostate cancer 2.64 times that of those eating the lowest amount. In fact, several studies have demonstrated a positive association between saturated fat intake, from meat and dairy products consumption, and prostate cancers. For most types of red meat, even when you cut away the visible fat, there is still fat between the muscle fibers. A 9- to 14-ounce piece of prime rib served in most steak houses and restaurants can be more than 1200 calories and 50 grams of fat. These are over half the calories needed by an average man five-foot-ten-inches tall. When the USDA talks about a serving of meat, it is referring to a 3-ounce portion. Do you know how small 3 ounces is? A quarter-pounder at fast food restaurants is bigger.

Consider making red meat a rare part of your diet or consider even giving it up entirely. You may have been told you need red meat for its iron content, but it's better if you get the iron in a multivitamin.

Fish To Avoid

Among the food choices classified as seafood, you should consider giving up salmon, trout and catfish. These are high-fat, farm-fed fish that sit around all day in fish ponds eating fishmeal. They don't swim a lot or catch other fish. They just sit around and get fat. (Hmmm—sounds familiar). However, ocean-caught salmon are lower in fat but are available only in some stores for part of the year. Most of the salmon you can purchase in stores is farm-fed.

Nuts to Nuts

As said earlier, it's important to reduce the fat in your diet. To do this, begin by minimizing the intake of nuts of all kinds, including peanuts, macadamia nuts, peanut butter and pistachios. These are high in fat. It is true that they contain monounsaturated fatty acids but to cut fat calories, you have to eliminate the fat. I love nuts. My biggest problem is I find it impossible to get by with just a handful. I can usually inhale an entire jar or can. Rather than get started (and feel guilty afterwards), I don't buy them.

If you have more self control, go ahead and enjoy. But eat just a handful, and only on occasion.

Give the Slip to Oily Salad Dressings

Consider giving up salad dressings made with oil. Switch to wine vinegar, rice vinegar or balsamic vinegar which is quite tasty. You may also mix mustard and rice vinegar to make a Dijon-style dressing. Some vinegars now have various spices mixed into them to enhance their flavor. (There is even a raspberry wine vinegar.)

The key to using fat-free vinegar is to make the salad out of dark green leafy lettuce with plenty of taste while adding different ingredients such as red pepper, green pepper, alfalfa sprouts, cucumbers, etc. In so doing, you won't rely on the taste added by the salad dressing. Iceberg lettuce can be considered "Italian dressing-deficient" lettuce, because you have to douse it in dressing to get rid of its watery taste. It is also not a good source of micronutrients such as folate, which are found in great amounts in darker green lettuces.

Remember to exclude croutons and other toppings from your salad as they add extra calories. Be especially careful when visiting a salad bar. There are often things there that defeat the whole purpose of a salad, like bacon bits. Also, hold the mayo. Consider giving up mayonnaise, margarine and butter. Did you know that Ultra Fat-Free Promise Margarine is 100 percent fat? There are 5 calories per serving and 5 calories from fat. The U.S. Department of Agriculture says that if something has less than 1 gram of fat per serving (which is 9 calories), it can be called fat-free. This is the only place in mathematics that you can round down from 0.99 to 0.

You can substitute fruit jam for margarine in the morning and eat your bread warm so that it is moist. The taste is different, but remember, margarine, butter and mayonnaise are also an acquired taste.

Shake the Salt Habit

The only real benefit of salt is when you throw it over your shoulder for good luck. Health experts all say salt should be minimized in your diet. Yet some of us douse our food with it every day.

Foods high in salt are often high in nitrosamines which by them-selves cause cancer. Even smoked and pickled foods are loaded with salt. Foods like bacon, sausage and ham have a double whammy. Besides high salt content they're also high in fat.

Instead of salt use a salt substitute that is rich in potassium rather than sodium. Cosalt, light salt and other salt substitutes are widely avail-able in food stores. Make sure their labels indicate they contain potassium chloride. (Only patients with kidney disease need to be concerned about excessive potassium.)

Squeeze Out Cheese

You should give up or at least cut back on cheese (sorry, but that includes cheese pizza). Cheese is between 60 percent and 80 percent fat. There are fat-free cheeses, but they have the same problem as fat-free margarine. Besides, these are cheese foods, not cheese.

Desert Some Dessert

Consider minimizing or giving up on desserts and ice cream. Yogurt couldn't sell in this country until it was made to taste like ice cream. The fruit added to the bottom of nonfat yogurt has the equivalent of sixteen teaspoons of sugar that the body turns into fat. Sadly we've been taught that by eating nonfat yogurt we're doing a good thing; you know, if it's nonfat it must be better than the regular stuff. Not so. It's the so-called nonfat yogurt that you should avoid. Plain yogurt in a baked potato as a substitute for sour cream is fine.

Then there's our old friend ice cream. We reach for it both in cele-bration and when we need comfort. Again, it's usually loaded with sugar and of course, fat. (It's cream, right?)

You can eat ice milk or the low fat variety, but the taste won't be quite the same. Again, be careful. Often low fat or "lite" is more of a marketing term than what's truly inside the carton. Read the label to make sure. When they refer to Lite, they could mean the weight.

You're probably thinking at this point, what's there left to eat? What am I supposed to do, head for the nearest patch of grass and graze?

If you think these suggestions leave you with nothing to eat, here's the good news: Following the above strategies, you can still have the white meat of chicken or turkey (just breast, not dark meat), any white fish (halibut, swordfish, scrod, cod, sole, ahi tuna, canned tuna in water, etc.) and shrimp, scallops, crab, clams and lobster. That is, as long as they're not deep-fried. You can broil or roast these or cook them on a skewer over the barbecue in the summer.

No question, it will take time to add and to limit—and eventually eliminate—some of these items from your diet. You've had a lifetime to build your eating habits, and so it will take time to break them. Be patient with yourself. It's not going to happen overnight despite your vows and good intentions. (Remember what the road to hell is paved with.) If you falter, so what? Tomorrow is another day.

A SAMPLE DAILY MENU

Remember: Portion size counts as well.

For breakfast, try using pre-measured instant oatmeal and a full 8-oz. glass of nonfat milk and half a grapefruit. Another breakfast would consist of two hard-boiled or poached eggs with as little yellow added as possible (that's where the cholesterol and the fat are) along with an English muffin and fruit jam.

If you're one of those people who hates to eat breakfast, have a soy protein supplement. Keep a baggy filled with soy protein powder and some juice in a container in the back seat of your car and drink it in case you forget a meal or get hungry on the road.

For lunch, try a half to a full sandwich (depending on whether you are tall or short) made with any kind of bread (don't sweat the small stuff) and filled with tuna in water, white meat of chicken or white meat of turkey. You can use mustard and relish but no mayonnaise in the sandwich. For a change you can have a salad with white meat slices on top. Finish up with a sweet piece of fruit.

In the mid-afternoon, you should have another soy protein drink. This afternoon snack will counteract that low-energy feeling at that time of day and make you less likely to overeat at dinner.

Dinner is made up of three parts. Start with between 3 oz. and 6 oz. of white meat of chicken, turkey, white fish or shrimp, scallops, crab, clams or lobster. You should have one-half to one cup of rice, pasta, potatoes, beans, corn or peas (starchy veggies) and one cup of vegetables (such as carrots, asparagus, broccoli, brussels sprouts or string beans). Finally, add a large salad (sans croutons) and wine vinegar, rice vinegar or balsamic vinegar instead of salad dressing.

If you are hungry after dinner, either go for a walk or have some air popped popcorn with no oil and no salt. Don't buy the microwavable popcorn—there is a block of vegetable fat in each package. Don't buy the Weight Watcher's fat spray to spray on your popcorn. You will just be polluting your taste buds and making it harder to break your high-fat habits.

THE ADDED BENEFITS WHILE YOU
MAINTAIN YOUR PROSTATE

The nutritional changes suggested here are beneficial for other chronic diseases, such as heart disease, and should improve your overall quality of life. There is also the unmeasured benefit of recapturing control of your life. While your doctors oversee your medical and surgical therapy, nutrition and lifestyle are within your power to change.

QUADRUPLE YOUR IMMUNITY

Whew! We covered a lot of ground. You can pretty much eliminate all your prostate worries if you follow these simple guidelines:

Decrease percentage of dietary fat to 15 to 20 percent of total energy intake. Increase fruit and vegetable servings to between five and nine per day. The nutrients and fiber help protect against cancer.

Eat organic foods which are free of synthetic pesticides linked to prostate cancer.

Increase dietary fiber intake to 25 to 35 grams per day. Increase soy protein intake to 40 to 60 grams/day.

Every day eat tomato products.

Drink four large glasses of pure, filtered water each day (not at night, though).

Keep stress to a manageable level to stay healthy and maximize your immunity.

Eat soyfoods. These contain substances that protect against cancer and possibly BPH.

Don't smoke. Cigarettes are high in toxic cadmium and other bad stuff.

Avoid or minimize alcohol consumption, which contributes to BPH.

Cut back on coffee, which can aggravate BPH symptoms.

If you did all this, Mom would be so proud! Whether you tell her why is up to you.

CHAPTER THREE

NATURE'S REMEDIES

FOR A

HEALTHY PROSTATE

I can guess what you're thinking. There's no way you can follow all the recommendations in Chapter Two. Your life's too busy, too hectic to count the number of fruits and vegetables you eat every day. If anything, putting the kibosh on a juicy steak makes you crave one that much more.

Plus, there's some foods you just can't stand. You'd rather take your chances than have to eat THAT. Besides, in the words of the popular beer commercial:

You're not a "sally"

You're a "High Life" man.

Relax. First, the occasional cheeseburger is not going to give you prostate cancer or BPH. Sometimes we need to enjoy ourselves. Second, maintaining our health is not supposed to be punishment. If you're diligent most of the time—and the word MOST is the key—a fattening snack or a burger at a barbecue is not going to hurt you.

As for eating foods you hate. Well . . . There's got to be another way, and there is. Let me tell you a story.

The other day while I cooked spaghetti and tomato sauce I remembered I had a cake of tofu in the refrigerator. I thought I'd drop some into the sauce while it simmered.

Now, I'm no big fan of tofu. Not because it tastes or smells bad, just that it's so bland. Anyway, there it was, but it had expired. When I took it out of the package I could see why. You don't want the details, I assure you.

No big deal. The spaghetti and sauce were great, and I got a good healthy dose of lycopene. Still, I thought of all the benefits of soy that I'd missed because I had to toss the tofu.

Then I remembered. I went to the medicine cabinet and retrieved a bottle of soy germ tablets. I popped two in my mouth, and I had just about all of the benefits from the (doomed) tofu-ladened tomato sauce.

My point is, there are ways to "supplement" your diet while maintaining a healthy prostate. Notice I highlighted "supplement." I'm not condoning a "quick! Give me a pill" mentality.

Rather there are times when you just can't eat prostate-friendly foods. Or, if you're like me, there are some foods you just can't stand.

But don't fool yourself.

Naturally, it's easier to take vitamins, minerals and herbs than to change eating habits. Supplements make us feel we're caring for our health, and they remove the burden of healthy eating. It's not that simple.

Supplements are not a cure-all. Sorry, bud, there are just some eating habits you'll have to change. Supplements don't replace a balanced diet or "fix" a deficient one. They can only supplement what you eat and drink. Thus, their name. Still, adding a high-potency multiple vitamin and mineral supplement including antioxidants such as vitamins E and C, beta-carotene and selenium, will ensure that you're getting adequate nutrition AFTER you've eaten properly.

Then there are herbs—or botanicals, if you prefer. Herbs have been used as medicines for thousands of years. In fact, many of the pharmaceutical products sold today are synthetic chemicals based on herbal extracts. Herbal medicines may contain a whole plant, parts of a plant or extracts of either one or a combination of plants.

Many people prefer to use herbal medicines because in many cases they exert beneficial effects without the side effects caused by many pharmaceutical drugs, such as prostate drugs.

Doctors often prescribe two aggressively marketed drugs for BPH, including terazosin HCI (Abbott Laboratories' Hytrin®) or finasteride (Merck & Co.'s Proscar®). Unfortunately, their side effects include dizziness, impotence and loss of libido.

Herbs have played a significant role in BPH treatment for years. Specifically, alternative practitioners have recommended three safe, effective and inexpensive herbs for the treatment of BPH: saw palmetto (*serenoa repens*), pygeum (*pygeum africanum)* and stinging nettles (*urtica dioica*). Their value in BPH has been documented in European medical journals since the early 1970s, long before they were approved for use in the United States. These three herbs, along with pumpkin seed oil and pollen, have resulted in a drop in surgery rates for BPH and a safer, more cost-efficient approach for managing the condition. Moreover, there's evidence they can fight prostatitis and even prostate cancer.

Before you take any of the supplements mentioned here, I recommend you check with your doctor first, especially if you're on prescription medicine. There may be a conflict. Also, sometimes botanicals conflict with each other. For example, if you're on blood thinning medication, you may not want to take garlic or the memory enhancer, ginkgo biloba, since both also thin the blood.

NATIVE AMERICAN HEALERS WERE RIGHT

Long ago, Native American men knew that the dark, brownish-black berries from a small palm tree that grew wild in Florida, Georgia, Louisiana and South Carolina were an effective cure for "male problems." Then during the early part of this century a tea made from saw palmetto berries was commonly recommended in the United States for prostate and urinary tract problems. It was also thought to increase sperm production and sex drive in men and became a popular male tonic. As a result, saw palmetto has been recognized by the United States Pharmacopoeia as a remedy for prostate problems since 1905.

Research in Europe in the 1960s led to the discovery of the oil portion of the berry and its medically active free fatty acids, ethyl esters and sterols. Today, the extract is considered natural, safe, inexpensive, and has no known side effects in treating BPH.

Saw palmetto attacks BPH from several fronts. You may recall that the enzyme 5-AR is believed to be the culprit that speeds up the conversion of testosterone to DHT as men age. This increased 5-AR activity and subsequent increases in prostate levels of DHT appear to have a major influence on formation of BPH. The saw palmetto berries contain substances which actively inhibit this enzyme from making this conversion.

But that's not all. Other hormones may also contribute to formation of BPH, including estrogen, progesterone and prolactin. Saw palmetto reduces the effects of estrogen and progesterone on the prostate. It also "cools" inflammation in the gland itself and inhibits the formation of inflammatory substances that contribute to increasing the size of the prostate and can lead to prostatitis, too. Since high levels of DHT also correlate with prostate cancer, saw palmetto may also help prevent this disease.

Men suffering with BPH are generally offered drug therapy to control it in its earlier stages. As I've said, prescription prostate drugs have serious side effects including impotence. When compared to finasteride, the drug most commonly prescribed for BPH, the saw palmetto extract consistently shows higher effectiveness in improving prostate symptoms, with far fewer side effects. Saw palmetto works the same way finasteride does—it prevents the breakdown of testosterone to dihydrotestosterone. Plus, studies show this herb to be remarkably safe.

When Abe's doctor felt a ridge on his enlarged prostate during a routine rectal exam, he became alarmed. He recommended Abe, who was in his mid-50s, go to a urologist for a thorough assessment. Abe quickly made an appointment.

The urologist recommended a sonogram which uses sound waves to evaluate the overall health of his prostate and collected tissue samples with a needle that pierced the colon wall at high speed. Fortunately, the biopsy results were negative. Abe's next step was to decide what, if anything, to do about his enlarged prostate. The urologist sat Abe down and explained all the surgical options, the whole smorgasbord of T-based acronyms; TURP, TUIP, TUMT and TUNA. Abe wasn't thrilled with the prospects of any of them.

On the recommendation of his daughter, a student of herbal medicine, Abe decided to postpone surgery and try saw palmetto pills. While taking an over-the-counter standardized version of saw palmetto, an 85 percent to 95 percent concentration of fatty acids and sterols once and sometimes twice a day, his BPH symptoms dramatically decreased over the course of a year and a half. Abe had escaped the battle of the acronyms.

In 1984, Dr. G. Champault, a well-known British scientist, conducted one of the first double-blind studies to show that saw palmetto actually counteracts the hormonal imbalances which are the most common cause of prostate enlargement. The results of Dr. Champault's study were so impressive that he excited the interest of the medical community. As a result, numerous prominent scientists at nine medical research centers around Europe decided to conduct their own double-blind studies on the saw palmetto extract.

Since the mid-1980s, at least ten studies on more than 1,000 patients in Europe have confirmed the value of saw palmetto. Specifically, an amazing 90 percent of the patients who were given this extract experienced remarkable relief from their symptoms.

If you're the type of guy who needs proof, here are summaries of many of the studies performed on saw palmetto. Me? I like to know as much as possible about something before I start gulping it down. I want to know if I'm creating a whole new slew of problems, or if I'm just producing expensive urine.

However, if you're a trusting soul, or numbers bore you, you're not going to hurt my feelings by skipping over the numbers. But if you decide to do that, make sure you don't miss the important stuff!

That said, here's a quick summary of saw palmetto research:

German studies of up to 200 men with BPH, as well as those in British, French and Italian medical journals, have confirmed the value of saw palmetto extract. The dose of extracts in the studies typically was 320 mg per day, in two divided doses.

A one-year study in Hungary found that 320 mg of saw palmetto extract daily led to a reduction in residual urine (the urine left in the bladder after urination) and an increase in urinary flow rates. These results were considered significant by the sixth month of treatment.

One 28-day study with 110 BPH patients found 320 mg.-per-day was effective in reducing painful urination, nighttime urination and urine residue left in the bladder. There was also a significant improvement in urine flow rate. Forty-seven patients were then followed for 15 to 30 months and were found to have continued improvement.

In another study, researchers followed 305 BPH patients who took 160 mg of saw palmetto extract twice daily. At the end of 90 days, 88 percent of the patients rated the treatment a success. Their physicians' evaluations were equally favorable. Urinary flow rate improved significantly and there was a notable decrease in prostate size.

In one recent three-month study, 88 percent of the patients treated with saw palmetto and their physicians reported:

- Improvement in urinary flow,
- Less residual urine, and
- Reduced prostate size.

Other results noted included:

- Fewer nighttime visits to the bathroom, and
- (Ahh!) A stronger stream.

Not surprisingly, there is currently a huge market in Europe for saw palmetto. Guess what? It's popularity in the United States is growing by leaps and bounds, too.

So here's a summary of the good news about saw palmetto:

Besides being effective and free of side effects, saw palmetto costs about one-third as much as prostate medications such as Proscar.

Men who take saw palmetto for BPH usually notice results after two to six weeks, though most use the herb longer for more complete relief.

Many doctors are learning that saw palmetto is an inexpensive and safe way to maintain prostate health. For younger men, this herb can help prevent prostate problems later on in life.

In order for saw palmetto to be effective, it must be in an extract form (usually capsules, though tinctures are also used). Since the active ingredients are fat soluble, a tea made from the berries would not give much benefit.

Dr. Julian Whitaker, who practices alternative medicine in Potomac, Maryland, says to prevent BPH, men should start taking saw palmetto extract on a regular basis in their mid-forties. For those who do not yet have a problem, he recommends a dosage of 80 mg twice a day. For those who already have a prostate problem, he recommends taking 160 mg to 320 mg of the extract each day while under the watchful eye of a physician. He also says such men should have a urine flow check every 30 to 60 days.

OUT OF AFRICA, A NATURAL CURE FOR PROSTATE DISORDERS

High in the mountains of central and southern Africa, the bark of a large evergreen tree yields another herb that decreases prostate swelling. In fact, the powdered bark from *pygeum africanum* has been used by locals as a tea for relief of urinary disorders for ages.

European scientists exploring traditional herbal medicines were so impressed with reports of pygeum's actions that they began laboratory investigations. As was the case with saw palmetto, this led to the development of an extract of the bark. As a result, it's been used extensively in France and elsewhere in Europe, and recently has been imported into the United States.

Now, you may be asking, how do they discover these things? Who's the brave soul who first peels off the bark, tastes it and discovers it's a remedy for some ailment? I don't know. I'm just glad someone did.

Pygeum seems to work, like saw palmetto, by limiting the formation of DHT. It also lowers prolactin levels, a pituitary hormone related to prostate and sexual function. Pygeum has additionally proven useful for the treatment of chronic, non-bacterial prostatitis, a condition, you may remember, that leads to inflammation of the prostate and can affect males at any age.

In 1997, in the British medical journal *Lancet*, German researchers reported on a study of 200 men who had symptoms due to BPH. Half received a placebo and half 60 mg.-per-day of beta-sitosterol which is one of the main active ingredients extracted from *pygeum africanum* bark. It or similar compounds are also present in other herbs that are used to treat the prostate.

After three months, the men taking beta-sitosterol extract had a statistically significant improvement in the velocity of urine flow. Those taking the placebo did not.

Scientists are not exactly sure how beta-sitosterol works to improve prostate symptoms. One interesting tie-in is that it lowers blood cholesterol. It's believed that accumulation of cholesterol in the prostate increases the binding sites for testosterone and DHT. These researchers are also convinced high cholesterol is an important factor stimulating prostate growth.

Another good reason to watch your diet!

Here's a summary of other research on pygeum:

In several double-blind studies, a fat-soluble extract of this herb improved prostate symptoms significantly without many side effects (of these, stomach irritation was the most common). In fact, in one study sexual ability was increased as well. So, besides helping relieve BPH symptoms (and sexual disorders due to BPH), pygeum may work for those with prostatitis.

Pygeum extract (100 mg per-day) or a placebo was administered to 263 BPH patients for 60 days. The pygeum group showed marked clinical improvement with noticeable increase in urinary flow rate.

Eighteen patients with either BPH or chronic prostatitis were treated with pygeum (200 mg.-per-day) for 60 days. Urination performance parameters improved and there was a measured reduction in prostate size in BPH patients as well as reduced inflammation in the prostatitis patients.

Twenty BPH patients, ages 51-89, were given either pygeum (200 mg.-per-day) or a placebo for 60 days. Again, the pygeum group showed a significantly greater improvement of BPH symptoms.

An Italian study published in 1991 reported that not only did pygeum reduce urinary problems and prostate inflammation, but it also increased sexual desire. La dolce vita!

TAKE THE STING OUT OF PAIN

Another herbal treatment for BPH is the root of stinging nettles (*urtica dioica*). Stinging nettles, which can grow just about anywhere, have little prickly hairs that stick in your skin and sting and itch like crazy (thus their name). Aside from the stinging factor, the nettle is a very useful plant with uses as food and many medicinal applications; its minerals include iron, silica, potassium, manganese, sulfur and vitamins A and C.

The fresh green leaves may be cooked and eaten like spinach, or made into soup or tea. (Fortunately, the sting is not present in the cooked or dried plant form.) A tea made from the leaves is a powerful tonic that provides many important vitamins and minerals. The vitamin C content works to help the iron be absorbed by the body. There are many folk and homeopathic medicinal uses for nettles including stopping BPH. Like saw palmetto and pygeum, it blocks the formation of DHT.

There's been a limited number of double-blind studies supporting its effectiveness for use with prostate problems. One study of 67 men with BPH found that supplements of this herb reduced nighttime urination. A typical dose is 300 mg of an extract.

If these three herbs are so good, would taking more than one of them supergalvanize your prostate? As you might expect, some researchers say combinations of at least two of these herbs exert greater benefits at low doses.

Two recent studies looked at a combination of saw palmetto extract and nettle root to treat BPH. They were impressive because of the large number of patients followed in the first study, and the head-to-head comparison with Proscar in the second.

The first study followed 2,080 BPH patients for 12 weeks. Men in the study were treated with a combination of saw palmetto extract (160 mg) and nettle root extract (120 mg) twice daily. The saw palmetto/nettle root combination produced:

- 26 percent increase in maximum urinary flow,

- 44.7 percent reduction in residual urine,

- 62.5 percent reduction in painful urination,

- 53.6 percent reduction in post-urination dribbling, and

- 50 percent reduction in nighttime urination.

A recent one-year study comparing the saw palmetto and nettle root combination versus Proscar showed equal improvement in both groups after six months of treatment.

A French research study noted that a combination therapy of stinging nettles and pygeum led to dramatic improvements in BPH in only one month. Likewise, a combination of saw palmetto and nettle root has been the focus of two important clinical studies. Several studies have also shown that saw palmetto and *pygeum africanum* work well together.

It's up to you to decide if you want to take more than one. Remember, they all work well on their own. I've been taking 160 mg of saw palmetto every day for about 18 months. I'm happy to report my doctor told me I have had no prostate enlargement. Also, my stream and libido are just fine, thank you. (Knock on wood!)

However, if you're the type who believes two or more are better than one—and money is no object—go ahead. I do recommend, though, you start with just one. If you show no negative response, such as stomach problems, add another.

Saw palmetto, pygeum and stinging nettles extracts offer a safe and cost-effective approach to men with BPH or those who want to prevent it in the first place. Medical experts say patients using the first two usually begin showing effects within three to four weeks of use. However, men who already have BPH will need to stay on for at least six to nine months to determine true effectiveness.

Once you're convinced they work, doctors say you will need to incorporate either saw palmetto, pygeum or nettles into your daily supplement routine for the long term since many patients have noted a return of symptoms within one or two weeks of stopping any of the extracts. Face it, it's going to become part of your daily regimen. It's a good thing the herbs are considerably cheaper than the drugs they mimic.

You'll be able to find saw palmetto more easily than the other two. I've seen it in drug, food, discount and convenience stores while I've only seen pygeum and nettles in health food and vitamin stores.

MORE NUTRIENTS YOU NEED

The Three Aminos

Amino acids are the chemical units that make up protein, which gives all tissue its structure. Three amino acids—glycine, alanine and glutamic acid—seem to have a direct link with prostate problems.

In a double-blind study, a mixture of these amino acids was given to half the men in a group of BPH victims and a placebo given to the other half. Within the group taking the amino acids:

- 92 percent had a reduction in prostate size.
- 95 percent experienced fewer trips to the john at night (nocturia).
- 81 percent had less urgency to urinate.
- 73 percent urinated less frequently.
- 71 percent had reduced discomfort.

Bee Pollen

Bee pollen is a highly nutritious supplement. It contains all known water-soluble vitamins and a gonadotropic hormone which stimulates sex glands and helps production of testosterone and growth hormones.

Pumpkin Seeds

Pumpkin seeds are a natural source of zinc and linoleic acid (vitamin F). They are purported to be important in helping to decongest the prostate gland and lessen residual urine.

Selenium

There's lots of evidence that getting enough of this essential mineral cuts your risk of most kinds of cancer—including prostate.

Selenium acts as an antioxidant, which means that it helps protect cells from harmful free radical reactions. It acts together with vitamin E: selenium protecting within the cells and vitamin E protecting the outer cell membranes.

For cancer prevention, nutrition-oriented doctors recommend 50 to 200 micrograms of selenium a day (depending on what part of the country you live in and your personal and family history of cancer), taken in the form of l-selenomethionine. This is the organic form of selenium, which means it is more easily absorbed, with less possibility of adverse side effects.

Good food sources of selenium include whole-grain cereals, seafood, garlic and eggs. It's important to note that processed foods lose their selenium. Brown rice, for example, has 15 times the selenium content of white rice, and whole-wheat bread contains twice as much selenium as white bread.

Watermelon Seeds

Watermelon seeds have natural diuretic properties and are also an antioxidant. They are purported to help prevent excess build-up of urine due to prostatitis and BPH. They work well with uva ursi and buchu.

Jay didn't have prostate problems until he was in his sixties, and was preparing for retirement. As he planned a future of sailing and other pleasures, he gradually developed pain and urinary difficulties. When his BPH symptoms became too tough to bear, his urologist at the University of California at Los Angeles recommended surgery. That prospect scared Jay and he found himself finding excuses to postpone it. His condition worsened.

Although he was never much for herbal remedies, Jay figured he had nothing to lose to try a tincture he read about. Three times a day he took an herbal formula consisting of saw palmetto, stinging nettles, sarsaparilla root, wild yam root, echinacea, and pipsissewa. After only a few weeks, he starting feeling better and after a few short months his BPH seemed to disappear.

Still, he was nervous before his next visit to his urologist. To his surprise as well as his doctor's, Jay's condition had improved markedly. His doctor said he had never seen BPH virtually disappear without surgery. When Jay told him about his magic elixir, the doctor conducted his own investigation. Today, Jay—and his doctor—are herbal converts.

CAVEAT EMPTOR: BUYER BEWARE (PART I)

If you've been to your local pharmacy recently, or even the local K-Mart or WalMart, you've noticed that there's been a huge explosion of supplement choices. No longer do you need to go to a health food store to get something a little more effective than Flintstones. Just last week, at a Wal-Mart that recently opened near where I live, an entire wall overflowed with all sorts of vitamins, minerals, herbs and who knows what else. In fact, I counted seven different saw palmetto products, all with different strengths, added ingredients and capsule counts.

Although the variety and choices are greater than ever, that also presents some problems. Which is the best? Who's ripping consumers off? It seems like every Tom, Dick, and Harry is selling supplements of one sort or another. With popularity increasing it is definitely Buyer Beware.

It's probably a good time to fill you in on what's happening in the supplement market—consider this a sort of Supplement Primer.

Herbs, also known as botanical products, are part of a broad category called dietary supplements that also includes vitamins, minerals and amino acids. Botanicals have been around for centuries as herbal remedies and are still widely used in other countries. They fell out of favor in the United States during World War II when the public became enthralled with synthetic drugs. Today, some people are turning to herbs because they think they may be a safer, less expensive, more natural alternative.

Estimates vary on exactly how many people have used botanicals. Some surveys suggest that more than 30 percent of people in this country have taken an herbal product.

So far, the most popular ones include:

Echinacea to prevent and treat colds and flu,

Garlic to lower mildly elevated cholesterol, among other benefits,

St. John's wort to treat mild to moderate depression,

Ginseng to boost mental and physical resistance to stress,

Ginkgo biloba for age-related cognitive decline, and

Saw palmetto for the treatment of mild to moderate BPH.

Botanical sales have been rising for the past few years. In 1996, herbal supplement sales totaled $2.98 billion; in 1997, the number grew to $3.5 billion; in 1998, they topped $4 billion. It's predicted they will jump 12 percent to 16 percent every year for the next four years.

Supplements come in many forms, including tablets, capsules, powders, softgels, gelcaps and liquids. Though commonly associated with health food stores, dietary supplements also are sold in grocery, drug and national discount chain stores, as well as through mail-order catalogs, TV programs, the Internet, and direct sales. Surveys show that more than half of the United States adult population uses these products.

Supplements are not drugs. A drug, which sometimes can be derived from plants used as traditional medicines, is a substance that, among other things, is intended to diagnose, cure, mitigate, treat or prevent diseases. Before marketing, drugs must undergo clinical studies to determine their effectiveness, safety, possible interactions with other substances, and appropriate dosages. The FDA must review their data and authorize the drugs' use before they can be sold. The FDA does not authorize or test dietary supplements.

Just because herbs are "natural" doesn't necessarily mean they're safe. In fact some are downright dangerous.

Take the case of a 60-year-old woman who for 10 months took an extract of a desert shrub called chaparral, touted as an antioxidant. According to the February 8, 1995, issue of the *Journal of the American Medical Association*, the herb produced chronic liver damage and she required a liver transplant.

There are other herbs that can be toxic to the liver. There's evidence that Jin Bu Huan, germander, comfrey, skullcap, margosa oil, Gordoloba yerba tea, and pennyroyal oil, among others, have been implicated. Few of these substances have been extensively tested and their safety isn't well established. Also, labels may not be accurate and manufacturing procedures often aren't up to standards that make for a feeling of confidence.

For information about other potentially dangerous dietary supplements, see the Following Food and Drug Administration Web Site: **http://vm.cfsan.fda.gov/~dms/fdsuppch.html.**

KEYS TO BUYING SUPPLEMENTS

Can manufacturers claims be trusted? Are they safe? Does the Food and Drug Administration (FDA) approve them?

The FDA oversees safety, manufacturing and product information—such as product claims—in a product's labeling, package inserts, and accompanying literature. The Federal Trade Commission regulates the advertising of dietary supplements.

The 1994 Dietary Supplement Health and Education Act, or DSHEA, set up a new framework for FDA regulation of these products. The United States Congress recognized that many people believe dietary supplements offer health benefits and also that consumers want a greater opportunity to determine whether supplements may help them. DSHEA essentially gives the manufacturers freedom to market more products as dietary supplements and provide information about their products' benefits—for example, in product labeling.

Congress has created an office in the National Institute of Health to coordinate research on dietary supplements. It also called on President Clinton to set up an independent dietary supplement commission to report on the use of claims in dietary supplement labeling.

The Council for Responsible Nutrition, an organization of manufacturers of dietary supplements and their suppliers, welcomes the change. "Our philosophy has been . . . to maintain consumer access to products and access to information [so that consumers can] make informed choices," says John Cordaro, the group's president and chief executive officer.

Still, under DSHEA, the FDA's requirement for review of dietary supplements is less stringent than for other products it regulates, such as drugs and many additives used in conventional foods. Sadly, this means it's left up to the manufacturers to check the safety of dietary supplements and savvy consumers to determine the truthfulness of label claims.

Information currently required on the labels of dietary supplements includes:

- Statement of identity (what the product is, e.g., saw palmetto) and the net quantity of contents (number of capsules).
- Structure-function claim and the statement (e.g., This product is not intended to diagnose, treat, cure or prevent any disease.).
- Directions for use.

- Supplement Facts panel (lists serving size, amount and active ingredient).
- Other ingredients in descending order of predominance and by common name or proprietary blend.
- Name and place of business of manufacturer, packer or distributor.

Historically, dietary supplements referred to products made of one or more of the essential nutrients, such as vitamins, minerals and protein. DSHEA broadens the definition, however, to include, with some exceptions, any product intended for ingestion as a supplement to the diet. This includes vitamins, minerals, herbs, botanicals and other plant-derived substances. Amino acids and extracts of these substances are also covered.

DSHEA requires manufacturers to include the words "dietary supplement" on product labels. Also, starting in March 1999, a Supplement Facts panel will be required on the labels of most dietary supplements.

A product sold as a supplement with claims on its label as a new treatment or cure for a specific disease or condition would be considered an unauthorized—and thus illegal—drug. Labeling changes consistent with the provisions in DSHEA would be required to maintain the product's status as a dietary supplement.

As with food, federal law requires manufacturers of dietary supplements to ensure that the products they put on the market are safe. But supplement manufacturers do not have to provide information to FDA to get a product on the market, unlike the food additive process often required of new food ingredients. FDA review and approval of supplement ingredients and products is not required before marketing.

Under DSHEA, once a dietary supplement is marketed, FDA has the responsibility for showing that a dietary supplement is unsafe before it can take action to restrict the product's use. DSHEA also gives the FDA authority to establish good manufacturing practices, or GMPs, for dietary supplements.

Besides the FDA, individual states can take steps to restrict or stop the sale within their jurisdictions of potentially harmful dietary supplements. The industry also strives to regulate itself, says a spokesman for the Council for Responsible Nutrition. He cites the GMPs that his trade group and others—such as the United States Pharmacopoeia (see next page)—developed for their member companies.

WHOM CAN YOU TRUST?

What about product claims? Can we trust them?

Under DSHEA and previous food labeling laws, supplement manufacturers ARE allowed to use, when appropriate, three types of claims:

> Nutrient-content claims: For example, a supplement containing at least 200 milligrams of calcium per serving could carry the claim "high in calcium." A supplement with at least 12 mg per serving of vitamin C could state on its label, "Excellent source of vitamin C."

> Disease claims: Show a link between a food or substance and a disease or health-related condition. The FDA authorizes these claims based on a review of the scientific evidence, or an authoritative statement from certain scientific bodies.

> Nutrition support claims, which include "structure-function claims": Describe a link between a nutrient and the deficiency disease that can result if the nutrient is lacking in the diet, such as "vitamin C prevents scurvy." Nutrient content claims describe the level of a nutrient in a food or dietary supplement. An example of structure-function claims is "Calcium builds strong bones."

We as consumers need to be on the lookout for fraudulent products which can often be identified by the types of claims made in their labeling, advertising and promotional literature. Some possible indicators of fraud, says Stephen Barrett, M.D., a board member of the National Council Against Health Fraud, are:

> Claims that the product is a secret cure, and use of such terms as "breakthrough," "magical," "miracle cure," and "new discovery." If the product were a cure for a serious disease, it would be widely reported in the media and used by healthcare professionals, says Barrett.

> Pseudo-medical jargon, such as "detoxify," "purify," and "energize" to describe a product's benefits. These claims are vague and hard to measure, Barrett says. So they make it easier for success to be claimed "even though nothing has actually been accomplished."

> Claims that the product can cure a wide range of unrelated diseases. "No product can do that," he says.

Claims that a product is backed by scientific studies, but with no list or an inadequate list of references.

Claims that the supplement has only benefits and no side effects. "A product potent enough to help people will be potent enough to cause side effects," Barrett says.

Accusations that the medical profession, drug companies and the government are suppressing information about a particular treatment. It would be illogical, Barrett says, for large numbers of people to withhold information about potential medical therapies when they or their families and friends might one day benefit from them.

Still, it's difficult for consumers to determine which brand is best, which one comes closest to delivering the right dosage to treat what ails them, which has the best quality herbs. Despite the intentions of DSHEA, there still are no official standards yet for quality, purity and strength of botanicals, but that's changing.

The United States Pharmacopoeia (USP), a private, nonprofit organization that sets legally recognized standards for medicines and health care technologies, is trying to develop standards for herbs. Currently, USP has 18 standards for purity, quality and strength for vitamins and minerals, and is in the process of developing similar standards for 25 to 30 botanical products, says Jim Crandall of the USP. Eventually, that will mean that botanical manufacturers will have the option of meeting the group's requirements and carrying USP on the products' labels, indicating that it meets the group's standards.

USP also is performing research to determine the active ingredients in botanicals, Crandall says. And some drug and supplement companies are conducting their own investigations in order to find out exactly what components and what quantity produce the herbs' medicinal effects. In the past, most of the companies have standardized their extracts based only on a single part or component of the herb, says herbal expert Varro Tyler. But now many are conducting scientific checks for several of the active ingredients in their products.

For example, Susan Trimbo of Whitehall-Robins Healthcare, which is marketing Centrum Herbals, says the company is using a unique process developed by PharmaPrint that can identify the active components in herbs using a combination of chemical analysis and laboratory tests.

Poor manufacturing practices are not unique to dietary supplements, but the growing market for supplements in a less restrictive regulatory environment creates the potential for supplements to be prone to quality-control problems. To help protect themselves, consumers should:

Read product labels, follow directions, and heed all warnings.

Realize that the label term "natural" doesn't guarantee that a product is safe.

Avoid products sold for much less money than competing brands. The manufacturer had to scrimp somewhere, possibly in the quantity or quality of ingredients.

Look for products with the USP seal, which indicates the manufacturer followed standards established by the United States Pharmacopoeia.

If you see a supplement whose label states or implies the product can help diagnose, treat, cure, or prevent a disease ("cures cancer"), the product is being marketed illegally as a drug and as such has not been evaluated for safety or effectiveness.

Look for a familiar name. Though usually more expensive, supplements made by a nationally known food and drug manufacturer have a reputation to uphold, and its products are likely made under tight controls. Of course, this isn't fool proof.

That said, there are a number of other nutrients and herbs proven useful to the prostate. For most BPH and prostatitis sufferers a combination of only a few is all that is necessary. Use your best judgment. Here are some examples:

19 HERBS THAT CAN HELP

1. BACHU: Bachu is a small shrub native to South Africa where it is often used both as a flavoring agent and as a urinary antiseptic. It contains an oil that increases urine production. A natural diuretic that also has antimicrobial properties, it is purported to help strengthen and heal the genito-urinary system, and is used to treat acute and chronic prostatitis. This herb works well with couch grass and echinacea for prostatitis. Bachu should be used with caution if you also suffer from kidney disease.

2. BUCKTHORN: Buckthorn has been used by herbalists as a cancer treatment all over the world but is still a long way from being an accepted treatment. You should discuss using it with your doctor if you have cancer and would like to try this herb in addition to other therapy.

3. CERNILTON: This is an extract from a Swiss flower with potent anti-inflammatory actions. It's been proven effective in treating prostatitis in a number of clinical studies.

4. COUCH GRASS: Rhizome Herbalists have found this grass valuable for treating enlarged and infected prostates. It has a very soothing effect on the genito-urinary system. Couch grass works as a diuretic and also has demulcent and anti-microbial properties. It may be combined with saw palmetto, echinacea and bachu.

5. CRAMP BARK: This herb has antispasmodic, sedative and astringent properties. It is claimed to have strong antispasmodic effects on the genitourinary system for males and females. May be combined with chamomile or angelica root for genito-urinary cramping.

6. CRANBERRY: Juice from this berry is said to help prevent or cure urinary tract infections. It's also recommended for incontinence as it is purported to deodorize urine.

7. DONG QUAI: Dong quai has antispasmodic and diuretic properties and has been useful in treating prostatitis. Works well with cramp bark for genito-urinary cramping. Dong quai tends to increase blood sugar levels so it should not be used by diabetics.

8. ECHINACEA: This herb has antibacterial, anti-viral and anti-microbial properties that work well on the reproductive system. Echinacea is the scientific genus name of the coneflower; the purple coneflower is among the most popular and best-known herb extracts in the United States today. Traditionally the root has been used, but today, all parts of the plant except the stem are harvested to make liquid extracts, pressed plant juice, capsules and tablets. It may be combined in equal parts with saw palmetto and used as a suppository for treating prostatitis and enlarged prostates.

To be effective, echinacea needs to be taken in large amounts to fight infection. In some people, it can cause stomach upset and can cause the mouth to tingle and actively salivate.

9. GARLIC: As you may remember from the last chapter, garlic has tonic, stimulant, antispasmodic and anti-microbial properties. It's reputed to help treat infections and rid the body of parasites. It combines well with echinacea and goldenseal for treating microbial activity. It contains alliin, but needs to be chewed or crushed to bring out alliin's antibiotic properties. Studies have found that 1 medium clove pack has the anti-bacterial properties of 100,000 units of penicillin. Depending on the type of infection, oral penicillin ranges from 600,000 to 1.2 million units. An equivalent amount of garlic would be 6–12 cloves. That's a bunch!

10. GOLDENSEAL: Highly valued by North American Indians as a medicine, wild goldenseal is becoming increasingly rare. It has anti-microbial activity and is active against many disease-causing organisms. It prevents bacteria from attaching to cells, stimulates the immune system, lowers fevers, and has anti-cancer effects.

Goldenseal has tonic, astringent and antiseptic properties useful in treating and strengthening reproductive organs. It combines well with saw palmetto and echinacea for prostatitis. You should avoid prolonged high doses because this herb is known to diminish essential flora of the intestines. It can also affect your blood pressure; it contains both berberine, which may lower blood pressure, and hydrastine, which may raise blood pressure.

So if you have a history of high (or low) blood pressure, heart disease, diabetes, glaucoma or stroke, exercise extreme caution: don't use this herb. For otherwise healthy individuals, goldenseal may be used for brief periods of time at the recommended dosage levels.

11. JUNIPER: It's claimed that juniper berries are good for genitourinary infections and incontinence (gives urine the fragrance of violets). They have diuretic properties and the essential oil is used in the over-the-counter (OTC) diuretic Odrinil. Juniper may lower blood pressure.

High doses may cause kidney irritation and damage; therefore juniper should not be used by anyone with a kidney infection or a history of kidney problems. Even though juniper may aggravate kidney problems, the FDA still includes it on its list of "herbs regarded as safe." Nevertheless, it should be used in small amounts and only in otherwise healthy individuals. Also, it should not be taken for more than six consecutive weeks.

12. MARSH MALLOW: This isn't the stuff that turns gooey when you toast it in the fireplace. Rather it is a plant that grows near water in

Europe and the United States. It has diuretic, tonic and emollient properties that are purported to help soothe and protect the genito-urinary system. One study has shown that marsh mallow enhanced the ability of white blood cells to devour microbes. Has also been found to lower blood sugar in animals; therefore it may be beneficial in managing diabetes.

13. PIPSISSEWA: Has diuretic, tonic and astringent properties. Used mostly for genito-urinary system. Purported to be very effective for chronic prostatitis and other genito-urinary disorders. Has a gentle yet powerful soothing effect.

14. QUEEN OF THE MEADOW: Has diuretic, nervine, stimulant and astringent properties. Considered by herbalists to be very valuable for treating genito-urinary problems.

15. ROSEMARY: The extract from this fragrant herb is such a strong preservative that it's used in the food industry to keep foods fresh. Studies have found that animals eating even small amounts of rosemary each day are protected from cancer.

16. SKULLCAP: Leaves have nervine, tonic, sedative and antispasmodic properties. Purported to relieve stress and nervous tension, nervous headache, neuralgia, insomnia and restlessness. Combines well with valerian for treating stress and nervous tension, and with chamomile for restlessness and insomnia.

17. SIBERIAN GINSENG: (Not truly a Ginseng.) Claimed to be an immune system enhancer, it helps the body's acute defense system build resistance, expand blood vessels to increase circulation, regulate blood pressure, and boost physical energy. It can also be used as a reproductive and prostate tonic, and is purported to relieve stress of impotence and insure adequate penile circulation. More on all the ginsengs in Chapter Five.

18. VALERIAN: Has sedative, hypnotic, antispasmodic properties. Combines well with skullcap for tension and anxiety, with chamomile for insomnia, and with cramp bark for pain and cramping. Contains valepotriates, chemicals that appear to have sedative properties, with the highest concentration in the roots. On rare instances, valerian has been known to have stimulant effect rather than a calming effect. (More on valerian later in this chapter.)

19. PYCNOGENOL: Made from extract from the bark of the French Maritime Pine and skins from grape seeds. Reported to be a very powerful antioxidant. There are also claims that it's more effective than vitamins E, C and betacarotene as an antioxidant.

SLEEP THROUGH THE NIGHT

Long-term studies suggest that people who get seven to eight hours of sleep each night live longer, healthier lives. However, according to a Louis Harris survey, more and more adult Americans—50 percent—are getting by on less than the seven to eight hours' sleep considered ideal for most individuals. At least a third of Americans complain of insomnia, the inability to fall asleep quickly or to fall back asleep after awakening.

Chronic sleep loss can contribute to decreased coordination and ability to ward off infections, depression, irritability and other mood changes. But sleep deprivation can be even more serious. Drowsiness is blamed for 200,000 to 400,000 automobile accidents each year and almost half of all accident-related fatalities. Inadequate sleep can compromise productivity and erode personal relationships.

When James, a 45-year-old Midwest banker went to his doctor, he hoped he'd give him something for his insomnia. Turns out, James didn't suffer from insomnia at all, but from BPH. His lack of sleep was due to his trips to the bathroom every two hours during the night. His doctor recommended he suspend all fluid intake three hours before bedtime. At last report, James was sleeping through the night.

Americans' sleep deficit can be traced to a number of causes. Many people choose to skimp on sleep as a way of trying to squeeze more activities into their frenzied lives. But it's more than that.

For one thing, our sleeping patterns change as we age. People in their 50s commonly wake up two or three times during the night after the first two hours of sleep. Several factors may contribute to these problems. A greater incidence of aches and pains, heightened sensitivity to noise and temperature, medications, anxiety, bereavement, and depression can all disrupt sleep.

Others suffer from a sleep disorder, such as sleep apnea or periodic limb movements. Jet lag or shift work accounts for some cases of chronic tiredness.

Then there's BPH . . .

If you already suffer from BPH, you undoubtedly get up once, twice, maybe more, to "take a leak." Even after your prostate shrinks, your sleep pattern will take some time to return to normal.

Maybe so far your prostate is normal, but due to stress, good sound sleep is hard to come by. For some, a warm glass of milk does the trick. But that's not for everybody.

Sleeping pills or tranquilizers are certainly not the answer. They can become habit-forming; they make you groggy, not sleepy; some can leave you with hangover-like feelings. Plus, they can play havoc with your prostate and your ability to perform sexually. What's more, people who use sleeping pills may grow dependent on them and find it difficult to give them up out of fear they won't sleep at all.

Good ol' Mother Nature has provided us with some very effective herbs to give us restful, relaxing sleep. Here are a few I've tried with success:

1. CHAMOMILE: This flower tends to calm rather than sedate. It has anti-spasmodic, antiseptic, anti-inflammatory, and analgesic properties. It is purported to have calming effects on cramps or painful symptoms of the genito-urinary system.

This makes an excellent bedtime tea, but don't drink too much or you'll just add another trip to the john in the middle of the night. One warning though: if you're allergic to ragweed, you may have a reaction to chamomile.

2. HOPS: You know what this is, right? It's the stuff that gives beer its flavor. It's also a sedative. People in Europe sleep on pillows stuffed with hops flowers. You may prefer to take it as a tincture. There are natural sleep-aid products containing hops, so read your labels to see if it's included. Resist the temptation to get hops from a six-pack. You'll just have to get up even more during the night "to pee."

3. KAVA KAVA: This is a muscle relaxant and works well for anyone suffering from pain. It can also quiet your mind if you suffer from anxiety. Since it makes you drowsy, don't take it if you plan to drive afterwards.

Try 300 mg at bedtime. Some experts recommend only taking it for a couple of weeks. I've tried it and it works well.

4. PASSIONFLOWER: Despite its name this isn't going to make you Joe Stud in the bedroom. Rather this sedative is a very effective muscle relaxant and reduces anxiety. The best way to take it is as a tincture. A dose of 150 mg should do the trick.

5. VALERIAN: Sometimes called "herbal Valium" because of its superior ability to relax muscles, reduce anxiety and bring on sleep quickly. Valerian is the root of *valeriana officinalis,* officinalis, a tall plant with showy white flowers.

When volunteers in a placebo-controlled trial used this popular European sleep aid, 89 percent reported improved sleep, and 44 percent reported perfect sleep. Unlike prescription sleep aids, valerian isn't habit-forming and is safer than chemical drugs because it has no synergism with alcohol or other depressants. In fact, valerian is used in Europe to help break addictions to sleeping pills. Because of its notorious bad odor, most people prefer to take it in capsules or tablets, though liquid extracts and teas are also available.

Recommended dosage is 300 to 400 mg at bedtime in capsule form, or you can use it in tea or as a tincture mixed with water or juice.

WARD OFF PROSTATE WOES WITH ZINC

One of the nutrients most critical for prostate health is the mineral zinc. Why? Because it can reduce prostate problems such as swelling while boosting male virility.

Zinc has been recognized as an essential trace mineral for plants, animals and humans since the 1930s. The average adult body contains between 1.5 and 3g. of zinc with approximately 60 percent of this in the muscles, 30 percent in the bones and 6 percent in the skin.

The prostate needs 10 times more zinc than any other organ in the body. In fact, this mineral is more concentrated in the prostate than in any other tissue. It makes sense, therefore, that zinc is vital for preventing prostate problems, including those of BPH sufferers.

In thwarting BPH, zinc, along with vitamin B6, inhibits the production of 5-alpha-reductase, thus reducing the levels of DHT which causes overproduction of prostate cells. In addition, it also helps the body dump excess DHT.

Zinc also acts to lower levels of another hormone, prolactin, which controls the development of testosterone in the prostate. When men reach their 40s, prolactin levels tend to increase, which, in turn, cause production of more 5-alpha-reductase. Scientists believe that zinc controls secretion of prolactin by the pituitary gland. In fact, the combination of zinc and vitamin B6 is so effective in reducing prolactin levels that many researchers believe that a deficiency in either one might be a main cause of prostate enlargement. Increasing zinc levels, therefore, restricts the actions of the hormones and leads to a reduction in prostate size.

In several controlled studies, zinc has proven to actually reverse prostate enlargement. For instance, Irving Bush and Associates at Chicago's Cook County Hospital tested the effect of zinc on patients with BPH symptoms. All patients reported symptomatic improvements, and 75 percent had noticeable shrinkage of the prostate.

In a 1996 study, researchers investigated the relationship between zinc and testosterone in 40 normal men, aged from 20 to 80. After 20 weeks of zinc restriction, they found lower testosterone in young men, while normal elderly men who took zinc supplements for six months had a marked increase in testosterone.

Benny was 49 years old when, during a routine physical, his doctor discovered his prostate enlargement. For Benny who is a vegetarian, doesn't smoke and has only one alcoholic drink a day and thought he had been doing all the right things, his diagnosis came as a shock. In keeping with Benny's philosophy on health, his doctor recommended he take saw palmetto and a zinc supplement. His prostate responded quickly. "Now my prostate is back to normal and I hope I'll never have enlargement again," says Benny.

Zinc is also believed to reduce cancer risks. It is required to utilize carotenes, and therefore may be cancer-protective.

A good source for zinc is from animal and fish as these high protein foods contain amino acids which bind to zinc and make it more soluble. More specifically, good sources include liver, shellfish, oysters, meat, canned fish, hard cheese, whole grains, nuts, eggs and pulses. The zinc in grains is found mainly in the germ and bran coverings, so food refining and processing reduce it substantially. For example, flour refining causes a 77 percent loss in zinc, rice refining an 83 percent loss, and processing cereals from whole grains an 80 percent loss.

Vegetables contain smaller amounts of zinc and also contain compounds such as phytates and oxalates which bind zinc, leaving less available for absorption. Also food additives and chemicals such as EDTA, which are used in food processing, reduce zinc absorption, as do large amounts of textured vegetable protein.

Unfortunately, 90 percent of us consume diets deficient in zinc, which is lost in processing, or never exists in a substantial amount due to our nutrient-poor soils. Also, zinc does not store well in the body and a reduction in dietary intake leads to deficiency fairly quickly. Excretion of zinc is mainly via the feces but some is lost in the urine. Excessive sweating can cause losses of up to 3 mg per day.

Zinc is poorly absorbed by the body on its own. Unless it is combined with vitamin B6, zinc cannot be converted into a form that is readily used by the prostate. Therefore, any therapy using zinc supplementation must also include adequate intake of this vitamin. You should know that zinc absorption decreases with age. People over 65 may absorb half as much as those between 25 and 30 years old.

Symptoms of zinc deficiency include eczema on the face and hands, hair loss, and apathy. Deficiency may also lead to loss of the senses of taste and smell, anemia, poor appetite, impaired conduction and nerve damage, white spots on the nails, mental disorders, susceptibility to infections, delayed wound-healing and impotence in men.

The recommended dietary allowance (RDA) is about 15 milligrams per day for adult males. Zinc is widely available as an over-the-counter dietary supplement. Specifically, these supplements, especially in the form of zinc picolinate or zinc citrate, may be beneficial in reducing the enlargement of the prostate and in reducing the symptoms.

If you decide to supplement your diet, here are some important points to remember:

Zinc supplements are available in various forms such as zinc gluconate, zinc sulfate, zinc picolinate or chelated zinc.

Zinc supplements may be best taken first thing in the morning or two hours after meals. However, taking them with meals helps to reduce the nausea which occurs occasionally when the stomach is empty.

Zinc and copper have related roles in many body functions and the balance between the two nutrients is important. If you take zinc regularly in doses of 25 mg or above it is wise to take 2 to 3 mg of copper to avoid imbalances in the copper-to-zinc ratio.

While toxic effects of zinc are rare, high doses—around 200 mg—can sometimes cause abdominal pain, nausea and vomiting. Other symptoms include dehydration, lethargy, anemia and dizziness.

THE INSURANCE VITAMIN

Vitamin E is an important antioxidant, and has been touted as a help for almost any condition from acne to wound healing. Now there's evidence it can cure prostate cancer.

A study published in the *Journal of the National Cancer Institute 1998* suggests that alpha-tocopherol—the most common form of vitamin E—may reduce the risk of advanced prostate cancer.

A placebo-controlled, double-blind trial carried out by Olli P. Heinonen and his colleagues at the University of Helsinki, Finland, studied 29,133 men ages 50 to 69. The subjects received either alpha-tocopherol (50 International Units—or I.U.—daily), beta-carotene (20 mg daily), both supplements together, or a placebo. The treatments were continued for five to eight years.

NOTE: To convert International Units (I.U.) to milligrams, multiply the number by .66 (or two-thirds) to roughly get the dosage in milligrams (mg). For example, 15 I.U. equals 10 milligrams.

Multivitamins generally contain about 30 I.U. of vitamin E while single supplements most often have a minimum of 100 I.U. of vitamin E. The dose of 50 I.U. in the Finnish study is about five times the Recommended Dietary Allowance of vitamin E for men, and about three times what most people get from food.

Compared with the placebo group, the men taking only alpha-tocopherol developed 36 percent fewer prostate cancers. The men taking both supplements had a 16 percent lower incidence, while those taking only beta-carotene had a 20 percent higher incidence than the placebo group.

Combined, the two groups receiving alpha-tocopherol developed 32 percent fewer prostate cancers than the two groups that did not receive it. Their incidence of advanced cancer was 40 percent lower, and their mortality from prostate cancer was 41 percent lower. Researchers found these differences statistically significant.

However, they found alpha-tocopherol had no significant effect on the incidence of late-stage cancer. Nor did it affect survival time after diagnosis, indicating that once advanced cancer had developed, alpha-tocopherol did not influence its course.

These results suggest that vitamin E may help prevent prostate cancer from moving from the latent to the progressive stage. How it might do so is uncertain, but several mechanisms are possible. Its antioxidant properties may prevent free radical damage, or it may protect against cancer by increasing immunity. Vitamin E also has been reported to depress the activity of protein kinase C, an enzyme that regulates cell proliferation.

Despite the striking results, this study has some potential sources of bias and must be interpreted cautiously. For one thing, the study was designed primarily to investigate alpha-tocopherol and beta-carotene in the prevention of lung cancer. Therefore, all the subjects were smokers.

Also—and I hope you can follow me here—since there is evidence that alpha-tocopherol may also reduce BPH, men who take vitamin E would have fewer symptoms, and would therefore be less likely to receive tests that might lead to cancer diagnosis. In addition, it is suspected that vitamin E supplements may also create other risks. Among those taking it in the study, there were 66 deaths from cerebral hemorrhage compared with 44 such deaths among the men not taking it.

Further clinical trials are obviously needed, and are planned, before vitamin E can be recommended for prostate cancer prevention.

Foods rich in vitamin E include vegetable oils (particularly those from safflower, sunflower and cotton seeds), grains, and nuts. The leading sources in the United States diet include salad dressings and mayonnaise, margarine, cake, cookies, doughnuts and eggs. To ingest 50 International Units of vitamin E from such foods would mean also taking in a great deal of extra fat. Therefore, supplements are a good idea.

Vitamin E is actually a general name for eight different compounds called "tocopherols" and "tocotrienols." There are four tocopherols called "alpha, beta, gamma and delta" and four tocotrienols with the same designations.

Vitamin E comes in both a natural and synthetic form. Natural types are given the name d-alpha (or d-beta, d-gamma, or d-delta) tocopherol. Synthetic vitamin E can be given the same name except there is a small "l" next to the little "d". So while natural vitamin E would be "d-alpha tocopherol," a synthetic type would be "dl-alpha tocopherol."

According to Mark A. Moyad, M.P.H.-Basic Science/Clinical Prostate Cancer Supplement Researcher and Lecturer-University of Michigan Medical-Urology/Oncology Dept., recent studies along with some past studies have demonstrated that natural vitamin E is not only better absorbed by the human body than the synthetic type, but the liver does a better job of recognizing it and putting it into the blood.

Vitamin E should always be taken with a meal for better absorption and to prevent an upset stomach. Also, you should know that the following can decrease vitamin E blood levels:

- a high level of vitamin A (from supplements)
- a high intake of wheat bran
- a high intake of pectin
- a high intake of alcohol
- smoking

Also, you should be cautious about taking vitamin E if you have high blood pressure since it may cause an initial increase in your reading. You should also be careful if you're already taking anti-coagulants or aspirin since vitamin E also can thin your blood.

The RDA for Vitamin E is about 10 milligrams or 15 International Units a day which many multivitamins seem to contain. However, as you've already read, this dosage is far too low to prevent or even have an effect on prostate cancer.

John Hathcock, Ph.D., Director of Nutritional and Regulatory Science for the Council for Responsible Nutrition, says Vitamin E, in all forms, is one of the safest of all vitamins. He has found no adverse effects demonstrated with alpha-tocopherol at intakes of 1,200 International Units (I.U.) or more.

IS BIGGER BETTER?

Up until now, the herbal products business has been dominated by independent supplement marketers. But now several big drug firms are introducing herbal supplement lines. Among them are:

1. Warner-Lambert has recently released two botanical supplements, Quanterra Mental Sharpness, which is made from ginkgo biloba to promote and maintain concentration and focus, and Quanterra Prostate, made from saw palmetto.

2. Bayer™ Corp.'s One-A-Day™ herbal products came out in September, 1998, and include "Cold Season" tablets with echinacea, zinc and vitamin C; and "Cholesterol Health," made with garlic, soy extract, vitamin E and lecithin. Also in this new product line is "Prostate Health," which I'll discuss shortly.

3. Whitehall-Robins Healthcare, a division of American Home Products Corp., has launched a line of six botanical products called Centrum Herbals™.

4. Pharmaton, a division of Boehringer Ingelheim Pharmaceuticals, has sold the popular Ginsana™ (ginseng) and Ginkoba™ (ginkgo biloba) for several years now. New products this year include Venastat™, a horse chestnut seed extract to promote circulation in the legs, and Movana™, a St. John's Wort product for mild to moderate depression.

5. Smith Kline Beecham has test-marketed four herbal products under the Abtei brand name.

Industry watchers expect these moves by the big drug firms to have dramatic effects on the testing and marketing of herbal supplements. They are expected to affect the way these supplements are viewed by the public, perhaps adding legitimacy to the burgeoning industry.

But just because the major drug companies are entering the market does not guarantee that they will make any better or more effective products. The only certainty is that you'll probably pay more for their offerings. For example, Bayer says it has a $25 million marketing budget this year for the new herbal line; most is going to advertising.

Still, botanical supplements from well-known drug firms will attract consumers who were hanging on the edge, unsure about whether to take the products, says Mark Blumenthal, founder of the American Botanical Council, a scientific and policy group. "You're going to have more people using herbal products, and you're going to have more pharmacists and physicians willing to recommend products because they are going to have the assurance that the products are well-manufactured," he says.

Whether the drug manufacturers are introducing products that are really any better quality than those already on the market is an open question. "I don't think anyone knows," says Robert Moore, an FDA senior regulatory scientist. Having drug companies make botanicals doesn't necessarily translate into a product that is inherently safer or more effective or that it's manufactured to any standards "because there are no standards," he says.

But others are confident that consumers can expect to buy quality botanical supplements from the drug companies. John Troup, president of General Nutrition Centers, says he thinks the pharmaceutical companies are going to increase consumer awareness of the use and benefits of herbs. He also says they're going to weed out the companies that don't have "good quality control and good marketing."

CAVEAT EMPTOR: BUYER BEWARE (PART II)

Because of the growing concern by men, supplements with ingredients specifically for treating prostate diseases are suddenly appearing on the market. If anyone had any doubt that prostate disease was a serious problem, all one had to do was look at what a leading pharmaceutical company recently did. The Bayer Corp.'s "One-A-Day™" division has recently introduced a new line of specialty supplements, one specifically for prostate problems. Called "Prostate Health," this product, which comes in a 30-count bottle, combines 15 mg of zinc (the U.S. RDA), 80 mg of Pumpkin Seed Oil Standardized Extract, and 320 mg of Saw Palmetto Standardized Extract. Its marketing material states, "Use One-A-Day Prostate Health alone or in addition to your One-A-Day multivitamin to help you feel your best." Bayer recommends that you take two softgels per day.

Now Bayer is a fine company and makes excellent products. But at 30 tablets per bottle, there's only a 15-day supply. Plus, it's missing some key ingredients, most notably, vitamin B6. As you may recall, zinc is poorly absorbed by the body on its own. Unless it is combined with Vitamin B6, zinc cannot be converted into a form that is readily used by the prostate. Therefore, any therapy using zinc supplementation must also include adequate intake of vitamin B6.

In order to get B6 and other helpful vitamins and minerals, you've got to buy ANOTHER of Bayer's products, namely One-A-Day multivitamins (or something similar.) You probably would want to anyway, but I find it surprising that B6 isn't included in Prostate Health.

I'm looking at *Parade,* the magazine insert that comes with my Sunday newspaper, in which there is a mail order ad for a product named ProSina. ProSina's ingredients include 30 mg. of beta-sitosterol, and 0.1 mg. of beta-D-glucosidase. Fine. As you may recall, beta-sitosterol comes from pygeum, and the ad mentions an article in the medical journal *Lancet* which touts beta-sitosterol. The ad even says ProSina conforms with DSHEA. Excellent!

Now ProSina is being sold by a company named Gempro in Linthicum, Maryland. I have never heard of Gempro. Second, ProSina has the official "Seal of Approval" from the American Prostate Society (APS.) Now I'm confused. With a little digging I've discovered that the American Prostate Society is a relatively new organization. Its web site has some good information (culled from other sources) but there's no mention of who's behind the organization; there are no doctors or medical institutions mentioned at all. I did notice that the organization is based in Hanover, Maryland. Is it just coincidence that the APS and Gempro are from the same state? Maybe so.

Assuming that everything is on the "up-and-up," let's look at ProSina a little more closely. For a 60-tablet trial size, ProSina costs $24.95 plus $1.50 for postage and handling. Now, even if you only take one tablet per day, that's pretty steep. At my local General Nutrition Center (GNC), where prices generally run high, I can buy sixty 1,000-mg pygeum capsules for $18.00.

You do what you like, but I think I'll pass on ProSina.

I'm on the Internet. There are scores of prostate products for sale here. One that's been around for a while is Proslan, which contains many good ingredients such as saw palmetto, bee pollen, hydrangea root, panax ginseng, glycine, l-alanine and glutamic acid, zinc gluconate, vitamin B6 (pyridoxine), copper gluconate, vitamins A, C and E, and silica. Unfortunately, it doesn't state how much of each is in the product. Also, prices are quoted in British Pounds. If you're in the United States, unless you can convert, you won't know how much it will cost in good' ol' Yankee dollars. If you can, you'll find that it costs about $33.

Now, maybe that's not too much to pay for a healthy prostate, especially when you calculate what the alternatives cost. Still, this is something you should be prepared to take for the rest of your life. The differences in price can add up.

Again, the choice is yours.

But it's not just mail order or on-line products you should be careful buying. If you venture into your local drug store you'll see myriad offerings for the same substance, all in the same size bottle. Look closely; not all have the same quantity of capsules or the same amount of milligrams. Some companies are ingenious when it comes to jamming cotton into a tiny bottle.

Then there's price. If it's much lower than a comparable product, it's probably some sort of gimmick. Study the label. It may be loaded with other unnecessary stuff, or inferior ingredients.

MORE TO COME . . .

You've probably noticed that you are near the end of the chapter, and you may be thinking, "Hey! I've heard of some other things that can help my prostate. This joker hasn't mentioned beta-1, 3-glucan, or vitamin C."

You're right. There are a number of other substances that can help your prostate. For example, evening primrose oil has proven helpful. There's also a Swiss extract of flower pollen (Cernilton) which has potent anti-inflammatory actions and has been effective in prostatitis in a number of clinical studies. And we've barely covered vitamins A, B6 and C.

Don't worry, we're not done yet—not by a long shot.

CHAPTER FOUR

EXERCISE YOUR
WAY TO
PROSTATE HEALTH

You're probably asking yourself what exercise has to do with your prostate. In a word—plenty.

Men who exercise have lower testosterone levels immediately following the activity. You may recall that reduced testosterone levels mean a reduced risk of prostate cancer. In fact, a standard treatment of prostate cancer is to reduce the amount of testosterone circulation in the body.

Without testosterone, prostate cancer cells cannot replicate nor can the cancer metastasize. Remember also, with lower levels of testosterone there's less conversion to harmful DHT. That means besides cancer, you're less likely to develop BPH.

It's not known whether the low levels of testosterone are a result of diminished production or of greater metabolism. It doesn't matter. In either case, the result is definitely beneficial to prostate cancer-prone men.

GETTING OFF ON THE RIGHT FOOT:
WHY IT'S IMPORTANT TO EXERCISE

Need proof to get you up and off the sofa? Consider the data gathered over 15 years in a Harvard University Alumni health study. Results gleaned from nearly 18,000 men strongly suggest that a consistent exercise program over many years may lessen the risk of developing prostate cancer. In the study, while 419 men did develop cancer, only one case was reported among the men describing themselves as highly active.

Still not convinced? Besides the Harvard study there have been at least nine others looking into a prostate-exercise connection. Seven indicated that exercise may offer some protection against prostate cancer. The largest of these was conducted at the famous Cooper Clinic in Dallas, Texas. It involved 12,975 men over an 18-year period and concluded that moderate to high levels of cardiorespiratory fitness may protect against prostate cancer. In addition, it showed that men who burned 1,000 or more calories a week in physical activity consistently had a lower prostate cancer risk compared with those who were less active.

You should know that there were three studies that did not show a correlation between exercise and prostate cancer. In those, two used only college athletes as subjects and the third simply considered those who had either sedentary or active occupations.

By the way, burning 1,000 calories doesn't require a whole lot of activity. Walking about 30 minutes a day five days a week will burn about that many. If you're more active than that—say you burn between 1,000 and 4,000 calories a week through exercise—you'll have even lower risk.

Ideally, you should do some sort of aerobic exercise, that is, any rhythmic activity that involves large muscle groups, like those of the legs or arms. Aerobic exercises include walking, jogging, cycling and swimming. Unlike anaerobic exercise, which is done at high intensity, aerobic exercise is performed at low to moderate intensity for an extended period of time. If a man is unable to talk during aerobic exercise, he is probably pushing too hard and is not in his aerobic training zone.

Be warned, though: extra exercise one week won't help you the next. The lowered post-exercise level of testosterone is only temporary and will return to normal within 24 hours.

Let's face facts. As we age, many of us get in worse and worse shape and, naturally, we like to blame it on our age. Sorry. That just doesn't hold water. Our shape (or lack thereof) is often not so much from the aging process itself, but from our sedentary lifestyle; we use our muscles less. Inactive adults lose approximately one-half pound of muscle per year, or five pounds per decade. Muscle weakness, bone loss and sluggish metabolism normally accompany aging but are not solely caused by it.

Since most people continue to eat as much as usual, what's going to happen? If you take in more calories than you burn, the extra calories are stored as fat. Fat is less dense than muscle; a pound of fat takes up more room than a pound of muscle. This means that as you lose muscle and gain fat, your weight might remain the same over the years, but your waistline continues to expand. So as time passes we gain weight, our muscles get weak, our joints lose flexibility and we increase our risk of disease.

There is one simple solution—get moving, and keep moving. Even lawn work, gardening, bicycling, hiking, golf, tennis—any activities that are just part of your life, but aren't formal exercise—are nevertheless exercise.

For example, when at an office building or a hotel, take the stairs instead of the elevator. Park at the far end of a parking lot, and walk a little. Anything is better than nothing. Remember that even a daily walk, at a brisk pace, will help your prostate.

If walking is not for you, there are many other ways to increase physical activity. One may even be more enjoyable than others: simply, more sex. Think about it. Besides the physical activity which reduces your testosterone, you'll lose more from ejaculating. Explain it to your partner. Tell her you need her help. It's not romantic but it just might work.

Let's get back on track. There's another positive for your prostate when you exercise: weight reduction. According to a study at Loma Linda University in California, obese men are more than twice as likely to develop fatal prostate cancer than men closer to their ideal weight.

Now granted, we have already spent a lot of time covering food. But as we all know, permanent weight loss from diet alone is pretty futile. Most, if not all of us, have suffered from the yo-yo effect after taking on some gimmick diet. I'll bet a pound of tofu that if you lost ten or more pounds in a month, you gained it back rather quickly. Am I right?

Now, before you go dashing off to the mall, let me ask you one simple question. Where do you think is the best place to buy exercise equipment? Discount stores? Sporting goods stores? Mail order? The answer is, none of the above. From my experience, the best place to buy exercise equipment is at garage sales or flea markets.

When it comes to physical fitness we all have the best of intentions. For many of us that means buying something to help us recapture that head-turning bod we had in high school. Or, if we didn't have it then, we swear that now is the time . . .

And so we go out and buy the hydromatic dual quad lifecycle, or the 12-speed treadmill with overdrive and chrome headers. We hurry home, set it up, put on our designer warmup suit and $250 "running shoes" and have at it. The next day we're stiff as hell, and decide to ease up a bit. Then, after a week or two we look in the mirror, climb on the bathroom scale and get depressed because the drastic changes we crave aren't coming fast enough. Still, we plug on, but the exercycle-slash-treadmill is getting more and more boring, and before long it's stored away. Next stop? Garage sale.

A successful exercise program is NOT directly related to how much money you spend on gear. It's about patience. It's about patiently working toward your desired goals. In our case, a healthy prostate.

We need to be realistic. Just like you're not going to bulletproof your prostate overnight, you are not going to get meaningful results on an exercise program right away either. You've probably "worked" a long time developing your flab. Give your body equal time to counteract it.

As I said earlier, exercise must be an integral part of any permanent weight loss program. The two go hand-in-hand: a sensible, healthy diet (often referred to as a low-fat diet), and exercise seem to be the only successful way to maintain long-term weight control.

Since the 1970s, the American College of Sports Medicine has recommended 20 to 60 minutes of aerobic activity three to five days a week at 60 to 80 percent of a person's maximum heart rate. But clearly this advice has gone unheeded. "People were overwhelmed," explains Tammy Griffin, fitness coordinator at the Central Health Improvement program at Central Michigan University in Mount Pleasant. "They felt they had to count their heart rate, join a health club, get a personal trainer."

Then in 1993, Dr. Stephen Blair of the Cooper Institute of Aerobic Research in Dallas released a study of 13,000 patients he had tracked over eight and a half years. Blair found that the least fit people had death rates three to five times higher than those considered moderately fit. But "moderately fit" people weren't the people entering 10K races or taking Jazzercise classes. They were just a tad more active than the average couch potato.

In response, the American College of Sports Medicine and the Centers for Disease Control (CDC) amended their fitness guidelines to call for 30 minutes of moderate, intermittent exercise most days of the week to improve our health. The new guidelines quickly became dubbed "Exercise Lite."

To meet this goal, exercise can include such things as a brisk walk, climbing stairs, and yard work. What's more, the 30 minutes could be accumulated throughout the day, rather than in one concentrated burst. But experts also say that the more you work out, the more you benefit. Even very intense exercise was shown to be better than moderately intense exercise. For instance, runners who covered 40 miles a week had a lower heart-disease risk than those who ran 30 miles a week.

Now some of us don't even drive 40 miles a week, so jogging that distance is out of the question. Even meeting the minimum fitness guidelines, though, seems a challenge for many of us. Fact is, most Americans flat out don't exercise, indoors or out. In a 1991 survey by the Centers for Disease Control, only 12 percent of adult Americans reported regular, vigorous exercise, defined by the CDC as the equivalent of a brisk 20-minute walk three or more times a week. Six percent of adults said they devoted little or no time to physical activity.

So how much exercise do we really need to galvanize our prostate against disease? Is it worth the extra effort to, say, join an aerobics class, or should we just be content with taking the stairs instead of the elevator?

The answer, it turns out, depends on what benefits you want from a fitness program, how safe you want to be. Everyday activities, if done frequently enough and with vigor, can indeed provide substantial health benefits. But if your goal is thwarting prostate disease, shedding some recalcitrant pounds, changing your body shape, or reaching peak condition, you'll need to work a lot harder.

How do you know if you're doing enough? Well, first you've got to exert yourself enough to work up a light sweat. Your heart rate should be elevated, although you should be able to carry on a conversation without gasping for air. Also, while you can spread your activities over the course of a day, Dr. Gregory Heath, an epidemiologist at the CDC suggests that you try to exercise in increments of at least 10 minutes. So one run up the stairs from the basement may not fill the bill, but climbing perhaps 10 flights at the office would work.

You needn't be a fanatic, though, about keeping track of time and activity. Tammy Griffin says the goal of Exercise Lite is "to get someone into a regular routine where they're at least going out and walking." People should "just become more aware of changes they can make in their overall amount of activity."

Both Griffin and Heath also recommend some weight- or resistance-training at least twice a week. "It doesn't matter how they do it, be it carrying in their groceries, taking some cans of food and doing biceps curls, or a formal weight training program," says Griffin. "Just work against gravity."

Besides benefitting your prostate, exercise can do quite a few other great things for you. It can improve skeletal-muscle strength and endurance, cardiopulmonary fitness, flexibility, and enhance feelings of well-being. Aging is normally accompanied by loss of muscle strength and bone density. Both problems are helped by exercise. Tendons and ligaments are also strengthened by exercise, which helps to stabilize joints, which reduces risk of falls. And stronger joints enhance overall mobility as well.

Exercise can help to improve posture, and poor posture can cause lower back pain. It can also help sufferers of arthritis, and other musculo-skeletal problems. Even if you end up in a hospital for surgery, the fitter you are, the better your chances of a successful recovery.

There is some evidence that exercise enhances the immune system. It definitely helps prevent development of diabetes in adults, and improves digestion, since it is a natural laxative. There are numerous other potential results: improved self-image and self-confidence, perhaps improved mental acuity, increased sociability, and an aid in overcoming insomnia.

It also can reduce your mental stress, which can put pressure on your prostate. In fact, reducing stress should be high on your list of reasons to exercise.

Exercise is important not just for immediate calorie burn, but for increasing the Resting Metabolic Rate (RMR—formerly known as basal metabolic rate, or BMR) so that we expend more calories all day long, even during sleep. Exercise can perform this little miracle by increasing muscle tissue, which is more metabolically active than, say, "fat." That is, muscle burns more calories than fat does.

In addition, older, sedentary individuals tend to rely more on carbo-hydrate utilization than do younger individuals. This does not imply that older people can't lose fat weight as a result of training. It does mean they may need to exercise at a lower relative intensity to keep going longer, thus enhancing duration and total calorie expenditure. Exercise training stud-ies on an elderly population have demonstrated that over time the elderly can increase the ratio of fat to carbohydrate use.

SHAPING UP—NOT SHIPPING OUT

Don't think you're too old to start. Exercise can help you at any age, if you're suitably cautious. It is a good idea to get the approval of your physi-cian before starting an exercise program.

There are several health risk factors which you should either elimi-nate or at least discuss with your physician as part of your pre-exercise medical consultation. They are:

- Cigarette smoking,
- Obesity (30 percent or more overweight),
- Diabetes,

- High blood pressure,
- High blood cholesterol level, and
- Family history of death under age 55 from heart or other health-related reasons.

The American College of Sports Medicine recommends at least 30 minutes of moderate exercise most days of the week. Sadly, about half the people who start an exercise program quit within the first year. In spite of all the information on the health and longevity benefits of regular exercise, most Americans moan and groan when it comes to moving their bodies.

Here are some of the most common reasons why good exercise intentions fail. Do any of these sound like you?

"There's Just Not Enough Time."

Solution: Make fitness a priority and schedule time to exercise.

"I Have Demands from My Job, Family and Other Commitments."

Solution: Everyone wastes at least one hour a day, so blocking out 30 minutes to do something pleasurable for ourselves isn't unreasonable. We must learn that exercise needs to become a habit and then part of a lifestyle.

Still think that's impossible? Try planning your workout as you would any other important appointment, and don't let yourself miss it.

You don't have to do all your exercise at once. Those 30 minutes can be broken into shorter segments throughout a busy day and worked into your routine. You could park your car a 15-minute walk from your office, set aside 10 minutes in the evening for a jog with the dog, or volunteer your time each weekend with a local group that builds houses for low-income residents.

"I'm Too Tired to Exercise."

Solution: Sitting all day will make you feel tired and sluggish. A little physical activity will feed oxygen to your brain and muscles, revitalizing you.

"I HATE Exercising."

Solution: That's OK. Most sedentary people feel this way. Don't think exercise, think physical activity. And when you think of physical activity, think of a fun recreational activity that just happens to include moving your body.

"I Tried It, and I'm Too Sore. What's the Use?"

Solution: Start slowly and build incrementally from week to week. One of the biggest reasons people don't stick to a program is that they approach exercise too rigorously. They get sore, bored, or frustrated and end up quitting.

It might help if you kept a log to set goals and chart your efforts. An exercise journal can help you chart your progress and set fitness goals. It doesn't need to be anything elaborate—just keep track of what you do and when you do it. At the end of the week you'll see what you were able to accomplish. Plus, it'll help you plan the next week.

"This is Going to Take Forever."

Solution: Be patient. It takes three to six months to see noticeable changes and to develop exercise as a habit. Too many people don't see the results they want in the first few weeks, and then they decide that it's not worth it, says Dee Papathanasiou of Health and Sportworks, Inc. in Charlotte, North Carolina. Face it. Quick fixes just don't happen with exercise.

"This is Too Boring. What's on TV?"

Solution: Find an exercise program that complements your body type, your schedule, your interests and your goals. Make sure you really enjoy whatever exercise you choose. If you've always hated jogging or loathed exercise bikes, by all means do something else.

If an exercise program provides more punishment than enjoyment, do you really think you're going to stick to it? asks Jim Taylor, Ph. D., a sports psychologist based in Aspen, Colorado.

Taylor strongly suggests finding a workout buddy with similar abilities and fitness objectives. In fact, research indicates that your chances of sticking to a fitness program double if you work out with someone else.

You also need to select the right exercise for your fitness goals. The best results come from selecting activities that support your aspirations. Believe it or not, one of your goals should be to have fun. If you enjoy working out, you're far more likely to stick with an exercise routine.

Here are some ideas for matching your personality to a fitness plan:

Do You Like Team Sports?

Try rowing, softball, volleyball, or basketball. If you're into one-on-one competition, think about racquetball or tennis.

Do You Like to Socialize While You Exercise?

Try an aerobic class, ballroom dancing, or exercising with a friend or spouse.

Do You Prefer Exercising Alone?

Try running, biking, swimming, or working out at home.

Do You Get Bored Easily by Most Exercise?

Pick up a novel along with a stationary bicycle, listen to tapes while you walk, or try an activity such as yoga that requires mental as well as physical concentration.

Are You an Active Person Who Likes to Try New Things?

Think about in-line skating, rock-climbing, or cross-country skiing.

Do You See Exercise as a Chance to Escape from the Frenzy of Everyday Life?

Try yoga or one of the martial arts.

Are You Injury-prone?

Try water sports, such as lap swimming or water aerobics.

Still Unsure What to Do?

Get a personal trainer to design a fitness plan.

BOY, YOU'VE GOT TO CARRY THAT WEIGHT

Aerobic-type workouts are important, but don't forget strength training. Researchers at the Tufts University exercise lab say that strength training is a potent age eraser. It is their weapon of choice for fighting physical declines associated with aging.

More and more fitness experts are recommending strength training for health reasons, for older adults as well as younger adults. Strength training is extremely important in combating the age-related declines in muscle mass, bone density and metabolism. It is an effective way to increase muscle strength and to shed unwanted inches. Strength training also helps to decrease back pain, reduce arthritic discomfort, and help prevent or manage some diabetic symptoms.

Don't think that you need to work out in a gym for two hours to strength train. Significant gains can be made with a consistent 30-minute workout performed two to three times per week.

Okay. Have you got an idea what you'd like to do? Great! Now it's important that you heed a few simple rules.

FOLLOW THESE SAFETY GUIDELINES

1. Drink lots of water before, during, and after exercise. Keep hydrated.

2. If you experience dizziness, queasiness or nausea, extreme shortness of breath, or shakiness, slow down, or stop for a rest.

3. Exercise muscles to fatigue, but never to pain or collapse.

4. Increase activity level only gradually—about 10 percent at a time. Only make increases when your current level of activity feels easy. If you get too tired, back off a bit.

5. Take a day off if you are really tired, and don't exercise if you have an above-normal temperature.

6. Don't exercise right after heavy meals. Wait about two hours. Hard exercise should be limited to five days a week, about one hour at a time to prevent injuries.

7. Use good posture when you exercise: no swayback, keep your weight evenly distributed on both feet, flex your knees, tighten abdominal and buttock muscles, and keep your neck in line with your spine.

8. Warm-up and cool-down. Although your time may be limited, both are very important. If you must cut back shave time off each step, not just one.

Guidelines for a warm-up are:

- Limber up for 6–7 minutes. This may be slow walking, pedaling on a stationary bicycle, or some similar aerobic activity.
- Rhythmic exercise for 5–6 minutes. This is a series of movements designed for specific muscles, to get them fully prepared for the exercises you plan.
- Very mild stretching for 1–2 minutes.

A good warm-up should raise internal body temperature slightly, and elevate your heart and breathing rates slightly. A warm body is ready for more intense exercise; joints and muscles are loosened up and ready to go. Note that weights should not be used during a warmup.

A cool-down is designed to allow heart rate and breathing to gradually return to normal. An abrupt termination of an exercise session can result in pooling of blood in the lower extremities, straining your cardiovascular system. Your heart has to work especially hard to get the blood back up to the trunk, so a cooling down activity helps that task. It's important that when you cool down, do not drop your head below your chest; otherwise you might faint as a result.

A standing cool-down should last about 5-7 minutes. This may be easy walking, or a very gentle ride on a stationary cycle, or other aerobic activity.

This cool-down description is more applicable to an aerobic workout, and may be tailored for a calisthenics or weight workout, which won't normally raise heart rate and breathing to sustained high levels.

Working a muscle to fatigue helps it grow stronger, but don't go to the point of being completely "wasted." An injury can result from uncontrollable, exhausted muscles, especially as we get older.

Remember that "no pain, no gain" is not a good indicator of just working hard. You must learn to distinguish between real pain, and just being tired. Fatigue is one thing, and pain is another. As we get older, tissue injuries are slower to heal, so we should strive to avoid them.

If you experience joint pain, it is wise to avoid the movement that caused it, but some muscle soreness around a joint is okay; it will go away, and you will get stronger. Unless muscle soreness is really intense, mild exercise is better than simple rest to make it disappear.

9. Last, for gosh sakes, don't forget to breathe, especially if you're doing resistance training. Remember: exhale on the exertion phase, and inhale on the "return" phase.

WHAT TO EXPECT AND HOW TO STAY ON TRACK

Fewer than one-third of those who begin an exercise program are still exercising by the end of their first year. Typically people drop out after one week, by the end of the first month, or after three months. The pattern is strikingly similar between individuals.

Here are the typical stumbling blocks and strategies to overcome them.

Week One

The first week of any exercise program has an extremely high dropout rate. Attempting "too much, too soon" often leads to soreness, fatigue and/or injuries. Additionally, unfamiliarity with movements and equipment can prove so frustrating that you want to throw in the towel.

STRATEGY: Begin slowly, and always warm up, cool down and stretch properly to help prevent soreness and injuries. Work at your own level and gradually increase duration and level of difficulty. It's natural to feel awkward at this point.

Weeks Two to Four

Expect some problems "sticking to it." Enthusiasm often wanes when pounds don't drop or muscles don't develop overnight.

STRATEGY: Don't expect immediate dramatic changes in body shape or weight loss. (Doctors recommend losing a maximum of one to two pounds per week.) Although changes are happening internally, most external benefits won't become visible for a few more weeks. Add a second activity to your exercise schedule to help prevent overuse injuries and boredom.

Week Twelve Through Month Six

Finally! Physical changes are becoming apparent at this stage. Increased aerobic capacity, reduced blood pressure, mood elevation, muscle mass increase and weight loss are all possible benefits. Still, half of us give up by the end of the sixth month. Determination is often enough to get people through three months, but during months four through six, reality hits. Also, changes in schedule, emergencies, illnesses and the like crop up causing missed sessions, which can further weaken resolve.

STRATEGY: If you've been forcing yourself to do something you really don't enjoy all that much, you're likely to quit. To combat this tendency, find a type of exercise you like better. Focus on the pleasurable aspects of your routine, such as the early morning sun or class camaraderie. Concentrate on the many benefits your body is reaping, not just in appearance but in general health. These can carry you through this period.

Months Six through Nine

Here's where you normally see the greatest gains: stronger heart, lungs, joints and muscles; better stamina; reduced blood pressure, cholesterol, weight and body fat. But another stumbling block looms. Because improvements begin to level off as you become fitter, further progression requires greater intensity and/or frequency. Additionally, as the mental benefits—exercise "high," improved self-confidence, reduced tension—become routine, you may forget what NOT feeling good is like. So you become discouraged.

STRATEGY: Think long term. If you are not satisfied with your fitness gains, increase your intensity and/or frequency. Realize, though, that further gains will be incremental, since you have probably already achieved your biggest improvements. You could try a new sport, machine or class to add variety and interest. If you make it through the end of the year, you will probably become a lifetime exerciser.

EASY EXERCISES YOU CAN DO ANYTIME, ANYWHERE

Before our first child was born, my wife and I attended natural childbirth classes. Although some of us go there kicking and screaming, there are some devoted husbands excited about participating in the birthing exercise. That is, until they get to one of these classes.

Since the women do most of the work, they tend to pay closer attention than the men. (When their wives go into labor the men who went through these classes can be identified by their yelling, "the baby's coming! the baby's coming!")

Although we have the greatest intentions, our minds tend to wander. There was one thing the instructor said, however, that stuck with me. When explaining exercises for the women to do to prepare for childbirth, she said, "You men should pay attention too. Here's an exercise that could help you later in life with your prostate." She was talking about Kegels.

What's a Kegel, you ask? In the normal male, the internal sphincter muscle at the neck of the bladder does the lion's share of controlling urine flow. Any loss of sphincter function may prevent the bladder neck from closing fully. This usually results in some degree of incontinence. However, men also have a second external sphincter adjacent to the bottom of the prostate. In time, this sphincter can take over some of the control which is lost when the internal sphincter is damaged, but it is not strong enough to do the job alone. Thus it becomes very important to strengthen the pelvic floor muscles, which, by supporting the bladder and preventing it from sagging, can help to keep it fully closed.

Improving the muscle tone of the pelvic floor muscles can be of great help in preventing incontinence, or in regaining continence following a radical prostatectomy. Why wait? Doing them now will not only help you should you have prostate surgery, but will also help your control now.

Doing the Kegel exercises is an easy, convenient, and almost effortless way to gain this valuable pelvic floor muscle tone. They are fast, taking just 5 to 8 minutes maximum, once, or if you prefer, twice a day.

Kegel exercises are easy. Actually there is no need to learn anything new. You've known how to do the basic Kegel movement from the time you were potty trained as a toddler. The pelvic floor muscles are those you would squeeze shut to stop urinating in mid-stream, or to hold back a bowel movement. See? You already know the basic Kegel movement.

If you're still not sure you're doing them right, try this. Put a hand on one butt cheek and contract. If your cheek presses in, you're doing it right. (I suggest you don't try this test in public).

You can do Kegels while lying down, sitting, standing, working or while walking. In fact you can do them at almost any time except when you're engaged in physical activity.

Kegel exercises are completely invisible to others. They are also equipment-free.

Here's the exercise protocol recommended at the Pelvic Floor Training Unit of the Incontinence Clinic at Beth Israel Hospital in Boston, Massachusetts. It's divided into two parts: sets of "long" and "short" exercises. A complete set of the Kegel exercises will take about 8 minutes.

"Long" Kegels

Squeeze your pelvic floor muscles shut as tightly as you can and hold them shut for up to a maximum of 10 seconds.

Relax completely for 10 seconds (not less).

Repeat this cycle 15 times.

That's all there is to it.

If you find you can't hold a contraction for ten seconds, don't worry. As you practice daily, your muscles will gradually develop more and more strength.

After you have completed as many cycles of the long exercise as you can, relax for an additional 30 seconds. Then start on the "short" exercises.

"Short" Kegels

Squeeze and hold for one second.

Relax completely for one second.

Repeat this 5 times for a total of 10 seconds.

Relax completely for 10 seconds.

Repeat this entire cycle four or five times.

When you're doing Kegels correctly, you should not be tensing or straining your stomach or lower abdominal muscles. Remember, the pelvic floor muscles are the only muscles that should be involved in the Kegel exercises. If you find yourself tensing or stretching any others—in the stomach, lower abdomen, hips, thighs, or elsewhere—you're doing them wrong.

Stan was doing Kegels for years, he just didn't know it. All he knew was the sensation was pleasurable and so he did the exercises often, at least 100 times per day. After his doctor noticed a highly developed pubococcygeal (PC) muscle running from his pubic bone in front and his tailbone (coccyx) in back he asked Stan about his bowel and bladder control. Stan said he had never had any problems.

When his doctor found a very, very healthy and normal prostate Stan revealed an even more interesting fact. Though nearly 50 Stan had a highly active and satisfying sex life. And no wonder. Because of his highly developed PC muscle, Stan had been multiorgasmic for over 20 years.

Travelin' Man

Does your job take you out of town quite a bit? You may claim this disrupts your exercise routine, but it doesn't have to. Here are some suggestions.

Before you leave on your trip, call your hotel, or perhaps someone you know, and ask about gym facilities onsite or nearby. Ask if there are parks, running tracks, and jogging paths nearby.

A hotel with a health club is a must. But always ask about the quality and quantity of exercise equipment. What many hotels call a health club often is really a laundry room with only a treadmill and an exercise bike.

Airport delays are a waste of time. They don't have to be. Instead of reading why not get some exercise by walking the terminal? You could even store your bags in a locker and don your training shoes. Naturally, the longer and faster you walk, the better. But even ten minutes can make a difference.

Here are some other tips for getting a workout away from home:

- Pay a single day fee at a nearby gym.
- Sightsee on foot.
- Run, walk or jog in a local park.
- Rent skates or a bicycle.

- Take stairs instead of elevators.
- Racewalk the hotel corridors.

If you tend to lie on your hotel bed mesmerized by the tube, here are three simple exercises you can do. Do them consecutively, or if time is tight, do some in the morning and others at night.

1. Stand with your back against a wall, and slide down, walking your feet away from the wall so they stay right under your knees, until your thighs are taking your weight and you look like you're sitting on an invisible chair. Hold that pose, breathing normally, until your thighs tell you to stop.

2. Lie on your back, knees bent. Cross your arms over your chest or place your hands behind your neck, elbows out to the side. Do not pull on your head. Take a deep breath. As you exhale, pull your abdominal muscles in and let that muscle contraction lift your chest, then shoulders, then—if you can—shoulder blades. Hold at the top for two seconds before slowly releasing down. Keep your head and neck relaxed through the whole sequence.

3. Push-ups are the most effective all-purpose upper-body strengthener. Whether you do push-ups with bent or straight legs, keep your head, neck, and spine in alignment and the abdominals contracted through the whole sequence. Lead with the chest, not your chin or forehead. Go no faster than two seconds down and two seconds up, even slower if you're strong. You should exhale on the way up.

Isometrics

Do you remember Major League pitcher Steve Carlton? In the 1970 and '80s, Carlton led the NL in innings pitched and strikeouts five times each, won 329 games, and captured four Cy Young Awards. He trained by using isometrics (and twisting his hands in three-foot-deep buckets of rice). The powerful lefty made 30 or more starts in 16 seasons.

It's probably safe to say if you haven't made the Major Leagues by now you probably won't. But whether you play golf, tennis, or just push a lawn mower, you can improve your strength by practicing isometric techniques which can enhance muscle size and strength. They can be performed at any age to achieve a stronger and better proportioned physique.

You don't need any fancy equipment besides your own bod. Isometrics target a particular part of the body and take only 10 seconds each. A complete workout can be performed in only 5 minutes.

The principle behind isometric exercise is pretty simple: you press one or more parts of your body against an immovable object. For example, to stretch and strengthen your hamstrings, you could scissor your legs and push against a wall.

How about when you're sitting at your desk? You could press your feet against the floor, or simulate curling weights by pressing up underneath your desktop. (Make sure it's secured well. Otherwise it could go flying across the room.)

Stuck in traffic? Press against the steering wheel with both hands to strengthen your shoulders and arms.

Got the idea? Be careful, though. If you try to simulate lifting an immoveable object, you could do serious damage to your back. You should also note there is little aerobic benefit from isometrics. Also, the exercises are static, and there are no ranges of motion. That means they won't do much for your flexibility.

Reach for Better Health

There's no doubt that strength, aerobics, balance and agility are important components of fitness. But don't overlook something nearly as critical: flexibility. Just a few moments a day devoted to improved flexibility could reduce the potential for musculoskeletal injury that could occur no matter what your activity, be it bowling, tennis, golf or even carrying or lifting.

If your whole body feels tight and you think it's just too late in life to increase your flexibility, you're wrong. It's never too late to begin stretching and you will be able to see results in time. Just check with your physician to make sure the stretches you're planning are safe for you.

Stretching to maintain flexibility has three potential benefits:

1. Stretching helps to maintain range of motion, making all physical activity easier to do when we're young, and easier to continue as we get older.

Stretching increases flexibility by actually elongating the cells in the muscle fibers. Although the muscle returns to its normal shape in the resting position, the cells remain elongated, lengthening the muscle and allowing that particular muscle group greater motion. The tendons, which connect muscles to bones, can also be stretched to some extent. And the fascia, the connective tissue that covers the entire muscle group, also expands to accommodate a longer muscle.

Although we don't usually think of reaching down to pick something up off the floor or getting in and out of a car as "physical" activities, these are movements that are a part of our day. If flexibility is poor and movement becomes strained, reaching to the carpet and getting up again can become a strain.

Stretching exercises help to maintain the pliability and extensibility of the tissues that are associated with range of motion, says Daniel Kosich Ph.D., senior director of professional development for I.D.E.A., the International Association of Fitness Professionals. "Our suspicions are that connective tissues tend to become brittle as we get older unless we make that effort to keep them pliable."

2. Increased flexibility could potentially reduce injury when cold muscles undergo sudden jerky movements. For example, if you need to assume an unusual body position to protect yourself from a fall, you might be less likely to suffer an injury—either from the fall or from trying to protect yourself—if your muscles are stretchy and flexible.

3. Stretching is a great relaxer. Research has shown that muscle tension is relieved when the muscles are stretched and then released.

Yoga and certain types of martial arts that put great emphasis on stretching have been used as methods of relaxation for centuries. Not only do these workouts physically relieve muscle tension, but they also include a component of mental relaxation.

Stretching is not without its risks, however. Muscles and tendons can tear if you force your body to stretch beyond its limits. Stretch slowly just until you begin to feel a slight discomfort in the muscle group, and not beyond.

People get in trouble when they want to do competitive stretching, trying to outdo the person standing next to them in exercise class, points out Peter Bruno, M.D., consulting internist for the Nicholas Institute of Sports Medicine and Athletic Trauma in New York City.

Men should never compare their ability to stretch—especially with women. Men's muscle units are bulkier and stronger than women's, but they're just not as flexible. Women are just stretchier by nature.

If you'd like to improve your flexibility but don't know where or how to start, most experts recommend concentrating on the areas we most often have trouble with: muscle tension in the lower back and the neck and shoulders.

Lower-back and lower-extremity flexibility are particularly important in view of the number of injuries that often occur to the lower back. To stretch your lower back and hamstrings (the muscles at the back of your legs), sit on the floor with your legs straight out in front of you and reach toward your ankles. To stretch your hamstrings, keep your back straight. To stretch out your lower back, round your back just slightly. In either case, lean forward just until you feel a pull and hold for several seconds, then sit up and repeat. Don't bounce, and don't push yourself beyond discomfort to pain.

To stretch your neck and shoulder muscles, sit or stand straight and, keeping your chin parallel to your shoulder, slowly turn your head to the right and hold for several seconds. Then slowly repeat to the left.

With appropriate training, flexibility can, and should, be developed at all ages. This does not mean flexibility can be developed at the same rate by everyone. In general, the older you are, the longer it will take to develop your desired level. Hopefully, you'll be more patient if you're older.

Many experts say that why we become less flexible as we get older is because of changes taking place in our connective tissues. As we age, our bodies gradually dehydrate to some extent. It is believed that stretching stimulates the production or retention of lubricants between the connective tissue fibers, thus preventing the formation of adhesions. So exercise can delay some of the loss of flexibility that occurs due to the aging process.

There are some other changes due to aging:

- An increased amount of calcium deposits and adhesions,
- Changes in the chemical structure of the tissues, and
- Loss of suppleness due to the replacement of muscle fibers with fatty, collagenous fibers.

This does not mean that you should give up trying to achieve flexibility if you are old or inflexible. It just means that you need to work harder, and more carefully, for a longer period of time when attempting to increase flexibility. Increases in the ability of muscle tissues and connective tissues to stretch or elongate can be achieved at any age.

MAKING TIME FOR FITNESS

You know that becoming physically fit can enhance the quality—and quantity—of the years ahead. But you can't seem to find enough time to make fitness work for you.

Making time means setting priorities, sneaking extra activity into daily routines, and scheduling fitness time as you would other important events.

Five minutes of movement here and there does add up to a more active lifestyle. To activate your daily routines, try some of these tips:

Take the stairs when possible, or if you're at the top of a skyscraper, walk a few flights and then take the elevator.

Deliberately park your car at the far end of the parking lot.

Hand-deliver messages at work rather than picking up the phone.

Schedule your fitness time as you would an important meeting.

Walk on your lunch hour, or instead of a coffee break, try a stretching break.

Bring your walking shoes and turn your coffee break into a "stress reduction and revitalization break." It really isn't that hard to do. Remember, this isn't a cardio workout—you won't get sweaty and have to change your clothes if you walk at a moderate pace for ten minutes.

When watching television, use commercial breaks to climb the stairs five times. Take "physical breaks" from the desk or computer to tone your muscles for five minutes with some easy strength-training exercises.

Rather than joining friends for drinks, get together for a jog or a vigorous walk.

We all fall into the habit of using our cars for short trips in the neighborhood. If safety isn't a concern, then probably it's just force of habit. Wouldn't we be better off if we just hoofed it to pick up that loaf of bread?

Replace the "business lunch" with an exercise session at the gym. Sound dumb? Some business people do it all the time. They call it golf.

There's no reason not to do something good for yourself by making fitness one of your daily priorities. By setting aside 20–30 minutes three times a week for a vigorous activity, and by sneaking extra activity into your daily routines, you can become fitter, happier, and more productive. Why not start right now? What have you got to lose?

Besides exercise, there are two other things you should aim for. One is eight hours of sleep a night. Second, limit the stress in your life.

TEN SUPER STRESS REDUCERS

Numerous studies show that high levels of stress increase cancer risk. It's impossible to avoid daily stresses, but you can learn to handle them effectively and stay in control. Maintaining a healthy balance between yourself and your work and family commitments will help you get the most out of life as well as from your personal and professional relationships. You should make it your goal to enrich each day from physical, mental, emotional and spiritual standpoints.

1. Put Yourself on Your "To Do" List

You'll focus more clearly on goals, dreams and to do lists if you write them down. Keep things simple, but do give priority to relationships and obligations that are crucial. And don't create unrealistic aims by expecting perfection or trying to be something you're not. Be honest in evaluation of your skills and preferences.

Establishing priorities will make it easier to say no to less important demands. It will also enable you to objectively balance potential conflicts between your career and personal life. To avoid stress, figure out what it takes to leave work on time.

2. Aerobics

The results of a new study support the notion that aerobic exercise can help older individuals beat the battle of the bulge. "Regular aerobic exercise may counter the age-related tendency toward obesity and its associated risk factors," concluded researchers at the Baltimore Veterans Affairs Medical Center in Maryland.

For a variety of physiological reasons, the amount of daily energy required by the body begins to decline in early middle age. When this drop in energy expenditure is not met by a decline in dietary caloric intake, weight gain results. As I've said, weight gain can lead to cancer, especially cancer of the prostate.

To see whether exercise might counter this trend, the Baltimore researchers placed 32 sedentary men over the age of 46 on a 6-month program of regular aerobic activity. They report that the average daily energy needs of the lean, formerly sedentary men rose by 8 percent after exercise, while those of the obese, sedentary men rose by 5 percent. Obese men lost an average of 8 kilograms (almost 18 pounds) over the 6 months of the program, according to the researchers, and lean subjects experienced a nearly 2 percent drop in body fat.

"Regular aerobic exercise training allowed the lean sedentary men in this study to eat more without gaining weight," the authors conclude, "and aerobic exercise plus weight loss allowed the obese sedentary men to consume more energy while maintaining a lower body weight."

You're now convinced; aerobic exercise can contribute to your overall health. Your first step is to find your target heart range (THR) which is the safest range of heartbeats per minute during exercise. To find it, subtract your age from 220 and multiply the answer by 60 percent and by 80 percent. Aim for the low range when you first begin, gradually working up to the higher range.

Count your heartbeats by taking your wrist or neck pulse for 15 seconds and multiplying the count by 4. If you have an existing medical condition or family history of heart disease, your healthcare professional should determine your best THR.

Your next step is to select aerobic activities that fit your physical condition, personal interests, and environment. Finally, make a commitment to exercise aerobically for 20–30 minutes at least three times per week. In less time than the average TV "sitcom" you can actively enjoy yourself while you improve your health. You can also find ways to fit aerobics into your busy schedule walk during lunch, bicycle to work, invite a friend to a game of handball.

Here are some common aerobic activities:

Aerobics Dancing or Step/Bench: Good choice for those who enjoy group activity and music; aerobics classes and tapes are available for all fitness levels. Aerobic conditioning will strengthen and tone muscles of upper and lower body and increase your flexibility. Low-impact aerobics reduces general risk of injury, while high-impact aerobics can cause stress injuries of joints and back.

Cycling—Stationary or Outdoor: This is a good choice for most people and is especially helpful for those with joint problems. Cycling strengthens and tones the front muscles of the legs and there is little-to-no-risk of injury.

Jogging: Good choice for the well conditioned; not a good choice for the seriously overweight or for those with back, knee, or foot problems. Jogging provides excellent aerobic conditioning. It can strengthen and tone calves, thighs, and buttocks. It can also cause stress injuries of feet, knees, and back.

Swimming: Excellent choice for most people, and is especially good for injury rehabilitation and overweight people. Swimming offers both flexibility and total body conditioning. Injuries are few to none, maybe a little soreness at first.

Walking: Excellent choice for most people, especially for beginners and older people. Walking can strengthen and tone leg muscles. There are various styles you can use: toe-to-heel, power walking, or a casual stroll.

Who says you have to move the same way throughout the walk? I don't know about you, but I find that walking the same way all the time isn't very much fun. For variety, I like to do intervals of something different: walk faster, sideways, even backwards. Naturally, the faster you go, the higher your THR.

Sometimes you're under stress and you can't get away to exercise. When you find yourself tensing up at work or at home, take a few minutes to relax, stretch, and breathe deeply. Or, you could try relaxation techniques such as yoga and TM. These exercises have a calming, refreshing effect: they help lower your heart rate, improve blood circulation, and loosen tight muscles.

Here are some of these formal techniques in more detail:

3. T'ai Chi

If you've ever been to Asia, you may have noticed older people exercising around six in the morning. (Assuming you're up at that hour.) More than likely they're performing the exercise rituals known as T'ai Chi Chuan or T'ai Chi. In China tens of millions of Chinese people do these daily.

T'ai Chi was derived from Taoism. The most important practice of Taoism was concerned with tranquility of mind and improvement of temperament. Taoists had to search for isolated spots where they could lead the life of a hermit. Therefore, the Taoists developed techniques of Martial Art for not only good health but to protect themselves from the attacks of wild animals.

T'ai Chi is based on the concepts of the Yin Yang relationship, where everything in the universe is based on these two different forces collectively called Lian Yee. Taoists believe that since all matter in the Universe is formed from Yin and Yang, it follows logically that all things inherently possess Yin and Yang.

See if you can follow me on this. Yin and Yang exist in both spiritual and material states. In the animal kingdom, Yin and Yang exist in life and death. Yin and Yang also exist in the North and South Poles, in day and night, in the positive and negative charges in physics.

Yin and Yang are opposites, but they are in unity while in opposition. When in harmony, they will counteract and develop, but in an unsuitable and unharmonized condition, they will repel one another and destroy all matter.

Yin and Yang counteract and yet they react. When their reaction reaches its end, they revert in the opposite direction and start all over again.

All natural phenomena follow this pattern of variation in constant repetition. So annually there are the seasonal changes: from warm spring to hot summer, from cool autumn to cold winter, then from cold winter to warm spring again. Also each day exists from the light at dawn to the darkness at dusk, and then from dusk it reverts to dawn again. Similarly, plants grow from flowers to fruits, from fruits to seeds, then from seeds to flowers again. Even for animals, one generation propagates another, and the pattern is repeated continuously.

Therefore, Yin and Yang are involved in all phenomena and at all times in the Universe. Since T'ai Chi reveals the relationship between Nature and Man, Taoists believe no man can evade the effects of this universal variation. Nevertheless, man can still adapt to an environment by putting restrictions on his demands, activities and ambition; then man may live a longer, more balanced life of stability and peace.

The series of Movements of T'ai Chi Chuan comprises the "open and close" of the arms and legs, the "void and substantiality" of steps, the "continuity" of actions, and the "softness" of postures. All these obey the theory of T'ai Chi.

In T'ai Chi, the promotion of our health belongs to Yin while our self-protection belongs to Yang. Slow practice and avoiding the use of great strength is necessary for the improvement of our health, since this will make the actions softer and the muscles of the whole body will relax more easily. It also makes the nervous system relax, so that our emotions will be more stable.

As for the self-defense aspect, the principle of T'ai Chi Chuan concerning this is divided into two parts—the yielding force and the unbending force. Now, I'm not explaining this so you can hold your own in some parking lot brawl, but it does help explain the exercise.

The yielding force belongs to Yin and the unbending force belongs to Yang. When fighting, the yielding force is used to counteract our opponent's attack and the unbending force to counterattack. The change of forces from unbending to yielding or vice versa is achieved in the form of a circle.

Therefore the main pattern of T'ai Chi is like many circles spiraling continually without end. The main feature of this circle is that we use half of the circle as yielding force to counteract the opponent's attack, and the other half circle as unbending force to counterattack the opponent. When using such circles, we can use one hand by itself or both hands together to act upon our opponent directly or indirectly at angles horizontal, inclined or vertical, depending on the circumstances.

T'ai Chi looks like a classical dance with graceful movements and alert actions. It also offers a balanced drill benefitting the muscles and joints throughout the body. Besides exercising the muscles and joints, it gives rise to uniform breathing, especially in the movement of the diaphragm and so offers a good opportunity to exercise the stomach muscles.

You can find T'ai Chi classes in your local Yellow Pages. Many colleges offer adult ed classes, too. That's where I first learned about it.

4. Yoga

When some people hear Yoga they think of it as a Hindu or Buddhist method of religious worship. Often people who practice meditation have been labeled as spacey, emotionally impaired, oversensitive individuals, rushing to fix themselves with the latest New Age contraptions, or as antisocial escapists having no interest in the world.

The truth is, Yoga can be a method of emotional healing and stress reduction. Meditation, or Dhyana, is a powerful tool, one that not only provides us the opportunity to see our lives, but also to slow it down, to let it cool off. It helps us to remember and get in touch with what we really long for, to learn about our real needs, and to find and connect with our authentic life's calling, which is to follow our inner bliss.

In the last decade meditation has become an important, although still minor, healing modality of psychotherapists and rehabilitation institutions, and is being studied at the world's largest universities. Science is finally confirming what was known to yogis for millennia: meditation helps us to heal emotionally, has a calming effect on our nerves, balances blood pressure, has excellent stress reduction properties, and helps us to relax and to control pain.

The term "meditation" can mean both the process or technique of meditation, as well as the state "elicited" by meditation practice. Usually during meditation we concentrate on a particular object or idea, such as a flower, a candle flame, a sound, a word (mantra), an image of a deity, our breath, or, in its purest form, simply nothing.

A beginner would benefit most from the insight meditation style: simply concentrating on the breath and whatever "is." An advanced practitioner might use the style of meditation that requires a concentrated effort, such as focusing the mind on complex visualization and repeating a specially empowered mantra. Such advanced techniques must be acquired only via the process of initiation and only from a competent teacher/guru.

The method of meditation you choose should correspond to your personality, body type and sam'skara (karma). For this, it is best to place your confidence in a competent teacher. The practice of meditation will gradually reduce the stream of thoughts arising in your mind.

The lotus posture is considered the best posture for meditation. Like all "asanas," the lotus posture (padmasana) affects the glandular and bio-magnetic systems. The requirement for an asana for meditation is for the spine to remain straight. Padmasana is a beneficial posture for meditation because it literally locks the spine in a straight position. It is also easy to maintain the straightness for a long time without breaks in concentration.

According to Yoga theorists, our hands and feet contain more afferent and efferent nerves as well as exocrine glands than any other single part of our body. Our hands and feet are major ways bio-energy enters and leaves our bodies. When we sit with legs crossed and locked and our hands folded, the bio-energy, which usually gets dissipated through our hands and feet, forms a closed circuit. This helps prevent our attention from wandering and thus allows for deeper meditation.

Although the lotus posture is said to be the best asana for higher meditation, it may take some time to learn to maintain it properly. You should not be concerned if you are unable to remain in this posture due to your physical condition. Other sitting postures, even in a chair, where the spine remains erect are as good for meditation as Padmasana.

The following method from the Abhidhyan Yoga Institute is ideal for beginners. It's simple, effective and not too time-consuming. Despite its simplicity, many teachers, especially Buddhists, limit themselves to it because it is sufficient for attaining enlightenment. It also helps in coping with stress, learning how to relax and seeing reality as it is.

First, find a quiet, pleasant place and turn off the telephone. Arrange to not be disturbed. If you do not have a quiet, convenient place, then adjust the best you can. It's actually possible to meditate under any conditions.

Sit comfortably on a chair, armchair, floor, mat or a blanket, straighten your back, put your hands on your lap one on top of the other (palms facing up), close your eyes. Slowly breathe in and out deeply 3–4 times to relax a bit. Then examine your body from inside. How does it look? How do you perceive the inside? Where are the organs? What is their color? What is their condition—healthy, sick, tired, full of life?

Slowly, step by step, direct your attention to all the major parts of the body. Once you've covered your entire body, with an imaginary broom, sweep out the tension and fatigue starting at the bottom with your feet and finishing on top with your head; then gradually, gradually let a feeling of pleasant relaxation enter the body, as if a vast seascape has opened up before you.

Now let into this inner seascape all of the inner and outer "happenings"; allow all the sounds, thoughts, perceptions and emotions to enter. It's important that you do not judge or analyze them. Let these inner and outer happenings have a place inside you but do not dwell on them. Let them begin and end of their own accord without your participation.

Register the incessant chatter, fears and hopes that continually surface in your consciousness. Note how you ceaselessly scheme about the future, projects which will never come to be. Feel the eternal itch of worry that something bad will happen. Listen to the quiet, aching guilt about past mistakes best left behind.

Sit this way in contemplation—not judging and not lingering on anything—for about 15 minutes. After your meditation practice it is beneficial to read an inspiring book, to be alone or to go for a walk.

That's it. Simple, isn't it?

If you want to get more involved in Yoga, I've included a list below of the various forms. They all differ, some dramatically, so be careful choosing which one best serves your goals.

No style is better than another; it's simply a matter of personal preference. More important than any style, though, is the teacher, the student and how they relate to each other.

Most yoga centers teach a form of hatha yoga, which focuses on postures. Although there are many styles of yoga, the differences tend to be about emphasis, with all of the styles sharing a common lineage. In fact, the founders of three schools—Astanga, Iyengar and Viniyoga—were all students of Krishnamacharya, a famous teacher at the Yoga Institute at the Mysore Palace in India. Two disciples of the famous guru Sivananda went on to found separate schools: Integral and Sivananda.

ASTANGA: For those who want a serious workout, Astanga may be the perfect yoga. Astanga is physically demanding. Participants move through a series of flows, jumping from one posture to another to build strength, flexibility and stamina. It's not for beginners or for anyone who's been taking a leisurely approach to fitness. "Power" Yoga is based on Astanga.

BIKRAM: Participants in Bikram classes raise the thermostat up very high, then perform a series of 26 asanas, sometimes twice, that are designed to "scientifically" warm and stretch muscles, ligaments and tendons in the order in which they should be stretched. Be prepared to sweat.

INTEGRAL: Integral classes put almost as much emphasis on praying and meditation as they do on postures. It was developed by Swami Satchidananda, the man who taught the crowds at Woodstock to chant "Om."

IYENGAR: B.K.S. Iyengar is one of the best-known yoga teachers and the creator of one of the most popular styles of yoga in the world. His style is noted for great attention to detail and the precise alignment of postures, as well as the use of props such as blocks and belts. No doubt part of Iyengar's success is due to the quality of teachers, who must complete a rigorous 2–5 year training program for certification.

It's hard to appreciate how involved a simple thing like just standing can be, how much concentration and how many subtle movements and adjustments it takes, until you take an Iyengar yoga class. Of course, the point is that you're not just standing.

KRIPALU: Called the "yoga of consciousness," Kripalu puts great emphasis on proper breath, alignment, coordinating breath and movement and "honoring the wisdom of the body." In Kripalu, you work according to the limits of your individual flexibility and strength. Students learn to focus on the physical and psychological reactions caused by various postures to develop their awareness of mind, body, emotion and spirit.

There are three stages in Kripalu yoga. Stage One focuses on learning the postures and exploring your abilities. Stage Two involves holding the postures for an extended time, focusing and concentration. Stage Three is like a meditation in motion, in which the movement from one posture to another arises unconsciously and spontaneously.

KUNDALINI: Kundalini yoga focuses on the controlled release of Kundalini energy. The practice involves classic poses, breath, coordination of breath and movement and meditation.

SIVANANDA: Sivananda yoga follows a set structure that includes pranayama, classic asanas and relaxation. Sivananda is one of the world's largest schools of yoga.

VINIYOGA: Viniyoga is a gentler form of flow yoga than Astanga, with great emphasis on the breath and breath movement coordination. Rather than work toward idealized postures, poses and flows are chosen to suit the student's abilities.

5. Self-Hypnosis

In one form or another, self-hypnosis has existed in all ages and civilizations. Research shows that hypnotic phenomena have been known since earliest recorded history. More than 3500 years ago, in ancient Greece and Egypt, there were "temples of sleep" where religious and psychological hypnotic healing methods were practiced.

Today, self-hypnosis has achieved widespread acceptance as an approach to self-change. It is now widely practiced by those seeking self-discovery as well as lasting solutions to personal concerns. It is both a state of mind and a way of using your mind. In other words, it is a way to unify and harmonize your body, thoughts, and feelings so that you may achieve more personal successes in life, and achieve them more easily.

Like hypnosis, self-hypnosis activates the power of your mind to accept and hold to an idea so strongly through auto-suggestion, that it produces both immediate and lasting results. In hypnosis we move away from the environment around us and turn our attention inward.

In your lifetime of experience, your unconscious mind has learned a great deal and can apply that learning for you in hypnosis. Your conscious mind can only process so much information at one time. Your unconscious mind is not so limited. It can think dynamically and can find better solutions for you than your conscious mind. In other words, give your mind a suggestion and it will "automatically" act on it.

It is the conscious mind that says "I can't . . ." or "I don't know how to . . ." or "I'm not smart enough . . .". Self hypnosis is designed to keep the conscious mind occupied so that it won't interfere.

For some people, self-hypnosis has yielded the following benefits. Keep in mind, though, that, while most people can easily learn self-hypnosis, success in each of these areas isn't a sure thing for every person.

- Concentration: Centers your mind so that distractions do not interfere with performance.
- Habit Change: Change old attitudes, thought patterns, self-image, and behaviors. It can also help you develop new, better habits.
- Memory: Statistics show significant memory improvement.
- Motivation: Helps overcome the inner conflicts that impede success.
- Pain Control: Most people can easily learn to use self-hypnosis for dealing with pain. When mastered, this approach is far superior to the side effects of drugs.
- Relaxation: Safeguards important aspects of health and promotes longevity.
- Self-confidence: Self-hypnosis can give you a new relationship with yourself, in which you learn to trust and rely upon your own inner understanding. Other people can sense this and your new confidence generates respect from those around you.

Sound good? It's not my purpose here to teach you self-hypnosis. I can tell you I've used it for years to change some of my behaviors with great success. I believe you can too.

There are plenty of professionals well-versed in the techniques. Your local university may offer classes at night, or you may want to ask your doctor for a recommendation. Who knows, the doctor may also use it!

6. *Transcendental Meditation*

Transcendental Meditation—or TM—was founded by Maharishi Mahesh Yogi over 40 years ago. Since then over 4 million people world-wide have learned the technique.

TM comes from the ancient Vedic tradition,a universal system of knowledge preserved for many generations by a long line of teachers in the Himalayas. Maharishi Mahesh Yogi is regarded as the world's foremost teacher in the field of consciousness.

You may recall that in the 1960s the Beatles visited the Maharishi to gain enlightenment. Only George Harrison became a convert. John and Paul left because they gained nothing from the experience and because the Maharishi hit on the women in their group. Ringo mostly complained about the food!

TM is growing at a rate faster than at any other time in its history. Today TM is taught in schools, prisons, to the military and police forces in many countries around the world.

There is a great upsurge in interest, particularly among doctors who recognize it as a simple and effective antidote to disease and stress. Scientific research on TM has been conducted at 214 independent universities and research institutes. One five-year study of health insurance data of over 2000 people found that TM users required less than half the amount of health care as the control subjects studied. As reported in *Psychomatic Medicine* magazine, they also needed less hospitalization for 17 categories of disease, including 87 percent less for heart and vascular disease, and 55 percent less for cancer. Also, after examining scientific research data on TM, Holland's largest health insurance company, Silver Cross, now offers 30 percent reductions in health insurance premiums to people who practice TM regularly.

The benefits of TM for health are not limited to the cure and prevention of particular medical conditions. Proponents say it dissolves fatigue and stress and gives energy and clarity of mind. They say it is a simple way to recharge our batteries every day. Over time it allows our natural creativity and latent capabilities to blossom, enriching all aspects of our lives.

A study by the Swedish government found that, whereas the incidence of admission to psychiatric units in Sweden was 1 out of 20 for the general population between 1972 and 1974, it was only 1 out of 3,500 among people practicing TM. There's more.

According to a 1987 study reported in *Age* magazine, meditators who had been practicing TM for more than 5 years performed at a level 12 years younger than their chronological age in tests of blood pressure, sight and hearing.

In a nutshell, TM is all about the ability to let go of worries and relaxing. "Good rest is the natural way for the body to restore itself. TM gives extra deep rest, dissolves stress and so is highly recommended for its life-promoting value," says Dr. William Weir, Consultant in infectious diseases at the Royal Free Hospital in London who has recommended and practiced TM for many years.

Practicing TM will not make you so relaxed that you'll lose your drive and motivation. On the contrary, by getting rid of stress and increasing energy and clarity of mind, you will become more dynamic and successful in your daily activity.

How does TM compare with other types of meditation? TM experts claim other types involve some controlling of the mind, either through concentration or contemplation. TM is easy to learn, effortless to practice, and involves no concentration or contemplation.

TM also differs from self-hypnosis, which always involves some kind of control. Specifically you must give your mind a specific problem to work on. In TM, the mind experiences a calm and restful state in an innocent and natural manner. Scientific research carried out world-wide shows that the physiological changes during TM are unique and distinguish it from self-hypnosis.

The benefits of TM are cumulative. To ensure good progress it is necessary to practice regularly, twice a day, for 15-20 minutes. TM cannot be learned from a book or by listening to a tape. Although TM can be practiced by anyone, the technique must be taught individually. Practitioners say this is because everyone is unique and needs to learn TM at his or her own pace, in order to have individual experiences verified by a trained teacher.

You should be able to find a TM teacher locally, and local colleges probably offer evening classes. Be careful, though. Just because they say they teach TM doesn't mean they really do. TM is becoming a generic word like "Scotch tape™" or "Xerox™." Ask for references and check with the Better Business Bureau before you sign up.

Greg S. from Kentucky has had chronic prostatitis for 15 years further aggravated by a stressful lifestyle. Recently he found some unique help; deep relaxation tapes called "Muscle tense-relax" recorded by his therapist. "My therapist described how many people hold tension within the body, often gathering stress in a specified area," says Greg. He notes that typical results of this tension result in migraine headaches, backaches, stomach ulcers, and prostate disorders. "Something I had noticed within myself was a constant, involuntary feeling of contraction in and around my prostate," he adds.

Similar to relaxation tapes readily available in book stores and libraries, Greg says he uses his tapes twice a day, in the morning and at lunch time. "It helps dissipate my stress," he says. "Although I still feel tension, it doesn't head straight for my prostate area, as it had for my previous 15 years. This has resulted in a noticeable reduction in my symptoms."

---

7. Keep Your Perspective

As I've tried to point out in the above topics, mental attitude is just as important as physical condition. If T'ai Chi, Yoga, TM, and self-hypnosis are not for you, find other productive ways to deal with anger, depression, and other destructive emotions. Sometimes an activity as simple as a brisk 10-minute walk outdoors will work wonders.

Try to keep your perspective. Work hard to prevent minor aggravations or unimportant demands from getting the best of you. Concentrate on becoming flexible and practical. And learn to give in to compromise; sometimes it builds character.

Also, resist the natural tendency to take negative events personally. Random calamities do happen; fate doesn't single you out. It may sound corny, but it's important to Think Positively and to recognize how damaging destructive thoughts can be.

8. You're Not a Loner When You're Alone

Everyone needs some time alone. Learn to enjoy your own company. You could use this daily opportunity to practice those breathing and relaxation techniques. Or spend it "indulging" yourself; take a sauna or steam, read a bestseller, or visit an art museum. Indulge . . .

9. Relax Under Pressure

If you find you're obsessing over a stressful situation, tell yourself to stop and then think of something else that's pleasant. Distract your mind with memories of a recent vacation or time spent with a good friend.

Here are two simple techniques you can do whenever you have a few minutes and need some relaxation. These may only provide a short-term respite, but will help you to cool off so you can gain some perspective.

SCANNING   Inhale and slowly "scan" your body. Think about each muscle group (face, neck, shoulders, arms, abdominals, legs and feet) and search out tense muscles. As you exhale, relax the muscles that are tense. If possible, do some simple stretches to help release the tension.

IMAGERY   Stop what you are doing and close your eyes. Imagine a beautiful scene. Spend a few minutes examining and enjoying every detail of the picture. See, hear and smell your relaxing surroundings.

Look for other logical reasons for an upsetting situation rather than your personal failure. For example, if your boss didn't return your call, it could be because he never received the message. Rather than having anything to do with you personally, there's usually a reasonable explanation of why someone won't or can't fulfill your expectations. Also, try to get rid of unnecessary "musts," "shoulds," and "have-tos," and replace these absolutes with preferences.

10. Remember: It May Not be You

Sometimes other people may make you the target of their frustrations, but keep in mind that if you weren't there, someone else would bear the brunt of their stress. Most other people recognize the real source of the problem. When you find yourself in a situation like this, assert your right to be treated with respect, or walk away from the person and come back when things have calmed down.

Also, don't think that everyone has to like you for you to feel good about yourself; you may wish that they did, which is much easier to live with. Sometimes there's no reason for people treating you shabbily. It may not be you!

As I once told my son, sometimes people won't like you just because you're likeable. Go figure.

THE 5,000 YEAR OLD ANTI-AGING EXERCISE

When I first heard about Reflexology, I figured it was just another fad or gimmick designed to separate me from my wallet. What I didn't know was that it has been around for thousands of years.

Do you remember when acupuncture was considered a far-out non-sensical approach to health? It's close to being mainstream now. I grew up in a society where medical treatments consisted of three things: a stethoscope, a thermometer and aspirin. Oh, yeah, and a blood pressure cuff. That makes four.

We weren't big on prevention, only on symptoms of disease and treatment of disease after that. Our ancestors were wiser than that.

Reflexology was first practiced by the early Indian, Chinese and Egyptian peoples. In 1913 Dr. William Fitzgerald, an American ear, nose and throat surgeon, introduced this therapy to the West. He noted that pressure on specific parts of the body could have an anesthetizing effect on a related area. Developing this theory, he divided the body into ten equal and vertical zones, ending in the fingers and toes. He concluded that pressure on one part of a zone could affect everything else within that zone. Thus, reflex areas on the feet and hands are linked to other areas, glands and organs of the body within the same zone.

In the 1930s, Eunice Ingham, a therapist, further developed and refined the zone therapy into what is now known as foot reflexology. She observed that congestion or tension in any part of the foot mirrors congestion or tension in a corresponding part of the body. Thus, when you treat the big toes, there is a related effect in the head, and treating the whole foot can have a relaxing and healing effect on the whole body.

The body has the ability to heal itself. Following illness, stress, injury or disease, it is in a state of "imbalance," and vital energy pathways are blocked, preventing the body from functioning effectively. Reflexology can be used to restore and maintain the body's natural equilibrium and encourage healing.

A reflexologist uses hands only to apply gentle pressure to the feet. For each person the application and the effect of the therapy is unique. Sensitive, trained hands can detect tiny deposits and imbalances in the feet, and by working on these points the reflexologist can release blockages and restore the free flow of energy to the whole body. Tensions are eased, and circulation and elimination is improved. This gentle therapy encourages the body to heal itself at its own pace, often counteracting a lifetime of misuse.

Since reflexology treats the whole person, not the symptoms of disease, most people benefit from treatment. The therapy brings relief to a wide range of acute and chronic conditions, and is suitable for all ages. Once your body is in-tune, it is wise to have regular treatments in order to help maintain health and well-being. An increasing number of people are using this safe, natural therapy as a way of relaxing, balancing and harmonizing the body.

A REFLEXOLOGY WORKOUT

On your first visit there is a preliminary talk with the practitioner. The reflexologist then begins to work on your feet, or hands if necessary, noting problem areas. There may be discomfort in some places, but it is fleeting, and is an indication of congestion or imbalance in a corresponding part of the body. For the most part, the sensation is pleasant and soothing. Reflexology will relax you while stimulating the body's own healing mechanisms.

Usually a treatment session lasts for about one hour. A course of treatment varies in length depending on your body's needs. Your reflexologist will discuss this with you at the first session. After the first treatment or two your body may respond in a very definite way: you may have a feeling of well-being and relaxation; or you may feel lethargic, nauseous or tearful, but this is transitory. It is, however, vital information for reflexologists, as it shows how your body is responding to treatment.

It's important that your practitioner is professionally qualified and a member of a bona fide organization. If you're not sure, check with your local Better Business Bureau.

I've tried to show that to a large degree our bodies have the innate ability to prevent diseases and heal themselves, including our prostates. There's only one thing necessary. It is not some fancy piece of equipment, or tons of money. The only thing necessary is you and your cooperation.

I know, that makes two.

CHAPTER FIVE

SPICE UP YOUR SEX LIFE

It's been said that love makes the world go round. If that's true, I know what drives it—gives it its spin, if you will.

Sex.

Day or night, winter, spring, summer or fall, sex (no matter what your definition) has started wars, maybe even ended a few. It's the theme of most great literature and music, and the sure fire ingredient to get people to plunk down their money to watch a flick. Yep, sex is the WD-40 on the earth's axis.

You don't need a major research study to prove that men are usually the sexual instigators. From that first stolen kiss on the playground, to grappling in the back seat of dad's sedan, to corny pickup lines in singles bars, men seek sexual conquest. And what are we really after? An amazing biological trick, an erect penis and the euphoria only sex can produce. Money and fame can't duplicate it. In fact, you can't get the exact feeling from anything else.

That's right, men; we not only hold the secret to proliferation of our species and world domination right behind our fly but happiness, too. Talk about pressure. And for many of us, as you'll see, the root of unhappiness.

Our ability to make love plays an important role in our lives. According to a "USA TODAY" survey, 476 men reported their favorite home activities are:

Making love	64 percent
Spending time with family	56 percent

Listening to music	34 percent
Beautifying home	23 percent
Reading	23 percent

(Respondent could choose more than one activity.)

You read right. We are three times as likely to try to score than read ... and obviously not care what condition our home is in when we do it!

Because sexual intercourse is one of the basic functions in a man's life, his ability to achieve and maintain an erection can be vital to his self-esteem. The nagging thought of being unable to have or to sustain an erection causes thousands of men to avoid sexual contact.

NATURE'S GIFT TO YOUR LOVE LIFE

In many cultures, the penis was and is a focus, symbol or totem for sex; as such it is linked to sexual "performance" or power. From the male standpoint there are four components to a completed sex act:

- Libido, or sex drive
- Erection
- Emission
- Orgasm

From the time we first reach puberty, most of us have a very, very strong sexual drive or libido. This was and is driven by our old friend testosterone. When we're young we have tons of it. All we needed back then was a quick glimpse of a female student's thigh in Social Studies and to stave off embarrassment we'd stay glued to our seat well past the time everyone else left for their next class.

When things are going right, how does our body play that neat little gravity-defying trick? The penis is comprised primarily of two cylinders of sponge-like vascular tissue that fills with blood to create an erection. Despite the wisdom we gleaned from our friends in Junior High, it's impossible to get a boner since there are no bones.

Blood is pumped into the penis under great pressure and a series of valves keep it in the penis to maintain the erection. A third cylinder is the urethra, a tube that carries our urine and semen out of our bodies. Blood flows to the penis by two very small arteries that come from the aorta. These arteries are the same size as the arteries to your finger.

Getting an erection requires many different things to happen. There are numerous chemical transmitters involved in this including epinephrine, norepinephrine, acetylcholine, prostaglandins and nitric oxide. The exact mechanism by which this works is still unclear. Needless to say, input from the brain is extremely important.

An erection occurs when we're aroused and our nervous system dutifully responds by instigating a rapid increase in blood flow. The vascular muscle in the spongy area becomes engorged with blood, and outflow of blood is cut off. Once the male has an orgasm or the stimulation stops, blood drains out of the cylinders in the penis and the penis becomes limp again.

By the way, in addition to those times when we're sexually stimulated, most men normally have erections when they sleep.

As you should know by now, one of your prostate's main roles is to make, then squeeze, semen into the urethra. A healthy prostate makes about 90 percent of our semen. Our prostates also muscle the semen out during orgasm. So without a prostate there's no material for the discharge. Our prostatic fluid does something else; it guards your urinary system and genitals from infection.

But this leads to one of the biggest misconceptions about the gland—that prostate problems automatically mean no erections. Nonsense. Often prostate problems cause a waning libido, not a decrease in your ability to get an erection. It's your libido that causes your erections; maybe you are turned on by an erotic picture or you fantasize about that babe at the topless car wash. It's important to remember—a sagging libido doesn't always mean a lack of interest. Sometimes it's due to a health problem, so consult with your doctor to find out for sure.

Most men treated for prostate problems report no loss in the erection part of their sexual ability. Notice I said "most." Here are a few exceptions. Notice, though, how libido always comes into play:

- Because the urethra runs right through the middle of it, a prostate's growth spurt will squeeze the urethra and begin to choke off its ability to move things through. This can hamper your sexual performance, and desire, for that matter.

- A prostatectomy is the surgical removal of all or part of the prostate. Sometimes this needs to be done because of an enlarged prostate. This procedure rarely causes impotence. If a radical prostatectomy (removal of prostate gland) is used to treat prostate cancer, new surgical techniques may be able to save the nerves going to the penis and an erection may still be possible. Talk to your doctor before surgery to make sure you will be able to lead a fully satisfying sex life. Sadly, as many as 70 percent of prostate cancer patients become impotent after surgery.

- An inflamed prostate gland, or prostatitis, also robs sexual pleasure, mostly among younger men. Urgent, burning urination is one sign of prostatitis, as is pain that invades the groin, scrotum, anus, lower back, abdomen and legs. Painful ejaculation, associated with this disease, is responsible for dampening the sexual desires of many men.

- Congestive prostatitis can be caused by your level of sexual activity. A healthy prostate secretes between one-tenth and two-fifths of a teaspoon of fluid daily. When you're hot and bothered you produce four to ten times that amount. The best way to release it is through ejaculation. If you don't your prostate becomes congested. (Remember blue balls?) Also, if your sexual climaxes suddenly fall off— maybe you're between partners or your wife is ticked at you—your prostate can become engorged.

- Likewise, if after a long period of not getting any, you suddenly find yourself in the sexual Olympics, your prostate goes into overdrive producing secretion. In effect, you end up blowing a head gasket and your prostate becomes inflamed.

That brings us to orgasm. Orgasms are more of a feeling rather than an actual event. You can have your prostate removed via a radical prostatectomy, and still have an orgasm. How is that possible, you ask? You don't have to ask me, ask a woman you're particularly close to. She's capable of having orgasms and, unless she's a medical wonder, has never had a prostate.

Impotence occurs when something goes wrong, namely, that something interferes with the initial phase of excitement, or with the ongoing sexual arousal during the sex experience, and you can't get an erection. Nearly every man, at some stage in his life, will have difficulty having or sustaining an erection. When just a single incident occurs, the best thing to do is forget about it. Temporary loss of erectile ability is called secondary impotence. Men who are obsessed with "performance" may see this as the end of their sexuality. But that's simply not true. You are not impotent. These "dry" periods shouldn't be of major concern.

Problems arise when this difficulty starts occurring regularly. Men who have an ongoing difficulty getting and maintaining an erection suffer from primary impotence. It's a common problem affecting at least 10 million men in the United States.

Men afflicted with repeated impotence tend to be middle-aged and older, with such a condition most common in men 60 years of age and over. By the time most men are 40 they have already experienced impotence at some time in their lives. It can be a major cause of concern to men (and women).

The good news is that all causes of impotence can be treated successfully. Fortunately, the silence that has always surrounded impotency has lessened. More and more single men and couples are now interested in facing this disorder and are turning to professionals for help.

The most significant body part leading to impotence is not your prostate. Rather it's that semicircular globe that sits above your ears, that depository of geometric theorems, state capitals and the dirty lyrics to "Louie, Louie," that contributes a lot to our inability to perform. According to Stanley G. Korenman, M.D., from the University of California School of Medicine in Los Angeles, the brain is the main sex organ. Often what's stored there are untruths and misconceptions. One is our ability to have sex as we get older. So your sexual desire waxes and wanes depending on not just your physical health, but your emotions, mood, relationship dynamics, and personal need.

We put so much emphasis on sex—and spend so much time thinking about it—that many men, as they age, experience psychological and physical problems with sexuality. The truth is that as you grow older you will have fewer significant hormonal changes than women. Your hormone level will remain relatively steady and your testicles will continue to produce sperm as they have since puberty—just not as much.

Most men do have a gradual decline in testosterone production, and some organs and glands, such as the prostate and testicles, may show a reduced ability to respond to testosterone. The fact is, when we reach our 50s (sometimes earlier, sometimes later) we experience fewer erections; and they're not as stiff as when we were young.

You may also notice that you get an erection less frequently when you fantasize about sexual situations or when you see an erotic picture or object. You may find that it takes longer for you to get an erection when making love, and that your penis needs a few minutes of direct stimulation before it becomes erect. Sometimes you may even fail to get an erection. This is a normal part of aging and is not impotence.

Similarly you may notice that your penis is no longer as erect as it used to be, that it doesn't stand as upright, and seems not as eager. Again, this should not be a cause for concern. You'll find that if you don't become anxious over this minor change, you will continue to enjoy sex as much as ever.

There may be periods when you lose your erection during foreplay before intercourse. Don't worry. This is also normal. Stimulation will restore it. When you penetrate your partner's vagina you'll find that you might even last longer than when you were younger, which means you'll both enjoy the sensation for a longer period.

Some men become overly concerned if they do not ejaculate each time they have sex. They feel that this somehow questions their virility. Nonsense—you and your partner have both just enjoyed a mutually sensuous and pleasurable act. That should be enough. You will probably ejaculate the next time, or the time after that. If—after sex—you find that you are still aroused, then ask your partner to stimulate your penis again, or masturbate.

Many older men find that they either ejaculate less forcibly, or the message from their advance warning system that they are about to climax is not as strong. Others discover that it takes longer to become erect again after intercourse. These changes are also normal. Don't sweat it.

Tension and anxiety (about work, finances or love life, or even fear of not being able to have an erection) are very common causes of erection difficulties. Generally speaking, psychologically-based impotence possibly results from the man's feeling unsure about his ability as a lover. He may be under some form of external pressure or emotional upset, or may find that his partner is not providing the type or extent of sexual kick that he wants.

Some causes of impotence and erection difficulties are ingrained. Again, your brain. For example:

- In our youth, we may have had a difficult or traumatic sexual experience. Maybe we were caught masturbating or having sex.

- Some of us, in our early years, lived under the control of strict parents and were taught that sex is "dirty" and that masturbation is wrong.

- Early on, we may have had doubts about our sexuality, "manliness," or capacity to "perform." These doubts could have built into a fear of or anxiety about sex, inhibiting our capacity to initiate sex with potential partners.

It's not easy to block out these early experiences and influences. They're probably still there in our subconscious and they can strongly affect our sexual responses and feelings.

Feeling anxious about your own sexual performance can be a major factor in reducing or preventing your capacity to have and sustain an erection. Sexual myth would have us believe in the male's dominance in bed and his capacity to have sex at any time and as often as he or his partner desires. A man's self-image can be set against this incorrect stereotype.

Believe it or not, a lack of male hormones is an extremely rare cause of erection difficulties—so rare, that it's not even considered in the vast majority of cases. Depression and similar disorders, and grief after the death of a relative or close friend, can temporarily suppress many feelings of desire—be it the desire to eat or the desire to have sex and the capacity to get an erection.

The main physical problem that causes impotence, also known as erectile dysfunction (ED), is not due to your prostate. Rather it's caused when the blood vessels become blocked and the blood can't get to the penis. The other major problem is leakage of blood from the penis into the veins around the penis, called a venous leak. This is very common.

Occasionally, other conditions can prevent a man getting and sustaining a satisfactory erection. Chemicals—such as alcohol and some drugs—can also suppress erections. A limp penis is a frequent side effect of a heavy drinking session. Common temporary illnesses—the flu, for example, or fatigue—can sometimes reduce sexual desire and, therefore, the capacity to have an erection. Smoking appears to have a negative effect on a man's erection, while exercise and good diet help to enhance anyone's sex life.

TAKING CARE OF YOUR MANHOOD

Regardless of their age, most impotent men can be treated successfully. As with any other ailment, a person who begins having this problem repeatedly needs to see a doctor. The doctor will want to rule out the possibility of disease, injury or side effects from medicine. For example, cardiovascular problems, diabetes, injuries to the spinal column, and side effects from high blood pressure medicine are among the physical conditions that can lead to impotence.

If the problem is physical, there are several treatments available depending upon the cause and severity of the problem. A physician who does not believe your problem is physical may suggest seeing a psychologist, marriage therapist or psychiatrist. In such therapy, the emphasis will probably be on explanation, education and support. Sometimes both medical and psychological treatment are used together. If this therapy proves unsuccessful, a device can be inserted surgically that will assist in allowing the man to have intercourse.

Due to the many possible causes of impotence, it is impossible to provide a definitive therapy for its prevention; some causes are incurable. There are, however, a number of ways to minimize its possibility or frequency. When a physician prescribes medicine or recommends a surgical procedure, the patient should ask if there may be side effects or complications that could influence him sexually.

Since half of all cases of impotence are believed to be psychological, there's a simple test that can help determine whether yours is physical or psychological. Although usually unaware of it, most men have frequent erections while they sleep. You can obtain a specially designed plastic band from your doctor to wrap on your penis at bedtime. If the band breaks during the night, then you are capable of having normal erections and the problem is probably psychological. It's probably a good idea to tell your partner you're doing this. Should she discover you've wrapped your penis like a present, you may have some explaining to do.

BANISH IMPOTENCE

If medical treatment is required, there are several therapies available. Certain medications, when applied to the penis, have been found to assist in enhancing erection, such as nitroglycerin ointment and Minoxidil. New treatments are being developed all the time.

Early in 1998, a new ointment was tested: MacroChem Corp.'s Topiglan™, a topically-applied gel for treating erectile dysfunction. "Topiglan differs from other erectile dysfunction treatments in that it is a topical gel that is applied directly to the gland, thereby minimizing the potential for systemic side effects," said Irwin Goldstein, M.D., professor of urology at the Boston University School of Medicine.

Topiglan is comprised of alprostadil, an agent that is already approved for the treatment of erectile dysfunction, and Sepa, a patented drug delivery technology which permits the drug to be absorbed through the surface of the skin. It should be noted that alprostadil is a naturally occurring substance that is present in male semen. Topiglan is still undergoing testing and may be an approved treatment for erectile dysfunction in a couple of years.

In some patients, impotence results from obstructions in the blood vessels of the penis that prevent them from filling properly, leading either to partial erections at best or none at all. In such patients, success has been reported in the use of injections of papaverine hydrochloride, prostaglandin, phentolamine and atropine which the patient can inject himself. Where surgery is required to correct such vascular problems, research indicates that almost 80 percent of patients can regain potency.

There was a media frenzy in the spring of 1998, when a new drug to fight impotency gained approval from the U. S. Food and Drug Administration. You would have had to be on the Moon not to have heard about it. That's right: Pfizer, Inc.'s Viagra™. Taken orally about an hour before anticipated sexual activity, Viagra (sildenafil citrate) is a blue oval tablet that gives men erections with sexual stimulation. Since Viagra is effective for most men with impotence it's been flying off drugstore shelves.

Viagra is the first in a new class of medications known as phosphodiesterase type 5 inhibitors that improve blood flow to the penis. In clinical trials, Viagra had demonstrated to restore sexual function in most patients (approximately 7 out of 10 men overall) and was effective with patients whose ED was attributed to diabetes, spinal cord injury or psychological causes, among others.

Viagra was well tolerated by patients in the clinical trials. Its most common side effects were headache, facial flushing and indigestion. Viagra may help millions of men but it is not a sexual cure-all. Nor is it an aphrodisiac. It will not work without desire. Nor will it make a normal erection harder or make one last longer. Plus, there are some risks in taking Viagra that everyone, whether sexually dysfunctional or merely dissatisfied, should consider before rushing to the pharmacy:

> One out of 10 men in the clinical trials developed blinding headaches that grew more severe at higher doses.

> Because the eyes contain an enzyme similar to that on which Viagra works in the penis, about 3 percent of users have developed temporary vision problems, ranging from blurred vision to a blue or green halo effect. (This adds no credence to the parental warning about masturbation.)

> Viagra should not be used by patients taking nitrates in any form, including the heart medicine, nitroglycerin.

Viagra can trigger sudden drops in blood pressure, and there is a risk that men who take it in combination with nitroglycerin or other anti-hypertensive drugs could faint or go into shock.

There is a theoretical risk that men with sickle-cell anemia, leukemia or urethral inflammation could, when taking Viagra, develop priapism, defined as an erection that lasts four hours or more. Although that might sound appealing (or appalling to some), untreated, priapism can lead to tissue damage and more severe impotence.

Sometimes impotence is an early indicator of heart disease, diabetes and some types of cancer. Taking Viagra could mask these life-threatening conditions.

Men with coronary problems who have not had sex for many years should consult their doctors before putting too much strain on a weakened heart.

The long-term effects of large doses of Viagra have not been established, especially on men who take it for the wrong reason. Although it is a relatively safe drug, there is a possibility that users will become psychologically dependent on it, unable to achieve an erection without it.

In November, 1998, the U. S. Food and Drug Administration and Pfizer, Inc. changed the original drug labeling. It now advises consumers and doctors that consideration must be given to the cardiovascular health of patients and other risks, such as priapism, prior to prescribing Viagra. Your doctor can help you decide if Viagra is for you.

There are other drugs and techniques that seem to work. Urologists differ in the types of treatment they recommend for impotence, but many opt first for nonsurgical treatment.

Injections of the drugs papaverine (Pavabid™) and phentolamine (Regitine™) or prostaglandin E1 (PGE1) into the base of the penis before intercourse have been shown to be roughly 80 percent effective in producing "satisfactory erection" in impotent men who have tried it. The drug alprostadil also is available in an injection kit (Caverject™).

These drugs work by relaxing smooth muscle, causing the blood vessels in the penis to dilate, which then promotes an erection that can last for a few minutes to 45 minutes, depending on dosage. An estimated 300,000 men in the United States use this technique each year. Possible side effects include priaprism (prolonged, painful erections). Also, although the injections are done with a tiny needle, and are supposed to be painless when done properly (proper technique is crucial), this prospect is unappealing to many men.

Use immediately after radical prostatectomy or radiation therapy may prevent atrophy of the smooth muscle necessary for erection which is associated with non-use of the penis.

A less invasive technique, which involves instilling alprostadil into the urethra with a tiny plunger, is under development and is expected to become available in the near future.

Vasomax has been used for years as an injectable medication and is now being tested in pill form. It is another medication which works to dilate penile blood flow in men with mild vascular problems. Apo-Morphine is being evaluated for treatment of only psychogenic impotence.

Medical Urethral System for Erection (MUSE™) is a cream which is absorbed through the urethra and dilates the cavernosal spongy tissue of the erectile chambers. It has about a 66 percent success rate; its approval is eagerly anticipated because it will be able to replace injectable forms of therapy.

A multi-center study presented by Ronald Lewis, M.D., of the Medical College of Georgia used an adjustable penile constriction band (Actis™) to block venous outflow in conjunction with the use of the drug MUSE™ (alprostadil) from Vivus, Inc. It resulted in 102 of 144, or 71 percent, of patients reporting successful sexual intercourse. During home treatment, 75 percent of administrations of MUSE™ plus Actis resulted in sexual intercourse. Erections lasted approximately 25 minutes.

The October, 1998 issue of *The Journal of Urology* reported that, in a clinical setting, MUSE helped 70 percent of men with severe impotence to achieve an erection sufficient for intercourse. Of these men, 57 percent reported successful sexual intercourse during home treatment. All 384 patients studied had undergone radical prostatectomy at least three months before the study and had identified the surgery as the cause of their erectile dysfunction.

A number of vacuum devices are used to promote erection. With these, a cylinder is placed over the penis and a hand pump is used to create a vacuum in the cylinder. This, in turn, causes blood to flow into the penis, creating an erection. The user then puts a constriction band around the base of the penis, causing the erection to last up to thirty minutes. These devices are available by prescription only. Some 100,000 men in the United States choose this treatment each year.

While this eliminates the need for medication, it does require some preparation time, which decreases spontaneity. Still, a survey sent to patients who had been provided such devices over a 5-year period showed that both patients and their partners were quite satisfied with the results of using them. Problems abound with this technique, however.

Since the early 1970s, more than 250,000 American men have turned to inflatable penile implants to mechanically create erections. Penile implants are surgically installed devices that are made of silicone or polyurethane. One type is made of two semirigid but bendable rods; another type consists of a pump, a fluid-filled reservoir, and two cylinders into which the fluid is pumped to create an erection. Penile implants are now coming under FDA scrutiny. Since 1984, the FDA's Center for Devices and Radiological Health has logged more than 6,500 reports of problems with inflatable devices—a large number for a medical device, according to the FDA. However, in one survey, 80–90 percent of persons who received penile implants were found to be satisfied with the results.

With the development of more effective agents, implants are now considered to be a last resort, to be tried only when all other methods have failed.

ORIENTAL SECRETS TO GREAT SEX
AND PROSTATE HEALTH

Statistics show that Oriental men have 50 percent fewer prostate problems than do men from the Western world; they also boast a lively sex life that continues well into their 80s. Although generalizations are always dangerous, here are some of the factors contributing to their longevity:

Diet: Asians eat less red meat than their Western counterparts, and are more likely to down vegetables and spices.

Exercise: Asians are generally more dedicated to it than Westerners. (We covered Tai Chi, Yoga and other exercise techniques in the last chapter.)

Attitude: Culturally, Asian countries have a healthier attitude about sex. Although their treatment of women raises some Western eyebrows, both sexes realize the importance of sex, and are much less inhibited about it.

According to Chinese folklore, there once was a man who, sickly and impotent, had lived into his 60s without fathering a child. After many consultations with various doctors to no avail, he became depressed and drank himself into a stupor in the hills near his home. When he awoke the first thing he saw was the strange sight of two plants growing intertwined together in a symmetrical pattern.

Inspired by this he dug up the roots and took them to an old herbalist who divined that they had great restorative powers. After several days of taking the herb the man's virility was restored and after fathering four children he lived to the age of 132.

The man's name was Ho Shou Wu and the plant was named after him. Also known as Fo-Ti-Tieng, or simply Fo-Ti, this much-honored herb has been known in Asia for centuries for its longevity and beneficial rejuvenating effects. Its ability to increase energy, preserve youth and restore impaired sexual functioning has made it a favorite ingredient in Chinese patent medicine.

Raw Ho Shou Wu may cause a mild diarrhea so it's usually processed by soaking in black beans and water. Should you wish to give it a try, the usual dose is from 5 to 15 grams per day.

GINSENG—KEY TO A VIBRANT SEX LIFE

Another safe, effective herb to relieve impotence is the root of Asian ginseng, or Panax ginseng. Many clinical tests have shown that within a short period of taking it, libido and sexual potencies increase significantly. Panax ginseng works by helping the body use oxygen more efficiently, by maintaining blood sugar and cholesterol, and by helping manage stress.

So far, Panax ginseng is the only herb recognized by researchers to stimulate testosterone production, although it's believed Fo-Ti may also. In a thorough study of this ancient herb at the University of Nebraska School of Medicine, world famous scientists Drs. W.S. Fahim and Denham Harman showed that Panax ginseng does indeed offer extraordinary powers for men. Their studies showed that it increased the production of testosterone, and in so doing, had several benefits: First, it helped to reduce enlarged prostates. Second, it helped to prevent future prostate problems. Third, it greatly enhanced the subjects' sex drive and performance.

Some people find that Panax ginseng overstimulates them, even to the point of insomnia. The safest way to take this herb is two weeks on, one week off. If you're hypertensive, use ginseng cautiously and have your blood pressure checked regularly.

During a routine physical, and almost as an afterthought, Mark mentioned a minor urinary problem to his doctor and a decrease in his libido. Since he was nearly fifty, his doctor said they should monitor his prostate for developing symptoms. As for his waning sexual desire, well, Mark would just have to accept he was getting older.

After considerable research, Mark started taking saw palmetto for his prostate and ginseng to add stamina during his workouts at a local health club. As a side benefit, he found his sexual desire coming back. Encouraged, he conducted some additional research, and added yohimbe to his regiment. At last report Mark—and his wife—are very, very happy.

GETTING YOUR PROWESS BACK

As we've already discussed in an earlier chapter, vitamins, minerals and other nutrients are vital for hormone production and sexual function. Because nutritional supplementation is so effective, safe and inexpensive, I would recommend it to all men who are suffering with prostate discomfort, or who are concerned that they may have discomfort in the future.

Here are a few commonsense nutrients to start reviving your prostate:

L-ARGININE: This amino acid, found widely in dairy, meat, fowl, chocolate and nuts, works to enhance energy, increase libido and hormone secretion. It also improves sexual performance, primarily by enhancing levels of nitric oxide (NO) in the body. NO helps keep an erection firm.

NO is the subject of thousands of scientific studies and has been proven conclusively to be the key neurotransmitter facilitating erection. If sufficient NO is not produced, erection or sexual stimulation does not occur. Arginine is absolutely necessary for the production of NO, so be sure to include foods containing this amino acid in your diet.

VITAMIN A: This vitamin, found to be an antioxidant, is essential for the male reproductive organs and sperm production. There is much information available today about the supposed benefits of antioxidants against the damage from free-radicals.

VITAMIN C: This versatile vitamin is believed to contribute to healthy sperm cell production even in smokers. Nicotine and other byproducts of cigarette smoke reduce sperm count and speed by 20 percent. Also, cadmium, a byproduct of cigarette smoke, went hand-in-hand with low semen volume. When Earl Dawson, Ph.D., from the University of Texas in Galveston gave 75 heavy smokers vitamin C, the health of their sperm increased.

VITAMIN E: The antioxidant vitamin E is recognized as a nutrient for sexual ailments. Early studies found that animals couldn't reproduce and males' testicles shrunk without vitamin E in their diet. One sign of vitamin E deficiency in men is slow-moving sperm.

Many naturopathic doctors recommend vitamin E-rich foods such as vegetable oils, whole grains, seeds and nuts to help sexual problems. Remember though, many of these foods are also high in fat.

ZINC: The prostate gland is rich in zinc and magnesium, and these two minerals are important treatments for prostatic and other male complaints. Zinc, which is necessary for protein synthesis, is most often part of a comprehensive fertility program. In a Turkish study, infertile men had about half the semen magnesium as fertile men.

When zinc levels fall too low, the result is poor sperm production and reduced testosterone levels, according to *Modern Nutrition in Health and Disease*. Foods high in zinc include seafood, meat, root vegetables, nuts and whole grains.

Zinc supplementation is also useful in some cases of male infertility. Remember, if you supplement with zinc, make sure you're also getting adequate vitamin B6.

PACK AWAY THESE OTHER NUTRIENTS

Prostate problems can undermine not only the daily quality of a man's life, but also his confidence; yet it is scientifically proven that simple, nutritional support can offer tremendous relief for prostate sufferers.

Behind every great sex life is a healthy diet. A deficiency of some nutrients contributes to lagging sex. Too little protein, for instance, can decrease testosterone levels in men, thus lowering sex drive.

If you and your wife want to get pregnant, your fertility can benefit from a diet based on fresh fruits and vegetables, whole grains, low-fat protein (skinless poultry, fish, legumes and beans) and clean water. Research from around the globe reveals that specific nutrients also help assure healthy sperm. Antioxidants are effective, possibly because they protect sperm from damage from toxins.

Other antioxidants besides A, C, E and zinc, showing promise for male infertility, are coenzyme Q10, selenium, and glutathione. Glutathione, produced in the body with vitamin C supplementation, helped several infertile men in Italy. Also, when a researcher from the National University of Singapore checked 200 men for trace elements, he found higher sperm density was associated with increased zinc and selenium levels.

Two members of the B-complex family have shown potential in infertility treatment. Folic acid is needed for synthesis of the genetic material DNA. When Giorgio Bentlivoglio, M.D., of the University of Genova supplemented Italian men with folinic acid, folic acid's active form for three months, their sperm numbers and motility increased. Vitamin B12 may also improve sperm count.

LIBIDO INCREASED

Can botanicals electrify your sex life? Here are a few that some men swear by:

1. Yohimbe tree bark, a popular love drug in Africa and West India, has been around for centuries. The claim to climax fame is its ability to stimulate the central nervous system in the spine at precisely the area that controls erection.

Today, there are doctors prescribing yohimbine, an extract from that tree, to treat impotence. It is thought to energize a man's sexual response by stimulating portions of his nervous, reproductive, circulatory and respiratory systems by increasing blood to erectile tissue.

This stimulation can cause a strong aphrodisiac effect. It has been useful in treating certain cases of diminished sexual interest. By some estimates, one-fifth of men with impotence completely recover after using yohimbine. It is generally of no value when impotency stems from organic nerve troubles, and it can be harmful when used for impotency caused by chronic inflammation of the sexual organs. It has a long folk history of helping increase libido or sexual energy and desire. However, many of the claims surrounding it are merely folklore. Unfortunately, yohimbe has been recommended in sports medicine for male athletes, especially body builders, for its supposed content of the male hormone testosterone, which can cause an anabolic or muscle-building effect.

No scientific research, however, indicates that either yohimbe bark or yohimbine extract contains testosterone or increases blood testosterone levels, or produces anabolic effects. Among the symptoms caused by yohimbe bark are excessive adrenal or sympathetic nerve stimulation, hypertension, increased heart rate, irritability, water retention, anxiety, and hyperactivity.

In its pure form the extract has side effects such as increased blood pressure, racing heart rate, tremors and irritability, headache, nausea or vomiting, sweating, dizziness, flushed skin and frequent urination.

Yohimbe should not be used by people who have inflammation in their sexual organs, nor by anyone taking drugs—especially tranquilizers, antihistamines or narcotics—or significant amounts of alcohol. Yohimbe can produce significant side effects if taken over a long period of time. If you have a cardiovascular disorder, kidney dysfunction, diabetes, abnormal blood pressure, irregular blood sugar, or are taking cardiac or psychiatric medication, advise your health care practitioner of your condition before asking for a prescription for Yohimbe or before taking any yohimbine-based product.

Some doctors recommend combining herbal yohimbe with Siberian ginseng and saw palmetto for men with low sex drive. Nevertheless, if you plan to try this herb, use it under the care of an experienced health care professional.

2. Since impotence is often due to poor genital blood flow, ginkgo biloba is a logical and safer choice than yohimbine. Ginkgo helps increase circulation and blood flow thus helping erectile function.

Ginkgo's side effects such as upset stomach and headaches are rare and mild. This ancient tree is best known in this country as a decorative plant. Its leaves contain compounds so beneficial for circulatory and nervous system problems that it's among the most prescribed and well-researched herbal medicines in the world.

3. Gotu Kola is a tropical and subtropical herb that is reputed to help stimulate the central nervous system, decrease fatigue, manage poor moods and increase sex drive. It appears to improve the flow of blood throughout the body by strengthening the veins and capillaries Like ginkgo, gotu kola is also believed to help improve memory and brain function.

4. Siberian ginseng, which is entirely different from Panax ginseng, is also purported to be a reproductive and prostate tonic. Proponents say it can relieve stress of impotence and insure adequate penile circulation.

5. Damiana leaf has a historical reputation for building enhanced sexual activity, one that extends over hundreds of years. Its use as an aphrodisiac can be traced to the ancient Mayans, and in modern times it continues to be popularly used as a sexual stimulant. Damiana leaf contains beta-sitosterol and various aromatic oils that create a stimulant effect on the body's sexual organs, helping to build stronger and more consistent sexual responses, and providing better sexual health and reproductivity.

6. A study by the Institute for Advanced Study of Human Sexuality found that men who suffered from reduced sexual desire and diminished performance were helped by green oats. Likewise, Dr. Benjamim Frankt of Budapest University in Hungary found a great increase in sexual vitality and energy in men using a combination of two herbs, green oats (*Avena sativa*) and stinging nettle. Nettle is full of vital minerals and is good also for hypoglycemia, allergies, depressions, prostate and urinary tract disorders, and a host of other problems.

When we talk about herbs to help your sex life, we're not really talking about aphrodisiacs. An aphrodisiac is a food, drink, drug, scent or device that, promoters claim, can arouse or increase sexual desire, libido and performance. What we think of as aphrodisiacs are often urinary tract and genital irritants.

Named after Aphrodite, the Greek goddess of sexual love and beauty, the list of supposed sexual stimulants includes anchovies and adrenaline, licorice and lard, scallops and Spanish fly, and hundreds of other items. According to the Food and Drug Administration, the reputed sexual effects of so-called aphrodisiacs are based in folklore, not fact. In 1989, the Agency declared that there is no scientific proof that any over-the-counter aphrodisiacs work to treat sexual dysfunction.

The FDA's findings clash with a 5,000-year tradition of pursuing sexual betterment through use of plants, drugs and magic. Despite the FDA's determination that aphrodisiacs are ineffective—and sometimes even dangerous—people continue the quest for a magic bullet.

Several principles help demystify some cultural views about aphrodisiacs:

> Sometimes the reason for an item's legendary reputation is obvious. It's easy to imagine how the sex organs of animals such as goats and rabbits, known for their procreativeness, have achieved their esteemed status as love aids in some cultures.
>
> Chilies, curries, and other spicy foods have been viewed as aphrodisiacs because their physiological effects—a raised heart rate and sometimes sweating—are similar to the physical reactions experienced during sex. And some foods were glorified as aphrodisiacs based on their rarity and mystery. While chocolate was once considered the ultimate aphrodisiac, the reputation wore off as it became commonly available. (It is still a tool of seduction, however, especially around Valentine's Day.)
>
> The similarity of the shape of the rhinoceros horn to the penis is credited for its worldwide reputation as a libido enhancer. The horn contains significant amounts of calcium and phosphorus. The addition of the food to a deficient diet could improve general physical vigor and possibly lead to an increased sexual interest. But in most Americans' diets, which are usually not lacking calcium or phosphorus, the small quantities usually consumed would not affect physical performance.
>
> Because Aphrodite was said to be born from the sea, many types of seafood have reputations as aphrodisiacs. Oysters enjoy particular esteem. Well, oysters are low in fat and high in minerals, and thus a pretty healthy food. Phosphorus, iodine and zinc can do a lot of good, especially zinc, which is said to increase both sperm and testosterone production as well as the secretion of a vaginal lubricant. But oysters as an aphrodisiac? Nah.

Some substances may not actually have specific sexual effects, but may change a person's mood and, therefore, seem to be an aphrodisiac. For example, alcohol has been called a "social lubricant." People drink for many reasons—to relax, reduce anxiety, gain self-confidence, and overcome depression. Because sexual problems can be caused or worsened by psychological stress, moderate drinking might seem like a sexual enhancer. In fact, it merely lessens inhibitions. Alcohol is actually a depressant.

Spanish fly, or cantharides, is probably the most legendary aphrodisiac and the most dangerous; in fact it's poisonous in large doses. Made from dried beetle remains, the reported sexual excitement from Spanish fly comes from the irritation to the urogenital tract and a resultant rush of blood to the sex organs. But Spanish fly is a poison that burns the mouth and throat and can lead to genito-urinary infections, scarring of the urethra, and even death.

So be careful. A universal aphrodisiac may never be found, but experts agree that what's good for your overall health is probably good for your sex life too.

A good diet—carefully supplemented with proven herbs—and a regular exercise program are a more dependable path to better sex than are goats' eyes, deer sperm and frogs' legs. A good mental state is equally important. As John Renner, founder of the Consumer Health Information Research Institute (CHIRI) says, "The mind is the most potent aphrodisiac there is."

A LIFT FROM BEE POLLEN

For some men, bee pollen could be called "The Nectar of Relief" since it has been found to be very helpful in treating prostate problems. Some studies claim pollen—including cernitin or cernilton—has helped numerous maladies including fertility and impotence.

A report in a Swedish medical journal cited several studies using bee pollen extract: patients with inflamed prostates showed a marked improvement, with their prostate size returning to normal over a one-year period. Similarly, a Japanese study of 30 patients suffering from acute prostatitis showed that 16 of the 30 men (over half) who were treated with bee pollen, described it as "markedly effective." Thirteen of the remaining 14 men enjoyed some relief, classifying the treatment as "effective."

Since bee pollen is the male reproductive part of plants, it is a very concentrated source of nutrients. Pollen contains every vitamin known, although B12 is low. It is up to 40 percent protein, with a complete spectrum of amino acids. More than 25 trace elements account for 3.8 percent of pollen, including every essential element.

Bee pollen is extremely rich in protein. It also contains 23 grams of fat per ounce. Most of the fats are essential fatty acids including omega 3, omega 6, monounsaturated and saturated fats. It also contains numerous active enzymes and coenzymes. Pollen is uniformly rich in carotenoids, bioflavonoids and phytosterols, but amounts vary depending on the plant sources and growing conditions. Pollen also contains lycopene, beta-sitosterol and numerous flavonoids which have been shown to inhibit the growth of prostate tissue and reduce pain, inflammation and the risk of prostate cancer.

It has failed to gain broad acceptance, at least partially because bee pollen quality is inherently so variable. Still, standardized pollen extract has been judged an effective treatment for prostate enlargement and prostatitis without significant side effects.

On the negative side, bee pollen can cause an allergic reaction in some individuals. If you're concerned, start with a small amount, and discontinue use if a rash, wheezing, discomfort or other symptom occurs.

I have been taking bee pollen in tablet form for some time now. I believe it has increased my energy and—who knows—may have helped me in other "areas" of my life. Try it if you like. It's relatively safe.

LET YOUR HORMONES "RAGE"

Sex hormones, chemicals that help shape your love life, decline with age. A man's decreasing testosterone levels can also reduce his desire for sex. Testosterone replacement for men may help combat the effects of declining sex hormones. Research indicates that the hormone dehydroandrosterone (DHEA), the precursor to every hormone in the body, may also contribute to sexuality. Produced in the adrenal glands, it's the most abundant steroid hormone in circulation.

According to the *Journal of Endocrinology and Metabolism*, some men experiencing impotence have low levels of this hormone.

Studies on DHEA have been undertaken for more than 60 years. However, research led by Arlene Morales from the University of California School of Medicine in La Jolla helped launch DHEA into the spotlight when she gave it to 17 women and 13 men between the ages of 40 and 70. Within two weeks, her subjects reported feeling great both physically and emotionally. No clear relationship between DHEA and sexual behavior was determined. Yet, DHEA is a hormone of the androgen family, and according to researchers, androgens appear to be critical for the arousal stage of the libido.

Because the long-term effects of supplementing with DHEA have yet to be evaluated, it should be used only in case of deficiency. This is determined by laboratory tests ordered by your health care professional. DHEA is available from natural products stores in supplemental form. However, minimizing stress is the safest, most natural way to boost the body's naturally occurring DHEA levels.

COMMON DRUGS THAT SPOIL YOUR SEX LIFE

Diabetes is the most common cause of sexual dysfunction seen in men. It has been estimated that between 50–60 percent of diabetic men have erectile dysfunction. Other diseases causing similar problems include chronic renal failure, carcinomas, rheumatoid arthritis, hypothyroidism, herpes zoster, anemias, and breathing problems, such as chronic obstructive pulmonary disease. It's also estimated that fifty percent or more of the men with multiple sclerosis have erectile dysfunction.

Parkinson's disease and temporal lobe abnormalities are risk factors. Stroke and alcoholism has a very high risk because of damage to the testicles in chronic alcoholism and the loss of testosterone.

Illnesses including hypothyroidism (underactive thyroid gland) drag down desire. Many chronic diseases such as clogged arteries affect overall health and slow blood circulation to the genitals.

Ill health and increased medication use may explain why older men are most troubled by impotency. The Massachusetts Male Aging study, reported in *Urology*, found that half of the 1,290 men they asked between the ages of 40 and 70 suffered from some degree of erectile dysfunction.

If you're concerned about fertility, you should consider that the drugs you're taking—prescription, over-the-counter, and otherwise—may be interfering with your ability to have children. Many drugs reduce sperm quality and quantity. If you're on a long-term prescription, ask your doctor about the effects of your medication on fertility.

Recreational drugs such as marijuana, cocaine and alcohol are a major cause of erection problems. Alcohol decreases the body's ability to produce testosterone. Research at Chicago Medical School revealed that drinking alcohol may cause the hormonal equivalent of menopause in men. Alcohol not only affects sexual function, but also helps set the stage for a heart attack and other dangerous conditions.

The number one drug that can cause impotence is tobacco. Experiments show that even two cigarettes will markedly decrease the blood flow to the penis if smoked before sex. A study done at Boston University showed that men who smoked one pack of cigarettes a day for five years were 15 percent more likely to develop clogging in the arteries that serve the penis, a situation that can cause impotence. In addition, heavy smoking decreases sexual capability by damaging the tiny blood vessels in the penis.

Prescription drugs are also a major culprit, especially blood pressure drugs. (Caution: Do not stop taking a prescription drug or change the dosage without consulting your physician.)

The major problem drugs include:

1. Estrogens—used in men with prostate cancer.

2. Anti-androgens (flutamide)—used in men with prostate cancer.

3. Lupron—Prostate cancer drug.

4. Digoxin—a drug for heart failure.

5. Diuretics—used for men with heart disease and hypertension.

6. Methyldopa—older treatment for blood pressure.

7. Beta blockers—for heart disease and hypertension.

8. Calcium channel blockers—new treatments for hypertension.

9. Tranquilizers.

10. Decongestants.

11. Seizure medications.

12. Drugs to lower cholesterol.

13. The drugs cimetidine (Tagamet®) and ranitidine (Zantac®) which are used to treat ulcers and heartburn, also have significant side effects in some men.

14. To inhibit the growth of prostate cells medically, drugs such as Proscar® (finasteride) are prescribed. Proscar, a 5-alpha-reductase inhibitor, is designed to work by blocking out the normal formation of the male hormone dihydrotestosterone (DHT). Although doctors will readily prescribe them, many have significant side effects, including reduced sexual desire and performance.

Now maybe you don't use tobacco or alcohol, and basically you're in good health. Yet you're limp as celery. Check out number 10 on the above list. Antihistamines and decongestants can actually cause serious problems. In fact, taking large doses of cold medications occasionally leads to urinary retention, a potentially life-threatening condition in which you completely stop urinating. Decongestants—known as a sympathomimetic—cause the muscle at the bladder neck to constrict, restricting the flow of urine. Antihistamines can actually paralyze the bladder.

So if you have allergies, as well as prostate problems, ask your doctor about prescribing astemizole (Hismanal®) or terfenadine (Seldane®), two medications that have no antihistamines. If you must buy over-the-counter medication, take half of the suggested dose. If no problem ensues, move to the full recommended dosage. Needless to say, more is not always better. Follow the directions on the label and don't take more than is recommended.

There are two other things that may help; the herb echinacea and zinc. We've already discussed the importance of zinc for prostate health.

Echinacea's medicinal use began with the Plains Indians of the American Midwest, who used it for a variety of ailments, including venomous bites and external infections. In 1887, echinacea was introduced into United States medical practice, and it grew in popularity. Indeed, in the early part of the 20th century, nearly every medicine cabinet in the country contained echinacea. However, with the discovery of penicillin and other "wonder drugs," its popularity eventually waned.

The plant was rediscovered in the 1930s by Dr. Gerhard Madaus of Germany, who came to America in search of echinacea seeds. Madaus' research revealed that echinacea contains complex sugar molecules—polysaccharides—that stimulate the cells of the immune system, including white blood cells. Echinacea also supports the production of interferon, an important part of the immune response to viral infections that cause colds and flu.

Echinacea is available in several different preparations. Again, the most popular worldwide is the expressed juice of the flower. It can also be found in capsules and liquid extracts, frequently combined with the herb goldenseal, or vitamin C.

There are no known side effects to echinacea, although some believe that it may worsen the effects of auto-immune disorders. I know people who have made it a regular part of their cold weather supplementation.

GET IN THE MOOD

It's important to remember: stress, fatigue, inactivity and an unhealthy diet can create poor health, which often saps desire. I've already explained how a good diet and an adequate regimen of nutrients and herbs can boost your libido. Emotional health such as depression or stress can also affect sexual desire.

During the past decade, a link has been discovered between reproduction and emotions. Stress creates a familiar scenario: fast-beating heart, sweating, rapid breathing. The reproductive system isn't immune to this body-wide reaction. Adrenalin, for example, can decrease blood flow to a man's testes, penis and prostate.

Several studies show how mild-to-serious emotional pressure affects male fertility. Specifically:

Students at an officer-candidate school had lower testosterone levels when stress rose. Sperm formation almost came to a standstill in prisoners who were sentenced to death and then kept waiting. In addition, fatigue, family and business worries and other pressures may dampen a man's fertility, libido and sexual performance. So, as for number 9 on our list of drugs, if you need something to help you get through the day—or night—there are a few herbal supplements that may help. As described in Chapter Three, kava kava and valerian are particularly good.

Kava kava (*Piper methysticum*) has been used for many centuries in the South Pacific island communities of Micronesia, Melanesia and Polynesia. It was first described for the western world by Captain James Cook in the account of his voyage to the South Seas in 1768.

The South Pacific herb burst onto the scene in 1998 with impressive sales that continue to soar. In fact, supplies ran low as consumers discovered what South Pacific natives have known for 3,000 years: that kava can alleviate anxiety, depression, insomnia and tension while maintaining alertness, and has no known abuse potential.

In smaller doses it has a calming effect without slowing energy or thinking; in larger doses it acts as a sedative, without producing any morning hangover. Kava has undergone extensive scientific study, with favorable results. Standardized preparations of kava are now gaining greater popularity in Europe and the United States.

The appropriate dose of a kava preparation depends on the level of kavalactones it contains. On the basis of clinical studies using pure kavalactones or kava extracts standardized for kavalactones, the dosage recommendation for calming effects is 45 to 70 milligrams, 3 times daily. For sedative effects, a dose providing 180 to 210 milligrams can be taken one hour before going to bed.

No side effects have been reported when using standardized kava extracts at recommended levels. However, extremely high doses (e.g., more than 31,000 milligrams, or 310 grams, per week) have been associated with adverse effects and, therefore, are unnecessary and not encouraged.

Although the research is somewhat scarce, the largest study of kava's anti-anxiety effects, a placebo-controlled clinical trial, was published in 1997. Researchers from the department of psychiatry at Jena University in Germany evaluated 101 outpatients based on standard psychological tests including the Hamilton Anxiety Scale. The average score for kava-treated subjects decreased dramatically—from 30.7 before treatment to 9.9. After 24 weeks, researchers rated 53 percent of the kava group as "very much improved" vs. 30 percent for the placebo group.

This was the first long-term trial testing kava to treat anxiety. Although more clinical trials are needed, kava appears to help many people who experience this all-too-common disorder.

Then there's the latest MVP of tranquillity: St. John's Wort which acts as both an antidepressant and a sedative. Dubbed by some as "herbal Prozac," St. John's Wort (Hypericum) can take the "edge" off your day without making you drowsy, silly or dopey. In fact, you won't feel anything after taking it. You should notice you're more focused and little things don't bug you nearly as much.

St. John's Wort enjoys a long colorful history. Dioscorides, Pliny and Hippocrates all used it in ancient Greece to dispel evil spirits. In the Middle Ages there was a common belief that sleeping with a piece of the herb under your pillow on St. John's Eve would protect you during the following year.

St. John's Wort has been popular for the past 15 years in Europe as a natural remedy for depression. In Germany, where it's currently the leading treatment, physicians write some 3 million prescriptions a year—25 times the number they write for Prozac. In 1994 alone, St. John's Wort was prescribed for 20 million people in Germany.

There have been some 25 scientific studies done since 1994 involving thousands of people. One compelling study tracked the herb's effects on 3,250 patients battling mostly mild and moderate depression, and found that about 80 percent either felt better or became completely free of symptoms after four weeks. Then in 1998, the *British Medical Journal* published a review of 23 controlled studies involving 1,757 depressed patients. In that analysis, researchers from the United States and Germany found that St. John's Wort worked nearly three times better than a placebo.

Among other positive results, they found:

> St. John's Wort leads to an increase in deep sleep and does not impair cognitive functions or the ability to work or drive a car. One study showed an increase in the secretion of nocturnal melatonin, which aids deep sleep.
>
> It showed a positive long-term affect on anxiety.
>
> It has anti-inflammatory and antibiotic effects when applied externally.

Also, the respected *Journal of Geriatric Psychiatry and Neurology* aroused a good deal of interest in 1994 when it devoted an entire issue— 17 research papers in all—to "Hypericum: A Novel Antidepressant."

The herb shows "definite promise," says Dr. Cynthia Mulrow, a University of Texas internist who co-authored the study. "It's a reasonable alternative to consider."

In all the studies, St. John's Wort has shown no major side effects and costs much less than comparable antidepressant drugs. Only 2.4 percent in a German study showed slight side effects such as restlessness, gastrointestinal irritations and mild allergic reactions.

Purdue University herb expert Varro Tylor notes that prescription antidepressants, such as Prozac, cause more common and more serious side effects, such as insomnia, weight loss and sexual dysfunction. "The absence of serious side effects is one of Hypericum's biggest selling points," he says.

One side effect worth noting, however, is the potential for photosensitivity, or increased sensitivity to sunlight, which has been demonstrated in animals. This phenomenon, while theoretically possible in humans, has not been documented in the recommended doses for depression.

Despite the promising studies, researchers still know very little about the herb's active ingredients or how it works. They also aren't sure whether St. John's Wort can help the severely depressed or if it is safe and effective for long-term use.

Experts note that many of the products in the health-food stores contain overly diluted concentrations that render the herb impotent. The optimum dosage, based on the majority of medical studies, is 300 milligrams of

Hypericum extract containing .3 percent of the active ingredient Hypericin, three times a day.

St. John's Wort takes two to six weeks to take full effect. If you are already using a pharmaceutical antidepressant for mild to moderate depression and you want to try St. John's Wort, then consult with your doctor and professional herbalist. St. John's Wort is not sufficient for people with severe depression.

Does it adversely affect sexual performance? Not at all. If anything it will only make you more focused since negative thoughts are less likely to creep in.

Do you remember our vegetarian friend Benny who reduced his enlarged prostate by taking saw palmetto and zinc? At the time, Benny was also made aware that although his vegetarian diet would increase his possibility of avoiding prostate cancer, a healthy sex life was also important.

Specifically he uncovered a study by British urologist Anjan K. Banerjee at the Manchester Royal Infirmary who discovered that frequent ejaculations helped to keep the prostate healthy and cancer-free. Dr. Banerjee tested his idea on 423 men who ranged in age from 60 to 80; 274 of the men had prostate cancer and 149 did not. Each man was asked to estimate his ejaculatory frequency per week during the sexually active periods throughout his life. This included ejaculation by any means including masturbation.

The men with no prostate cancer reported ejaculating significantly more frequently than those with prostate cancer. Dr. Banerjee could not come to a conclusion about what caused the connection between ejaculation rate and prostate health, but he did suggest that reduced ejaculation frequency appeared to promote the development of the disease.

With Benny's saw palmetto and zinc regiment, he claims to have no problem in that department. "My erections are fine and I hope to have them until I'm 100!"

Points to Remember:

Eat a healthy, well-balanced diet. Include pumpkin seeds and bee pollen, or royal jelly.

Avoid alcohol, particularly before sexual encounters.

Don't consume animal fats, sugar, fried or junk foods.

Don't smoke.

Avoid stress.

Consult a urologist for testing to determine whether impotence is caused by an underlying illness that requires treatment.

Keep in mind that sexual function changes with age. As you age, you may require more stimulation and a longer period of time to achieve an erection.

If you suspect impotence may be related to a drug you are taking, discuss this with your physician. There may be satisfactory alternatives that will not cause this problem.

Investigate the possibility of cadmium or other heavy metal intoxication. A hair analysis can reveal possible heavy metal poisoning.

If you suffer from impotence, the important thing to remember is "don't wait." The longer you wait, the greater the worry, the more difficult the treatment and recovery, and you'll miss out on a lot of great evenings in bed, too. Your best bet is to find a qualified doctor who is knowledgeable of the latest medical therapies. If you need help in locating someone, one of the following organizations can help:

- Impotence Institute of America & Impotence Anonymous—1.800.669.1603. The Institute also offers anonymous groups where men can hear the experiences of other men which usually relates to what they are going through.
- Male Potency Centers of America—1.800.438.7683.

YOU CAN PROTECT YOUR PROSTATE

If you're baffled about testosterone and its effect on your prostate, it's probably a good idea for us to summarize. Testosterone is plentiful when we're young and as a result, our sex drive is strongest. As we get older, testosterone decreases, and so does our sexual desire. What testosterone we do have, if not released, runs the risk of being converted to DHT leading to BPH or cancer, thanks to the enzyme 5-alpha-reductase.

What to do. You want to build up your testosterone via diet and herbs, and release it via exercise and sex. And remember: the easiest, most reliable mechanism for erotic stimulation is one's own imagination. To quote renowned sex expert "Dr. Ruth" Westheimer, Ed.D.: "The most important sex organ lies between the ears."

Sounds simple, doesn't it?

CHAPTER SIX

HOW TO

DEFEAT

PROSTATITIS

Prostatitis is an inflammation of the prostate, which may be caused by the presence of a bacterial infection. Then again—as you'll see—maybe not.

Prostatitis causes intense pain, urinary complications, sexual dysfunction, infertility and a drastic reduction in the quality of life. It can be a one-time occurrence, or it can be chronic, persistent or recurrent.

Prostatitis affects 60 percent of all males from puberty on and can occur in any prostate regardless of size. In fact, it is one of the most common reasons men visit urologists. It's a non-age discriminatory ailment; unlike BPH and cancer, it can strike males at any age.

Common as it is, the lack of medical knowledge about its causes and cures has led some doctors to refer to it as "a wastebasket of clinical ignorance." First of all it's hard to pinpoint. Symptoms, as you will see, have its victims worried about diseases ranging from testicular cancer to a sexually transmitted disease (STD). If you do suspect that it's a prostate problem, many of the symptoms of prostatitis are similar to those caused by an enlarged prostate or cancer.

For example, the most common symptoms include pain or a burning sensation during urination, frequent urination (especially disturbing at night), the sensation of urgency that you must urinate right away, impotence, burning with ejaculation or discolored semen. It can also be accompanied by chills and fever if there's an acute infection. At times the symptoms may also include generalized malaise, joint aches, muscle aches, fever or pain almost anywhere within the pelvis and scrotum. These symptoms of prostatitis may be mild or they may be overwhelming.

WHAT CAUSES PROSTATITIS

As I've said, prostatitis is a common, yet confusing ailment, often used to describe a variety of inflammatory conditions of the prostate gland. Unfortunately, when an accurate diagnosis fails, it's used as a "catch-all" phrase for a number of different urinary-tract infections and conditions. Granted, with the prostate's proximity to the urethra and bladder, conditions affecting one or another often have similar or overlapping symptoms.

Prostatitis can be a one-time occurrence, or it can be chronic, persistent or recurrent. Bacteria or some other microorganism can cause the disease, or it can result from factors other than bacteria.

Basically there are two kinds of prostatitis:

- Non-bacterial (or noninfectious).
- Bacterial (or infectious).

Non-bacterial prostatitis isn't a disease, it's a condition. Doctors usually divide it into two categories:

- Congestive prostatitis (sometimes called prostatostasis).
- Prostatodynia.

Congestive prostatitis occurs when too much prostatic fluid, the milky fluid in semen, accumulates within the prostate gland rather than being ejaculated out through the penis. The gland is said to be "congested" or "engorged."

Congestive prostatitis can be caused by your frequency of sex—sometimes too much, sometimes too little. We've already covered this in other chapters but it's worth repeating. Every day a healthy prostate secretes between one-tenth and two-fifths of a teaspoon of fluid. When you're sexually aroused you produce four to ten times that amount. Normally (or at least ideally), you release it by ejaculating. If you don't your prostate becomes congested. Also, an abrupt fall-off in sexual climaxes—maybe your partner is mad at you—can engorge the prostate. Also, if suddenly your sexual activity picks up, your prostrate becomes inflamed trying to "tool up" for the new, debonair you!

Prostatodynia is a condition in which pain "seems" to originate in the prostate but is much more likely to be coming from the muscles of the pelvic floor, from an inflammation in one or more of the pelvic bones, or from a disease in the rectum. This malady is thought to be stress-related. Despite its name, prostatodynia really has nothing to do with the prostate.

Prostatitis is further classified as "acute" or "chronic." Acute infections come on suddenly and have some or all of the following symptoms:

- Fever and chills,
- Pain and burning on urination and ejaculation,
- Strong and frequent urge to urinate while passing only small amounts of urine,
- Lower back or abdominal pain, and
- Occasionally, blood in the urine.

Symptoms of chronic prostatitis are usually milder than those of an acute infection, and fever and chills are usually not present. Either infection may occur with a urinary tract infection.

Whereas acute bacterial prostatitis is rare, "chronic prostatitis" is very common; some reports estimate about half of the masculine population is affected at least once in their lifetime, with others reporting even higher figures. Chronic bacterial prostatitis (CBP) is the least frequent condition, affecting only about 5 percent of all patients. The occurrence of non-bacterial prostatitis (NBP) and prostatodynia (PDY) varies in different reports, but both share more or less half of the remainder.

The causes of prostatitis are sometimes well understood but are more often obscure. It is often caused by bacteria similar to those which cause other types of urinary infections. Sometimes infectious bacteria invade the prostate from another area of the body. Not to scare you, but the resulting inflammation can result in urine retention, which can cause the bladder to become distended, weak, tender and itself susceptible to infection. Infection in the bladder is in turn transmitted up the urethras to the kidneys. As you can see, although often annoying and painful, it can also be dangerous.

Some patients, however, have no evidence of bacteria in their prostates, yet are thought to carry microorganisms such as Chlamydia or Ureaplasma, which are harder to identify by standard culture techniques. Still other patients have no evidence of any microorganisms at all. The reasons for their prostatitis symptoms are poorly understood and are possibly related to stress and/or congestion. Sometimes certain medications such as cold remedies with antihistamines and decongestants may be the cause.

In addition to being tough to diagnose, prostatitis is sometimes difficult to treat effectively. Sadly, for some it never completely goes away. This is often frustrating for both patients and doctors.

FREE YOURSELF FROM PROSTATITIS PANIC

If you think you have prostatitis (or any other disease for that matter), see your doctor immediately. Although self-diagnosis is never smart you may want to take this simple test called the University of Washington Symptom Score (obviously developed at the University of Washington):

Questions 1–7 constitute the pain scale,

8–14 the voiding scale, and

15 to 21 the sexual dysfunction scale.

The higher the score the more likely that you have prostatitis. Here we go:

In the past week, including today, how much were you bothered by (rank from 1 to 5, 5 most bothered):

1. pain in the lower back

2. pain between the testicles and the anus

3. pain in the lower abdomen

4. pain in the rectal area

5. pain in the testicles

6. pain in the penis

7. pain during urination

8. bladder does not feel completely empty right after urinating

9. need to urinate again less than 2 hours after urinating

10. stopping and starting several times while urinating

11. difficulty postponing urination, hard to hold it

12. weak urinary stream

13. having to push or strain to begin urination

14. getting up to urinate one or more times a night

15. difficulty maintaining an erection

16. pain with ejaculation

17. difficulty getting an erection
18. blood in your semen
19. lack of interest in sexual activity
20. premature ejaculation
21. difficulty in reaching ejaculation.

Okay. You now may have a pretty good idea if you have Prostatitis or not. Off you go to the doctor.

When your physician examines you, a digital rectal exam may reveal a very tender prostate gland. At times, however, your prostate may not be tender at all. Your physician may choose to examine either your urine or the prostatic secretions following a massage of the prostate. Because there are so many symptom complexes and causes for prostatitis, many physicians approach it differently. All examinations, however, should include a digital rectal exam.

Prostatitis is most commonly treated with antibiotics. This may be effective when there is actually an infecting agent (bacteria). Many times, however, they do not work, either because they don't eradicate the infection or because there never was an actual infection. It is common for some patients to receive multiple courses of different antibiotics in an attempt to find one that works. Patients may respond to certain pharmacological agents (drugs) which have a tendency to relax the muscles of the bladder neck and prostate gland. The long-term use of such drugs can lead to bacterial resistance, which in turn necessitates more potent drugs, more expense, and more medical complications.

Prostatitis which is difficult to treat or stubbornly recurrent may be treated with surgery. A limited transurethral resection (called a Focal TURP) of the prostate removes the part of the prostate affected by prostatitis with the same technical equipment used to operate on BPH. Essentially, the prostatic tissue is removed through a scope placed in the urethra. This is only a last resort for troublesome prostatitis and is performed only if the spot is distinctly painful or if there is a heavy suspicion that it may be the cause of obstruction.

Usually with patience and care, a less radical treatment regimen can be found which will afford relief. Sometimes a change of behavior helps relieve symptoms. Take bike riding, for example. A recent report in the United States linked bike riding with impotence. Your prostate (sometimes called the "seat of masculinity") is fairly close to the surface of the area that touches the seat of the average road bike. So every bump from every pothole you go over is transmitted to that region.

Researchers are also investigating whether this might also cause prostatitis. Whether it does or not, biking can make your condition worse if you don't have your clothing and your seat configured properly. (See Chapter One.)

The last ten years have seen great strides in the treatment of prostate cancer and BPH (Benign Prostatic Hyperplasia), diseases which affect mostly older men. For the most part, prostatitis, a non-fatal but often disabling disease affecting men of all ages has been neglected.

BANISH PROSTATE PAIN WITH NATURAL BOTANICALS

There are botanicals which can help the body reduce inflammation and infection, promote urination, soothe irritated tissues, reduce inflammation and pain and curb the typical dull, aching throb. For example:

There are herbs with antibiotic and anti-inflammatory properties such as echinacea, goldenseal, and garlic, to help reduce inflammation and knock out infection. Couch grass, watermelon seed and pipsissewa are natural diuretics that help flush urine, prevent urine buildup, and provide support for other preventive methods.

Echinacea and Siberian ginseng are immune system enhancers that help the body's natural defense system build resistance. Comfrey, couch grass and marsh mallow have demulcent properties to help soothe and protect.

Buchu, saw palmetto and pipsissewa are great genito-urinary tonics and astringents that help strengthen and heal; they have anti-microbial actions as well.

Later I'll give you more detail on these and other botanicals that may help you deal with prostatitis.

BETTER THAN PRESCRIPTION DRUGS

As I've stressed throughout the book, eating right is very important for prostate health. This goes for fighting—and preventing—prostatitis.

Should you suffer from prostatitis, eat lightly. Also make sure you eat plenty of whole grains, steamed vegetables and fresh fruits.

Here are a couple of foods you may want to add to your diet:

Parsley is more than just a garnish. It is the foremost diuretic to be recommended when urination is painful and incomplete. This is due to a swollen or enlarged prostate squeezing the urethra so tightly that urination is difficult. The presence of apiol and myristicin, as well as other flavonoids, in parsley will stimulate urination and provide relief. There is much talk of overdoses of pure apiol being harmful to the kidneys and liver. However, you shouldn't fear poisoning from the plant itself. Parsley works best in blends with other herbs, such as buchu and corn silk. (SEE BELOW). So when you put a salad together, don't scrimp on the parsley!

Pumpkin seeds are a natural source of zinc and linoleic acid (vitamin F). They have a reputation as a non-irritating diuretic which can help decongest the prostate gland and lessen residual urine. This property makes the pumpkin seed especially well suited to treat a swollen or enlarged prostate. Native American Indians used it successfully for this purpose long before the settlers adopted it. Today, it is universally accepted.

They're really quite tasty and readily available in supermarkets. You can either add them to your salad or cereal or snack on them like peanuts.

There are also some things you should avoid. If you have prostatitis, skip spicy foods. Also alcohol, not just whiskey, but wine too, can aggravate your condition. Coffee is another culprit that can cause your inflammation to flare up. Heavy lifting, prolonged driving, and vigorous exercise are also to be avoided. Although it's important to exercise, try to focus on more aerobic workouts than strength, at least until your condition improves.

If you haven't already, you should also begin a daily regimen of vitamin and mineral supplements that include the antioxidants, vitamins A, C, E, beta-carotene and selenium. (More on vitamin C later). Also add 60 mg of zinc picolinate if you have prostatitis symptoms; otherwise, 30 mg are sufficient.

KNOCK OUT INFECTIONS

Here are medicinal herbs with antibiotic and anti-inflammatory properties which can help reduce inflammation and knock out infection. When a botanical is described as acting as a "demulcent," that means it can help protect or soothe the inflamed tissue.

Echinacea is used as an antibiotic and immune system stimulant. It has anti-bacterial, anti-viral and anti-microbial properties that work well on the reproductive system. It combines well with saw palmetto for treating prostatitis. In fact, it can be combined in equal parts with saw palmetto and used as a suppository for prostatitis and enlarged prostates. Echinacea should be taken in large amounts for infection. It can cause stomach upset and can cause the mouth to tingle and actively salivate.

Garlic has tonic, stimulant, hypotensive, antispasmodic and anti-microbial properties. It is purported to help treat infections and rid the body of parasites. It is also good for spasms and cramps.

Garlic combines well with echinacea and goldenseal for treating microbial infections. It contains alliin, but needs to be chewed or crushed to bring out alliin's antibiotic properties.

Studies have found that 1 medium clove pack has the antibacterial properties of 100,000 units of penicillin. Depending on the type of infection, oral penicillin ranges from 600,000 to 1.2 million units. An equivalent amount of garlic would be 6–12 cloves.

Goldenseal has tonic, astringent and antiseptic properties. The astringent and tonic properties are useful in treating and strengthening reproductive organs. Goldenseal combines well with saw palmetto and echinacea for prostatitis. You should avoid prolonged high doses, as this herb is known to diminish essential flora in the intestines. It can also affect your blood pressure.

Goldenseal contains berberine, which may lower blood pressure, and hydrastine, which may raise blood pressure. So if you have a history of high blood pressure, heart disease, diabetes, glaucoma or stroke, exercise extreme caution and don't use this herb. For otherwise healthy individuals, goldenseal may be used for brief periods of time at the recommended dosage levels.

We talked about this botanical previously, and we will again. Although best known as a BPH preventative, the saw palmetto berry acts directly on the prostate to reduce inflammation, pain and throb due to prostatitis. It also increases the bladder's ability to contract and expel its contents by toning it, thereby helping to relieve straining pains. Studies have shown that saw palmetto can increase urine flow by 38 percent for prostatitis and BPH, while helping to treat infection.

Saw palmetto combines well with echinacea and buchu for prostatitis treatment. It may also be used in suppository form. Credit for the discovery of these principles goes to the early American eclectic physicians who so effectively transformed native American flora into a medicinal storehouse.

GET IN THE FLOW

It's important to exercise care when using any diuretic-type preparation because they can cause serum potassium depletion if used in large doses for an extended period of time. I also recommend drinking as much filtered water as you can tolerate to help keep your system flushed. Spaced throughout the day you should consume six to eight, 8-ounce glasses per day minimum.

Cornsilk, couch grass, dong quai, juniper, kelp, pipsissewa, queen of the meadow, and watermelon seeds are natural diuretics that help flush urine, prevent urine buildup, and provide support for other preventive methods. Here's a brief synopsis of each:

CORNSILK: This is a diuretic, and acts much like parsley. It is both mild and non-toxic, and is contained in several over-the-counter (OTC) type diuretic products in Europe and America (where it used to be an officially recognized medicinal agent). It is also popular in China. Most herbalists around the world agree that cornsilk directly reduces painful symptoms and swelling due to several inflammatory conditions, including prostatitis.

COUCH GRASS: Rhizome herbalists have found this grass very valuable for treating enlarged and infected prostates. It has a soothing effect on the genito-urinary system. It works as a diuretic and also has demulcent and anti-microbial properties. May be combined with saw palmetto, echinacea and buchu.

DONG QUAI: Dong quai, a species of Angelica, has diuretic and anti-spasmodic properties useful in treating rostatitis. It works well with cramp bark for genito-urinary cramping. Dong quai tends to increase blood sugar levels so it should not be used by diabetics.

JUNIPER: Berries purported to be good for genito-urinary infections and incontinence (gives urine the fragrance of violets). Has diuretic properties and the essential oil is used in the OTC diuretic Odrinil. Juniper may lower blood pressure. High doses may cause kidney irritation and damage; therefore, juniper should not be used by anyone with a kidney infection or a history of kidney problems. Despite this, the FDA includes it on its list of "herbs regarded as safe." Should be used in medicinal amounts only in otherwise healthy individuals. Should not be taken for more than six weeks.

KELP: Kelp has been used for scores of years by Asian peoples to treat disorders of the genito-urinary tract, including kidney, bladder, prostate and uterine problems. Clinical documentation is available to show that kelp ingestion on a daily basis gradually reduces the prostate in older men to the point that urination becomes painless, even though it is not certain how that occurs.

PIPSISSEWA: Has diuretic, tonic and astringent properties. Used mostly for genito-urinary system. Claimed to be very effective for chronic prostatitis and other genito-urinary disorders. Has a gentle yet powerful soothing effect.

QUEEN OF THE MEADOW: Has diuretic, nervine, stimulant and astringent properties. Considered by herbalists to be very valuable for treating genito-urinary problems.

WATERMELON SEEDS: Have natural diuretic properties and are also an antioxidant. Purported to help prevent excess build-up of urine due to rostatitis and BPH. Work well with uva ursi and buchu and may be found in health food stores alone or combined with them.

"WAVE" GOODBYE TO PAIN

You may be able to soak away some of your discomfort from prostatitis. Hydrotherapy, or water therapy, helps increase circulation in the prostate while helping to relax and open the urinary tract.

Here's what you should do: sit for 15–30 minutes in a tub full of the hottest water you can tolerate. Hot sitz baths draw more blood to the area, increase local circulation and relax the muscles.

Cold soaks may also be therapeutic, and should be alternated with hot soaks. Also recommended are hot and cold packs applied to the prostate area (between the scrotum and anus). You should note that hot soaks are not recommended for acute infection or inflammation.

Unless you think it's too sissified, you can also concoct an anti-inflammatory oil to add to your bath or to rub directly behind your scrotum. By combining two ounces of St. John's Wort, four drops of chamomile, and one-eighth teaspoon each of lavender and rosemary oils, you may find your circulation has increased, your muscles are more relaxed and you have less inflammation.

It's also possible for you to reduce your pain if you just simply relax and try to reduce stress, especially if you are suffering from prosatodynia. We've covered stress management techniques and exercise in Chapter Four, so there's no need to go delve into them again here. I will remind you, though, to do your Kegels.

There are herbs like chamomile, cramp bark, skullcap and valerian that can help relax muscles. Here are capsule summaries of each:

CHAMOMILE: Chamomile has anti-spasmodic, antiseptic, anti-inflammatory, and analgesic properties. It is used as a mild sedative and works well for adults, children and the elderly. An infusion, or tea, is purported to have calming effects on cramps or painful symptoms of the genito-urinary system.

CRAMP BARK: Has anti-spasmodic, sedative, nervine and astringent properties. Claimed to have strong anti-spasmodic effects on the genito-urinary system for males and females. May be combined with chamomile or angelica root for genito-urinary cramping.

SKULLCAP: Leaves from this botanical have nervine, tonic, sedative and anti-spasmodic properties. Purported to relieve stress and nervous tension, nervous headache, neuralgia, insomnia and restlessness. Combines well with valerian for treating stress and nervous tension, with chamomile for restlessness and insomnia.

VALERIAN: Has sedative, hypnotic, anti-spasmodic and hypotensive properties. Combines well with skullcap for tension and anxiety, with chamomile for insomnia, and with cramp bark for pain and cramping. Contains valepotriates, chemicals that appear to have sedative properties, with the highest concentration in the roots. On rare instances, valerian has been known to have a stimulant effect rather than a calming effect.

To fight prostatitis pain, you may wish to try herb teas and tinctures, such as saw palmetto and Siberian ginseng; both are good for the male reproductive system.

We've already mentioned saw palmetto. Siberian ginseng, which is not truly a ginseng like its panax cousin, is reputed to be an immune system enhancer. It may help your body's defense system build resistance, expand blood vessels to increase circulation, and regulate blood pressure, while boosting physical energy.

Another substance that may help is that highly nutritious supplement, bee pollen. In studies, pollen extract has been judged an effective treatment for prostate enlargement and prostatitis in double-blind, placebo-controlled clinical trials. There were no significant side effects. Pollen contains lycopene, beta-sitosterol and numerous flavonoids which have been shown to inhibit the growth of prostate tissue and reduce pain and inflammation, as well as the risk of prostate cancer.

THE REAL REASON THE CHINESE LIVE LONGER

It seems we keep coming back to the Orient. And why not? People in the Far East have developed herbs, exercise and fitness regiments that seem to be geared towards prostate health and long life. One that I haven't mentioned yet is the exercise and body movement technique known as Qi Gong.

It's widely accepted that exercise can promote health and prevent illnesses. Our exercise in the Western World mostly concentrates on muscular/skeletal development through the application of stress and load to build up strength. In other words, it works from the outside inward. Qi Gong, on the other hand, works the body from the inside outwards. It connects the body and spirit, focusing on breathing, concentration, and physical movements.

Qi Gong (pronounced "Chee Gong") consists of techniques for dealing with human energy flow. In applying these techniques, one employs the use of the human body's chakras and meridians which are the body's focal points and channels through which its Qi Energy flows. In the view of Chinese medicine, many illnesses are caused by blockages in these channels. Through use of certain energies and techniques, Qi Gong can relieve pain, strengthen the body's constitution, improve intelligence, and prolong life. Correct use of these energies results in regulation of the internal functions of the human body.

Qi Gong views the human body as an individual universe: a microcosm reflecting the macrocosm. In this view, that of the human body as being the universe, Qi Gong views the organs of the body as the galaxies and planets. Its primary energy, the Yin and the Yang, are in constant evolution and revolution, opposing, yet supporting, each other in that constant change and equilibrium.

Disease and illness are caused by excesses and/or deficiencies in this delicate, yet evolving balance. Any excess or deficiency will result in the otherwise natural flow of these energies becoming harmful energy—hence illness. If this imbalance is properly addressed, then the body will remain healthy.

How does it work? Simply put, that much of our illness is caused, or at least influenced, by our minds. Qi Gong utilizes techniques that exercise and regulate one's mind and body, thus directly and immediately influencing a person's physiological state. It also enables one to make the most of latent powers within the human body. It increases the body's ability to adapt to and defend against the outer environment.

Qi Gong can be considered a "holistic" therapy, exercising the body and mind, and increasing self-regulation and self-control. The main functions of Qi Gong can be summarized as disease prevention, disease treatment, strengthening the body, improving intelligence and prolonging life, and finally, manifesting the latent power within us all.

Qi Gong combines all of the above attributes of physical fitness, exercise, yoga, and meditation, in such a way that it is accessible to persons of any physical state, gender, age and condition and is easier to learn than Tai Chi.

Practitioners generally experience increased stamina, better digestion, improved circulation, more restful sleep, balanced internal energy and reduced stress and anxiety. With regular practice you will learn to feel and increase your life-force energy while dissolving energy blockages. One of the benefits of Qi Gong is enhanced resistance to disease.

Research carried out in China recently, using Western scientific apparatus, has verified this. For example, a series of experiments carried out at Tientsin Chinese Medical Research Center on 68 patients showed that the proportion of white blood cells, which are responsible for the body's self defense, increased from an average of 57.7 percent to 78.1 percent after practicing Qi Gong for three months.

If you're interested in learning more, check your local Yellow Pages, or check with local universities. There's an excellent chance they offer night courses teaching it.

Will this help your prostatitis? Possibly. It certainly will reduce your stress and, if you believe its proponents, increase your resistance to disease.

A SOOTHING JUICE CURE

Cranberry juice has properties that dislodge bacteria from the bladder wall so that loose invading bacteria are washed away. It may help to prevent infection from spreading to the bladder from the prostate and vice versa.

Drinking cranberry juice is a common home remedy for a urinary tract infection or to fight one once it occurs. The berry's bacteria-zapper was thought to be its acid. If that were true, though, why wouldn't lemon juice or tomatoes be equally potent?

In a study funded by Ocean Spray Cranberries, Inc., a group of researchers believe they have found the answer: "The effect is due not to the highly acidic nature of cranberries but to specific compounds in cranberries that inhibit the adherence of *Escherichia coli* (bacteria) to uroepithelial cells"—cells lining the urinary tract. This was reported by Dr. Amy Howell of Rutgers University, New Brunswick, New Jersey, and colleagues in a letter in the October 8th 1998 issue of *The New England Journal of Medicine*. *Escherichia coli*, or *E.coli*, is a bacterium found normally in the digestive tract. However, if certain strains of the bacteria gain access to the normally sterile environment of the bladder and urinary tract, the bacteria can trigger an infection, with symptoms including a frequent, painful urge to urinate and blood in the urine. The condition can be readily treated with antibiotics, but recurs in 25 percent of cases.

In a new study, the researchers tested the ability of cranberry extracts to inhibit the binding of certain disease-causing strains of *E.coli* to cells taken from the lining of the urinary tract. This binding process is thought to be an early step in the initiation of an infection. During the course of the 5-year study, the team found that extracts containing compounds called "condensed tannins" or "proanthocyanidins," which are found in cranberries and blueberries, could inhibit the binding process. "We have identified condensed tannins (proanthocyanidins) as the compounds in cranberries that are responsible for preventing . . . *E.coli* from adhering to the urinary tract," they conclude. "We found that the condensed tannins in cranberries were capable of preventing the bacteria from attaching to the urinary tract, which would promote flushing of bacteria from the bladder into the urine stream, resulting in the prevention or reduction of symptoms," said Howell in a statement released by Rutgers. Howell estimates that the amount of condensed tannins in a 10-ounce glass of cranberry juice taken on a daily basis could help prevent urinary tract infections, which are more common in women than in men.

A 1996 study found that when cranberry juice is sweetened with corn syrup (most commercial "cranberry cocktails" and "cranberry drinks" are), the juice loses its bacteria-fighting power. So Rutgers used cranberry extracts, such as pure juice and cranberry powder in tablet form. Besides urinary tract infections, it is also recommended for incontinence and is purported to deodorize urine.

Vinegar or lemon juice in tea is a time-honored folk/home remedy for infections. Theory: the vinegar or lemon cured the affliction; the tea made it possible to swallow the medicine. Given the research, it's a credible prescription except that the medicine isn't the vinegar; it's the tannin in the tea.

FIGHT INFECTIONS NATURALLY

We've already mentioned some botanicals, such as echinacea and Siberian ginseng, which are immune-system enhancers that help the body's natural defense system build resistance. In addition, herbs such as comfrey, couch grass and marsh mallow have demulcent properties to help soothe and protect. Likewise, buchu, hydrangea and pipsissewa are great genito-urinary tonics and astringents that help strengthen and heal, and have anti-microbial actions as well.

Buchu comes from Africa and is considered to be a urinary antiseptic. It contains an oil that increases urine production and is excreted virtually unchanged by the kidneys, rendering the urine slightly antiseptic. So it's a diuretic but also has anti-microbial properties. Buchu is purported to help strengthen and heal the genito-urinary system, and is used to treat acute and chronic prostatitis.

By themselves, buchu leaves are seldom used for acute prostate problems, but they lend just the right antiseptic property to preparations used for acute as well as chronic prostate problems.

This herb works well with couch grass and echinacea for prostatitis.

Hydrangea is an old native North American remedy for urinary stones, adopted by settlers and later established in herbal medicine. This herb has also been used historically for effectively treating kidney and bladder stones, cystitis, urethritis, prostatitis, rheumatoid arthritis, gout and edema. Hydrangea is a sweet, pungent herb that is both antiseptic and diuretic, and has the ability to soothe irritated tissues and reduce the formation of urinary stones. The plant, whose leaves have white undersides, is occasionally grown for foliage effect. Its cultivars have some of the largest flower heads of the species, consisting almost entirely of sterile flowers.

Marsh mallow has demulcent, diuretic, tonic and emollient properties. It is claimed to help soothe and protect the genito-urinary system. One study has shown that marsh mallow enhanced white blood cells' ability to devour microbes. It has also been found to lower blood sugar in animals and, therefore, may be beneficial in managing diabetes.

THE 10 CENT VITAMIN CURE

Wonder drug, or fancy urine? That's been the question since vitamin C trailblazer, Dr. Linus Pauling began expounding its virtues back in the 1970s.

Today, vitamin C is promoted for numerous health benefits, including fighting infections, such as prostatitis. It plays a vital role in every major body system, and its importance in preventing disease and maintaining optimal health can't be minimized. In fact, vitamin C protects the bowel, kidneys and bladder on the way out when we urinate. So much for fancy urine.

Vitamin C, also known as ascorbic acid, is a water-soluble vitamin sensitive to degradation by oxygen, light, heat and air. Its primary function is to maintain the formation of collagen, a protein found in skin, ligaments, bones and many other body tissues. It is also required for wound healing, formation of red blood cells, maintaining capillary integrity, and healthy gums and teeth.

It may also help prevent or alleviate prostatitis since it fights bacterial infections. In addition, vitamin C reduces the effect of inflammatory prostaglandins, while increasing the effect of anti-inflammatory substances. It is also involved in the production of neurotransmitters.

Vitamin C has been shown to reduce the effects of histamines that are involved in many allergic and hypersensitive reactions. These actions may explain its beneficial effects in both preventing and treating the common cold and on many types of allergy, hypersensitivity and inflammatory conditions such as asthma and arthritis.

When fully saturated, the human body contains about 5,000 mg. of vitamin C. Stress, smoking, high fever, use of sulfa drugs or painkillers, and prolonged use of oral contraceptives, antibiotics or cortisone all reduce the body's ability to absorb it. Even common aspirin thwarts the absorption of vitamin C by white blood cells. Taking aspirin for more than four days can cause a fall in blood plasma levels of ascorbic acid comparable to those seen in scurvy.

Smokers in particular need to ingest more vitamin C than non-smokers, at least 100 mg per day. Even nonsmokers exposed to smoke need more vitamin C, according to a study at the University of California, Berkeley.

Many conditions increase the body's need for this vitamin. Growth, wound healing, bone fractures and damage to cartilage, soft tissue and teeth all cause the body to use more vitamin C. It also plays a critical role in healing surgical wounds, burns and other types of injuries. It is necessary for the metabolism and detoxification of alcohol and drugs because it activates the enzyme that breaks down alcohol in the liver.

Vitamin C acts as an antioxidant. It protects against the damaging effects of free radicals on body tissues, cells and DNA and has a sparing effect on other vitamins. It prevents the formation of carcinogenic nitrosamines from nitrites and nitrates and preservatives used in many prepared meats. It also significantly increases the body's absorption of iron.

It also affects brain function, according to Mark David Altshule in *Nutritional Factors in General Medicine.* Low plasma levels have been associated with fatigue, depression and paranoia, while increased blood plasma levels of vitamin C help increase alertness and improve work performance, according to Linus Pauling, Ph.D., in his landmark book, *Vitamin C: The Common Cold & The Flu* (W.H. Freeman & Co.).

It's believed that vitamin C benefits our immune system in many ways. It increases white blood cell (disease-fighting) activity, increases interferon (proteins that fight viruses) levels, antibody responses and antibody levels. A National Cancer Institute study showed that therapeutic doses of vitamin C (5 to 10 grams) increased production of lymphocytes, the body's disease-fighting white blood cells.

Studies have demonstrated that, when used in large amounts, vitamin C has antiviral and antibiotic effects. Other studies have shown that intakes of five times the RDA or more are associated with decreased incidence of lung disease, stomach cancer, gum disease and cataract formation. Increased amounts have also been shown to increase fertility by protecting sperm from free radical damage that can cause birth defects.

The adult Recommended Daily Allowance for vitamin C is 60 mg. per day—about the amount found in half a glass of orange juice. This amount, however, is far below the optimal amount needed to promote good health and provide effective disease protection. For example, Nobel Prize-winning scientist Linus Pauling recommended using 1 to 2 grams (1,000 to 2,000 mg.) of vitamin C per day as a regular maintenance dose and increasing that amount to 4 to 10 grams per day at the onset of a cold.

Increased intake of vitamin C is associated with few side effects, even at 200 times the RDA. However, consult your health care practitioner before taking large amounts of any supplement. The most common side effect is loose stools, gas and sometimes heartburn. Most people can tolerate at least 1,000 mg/day. They can take more if they're ill. For example, people with HIV are often told to take 6 to 20 grams of vitamin C and may tolerate that level with no ill effects. Why are people advised to take so much? Because the body needs more vitamin C when combating disease. Also, vitamin C doesn't stay in the body long; ingested vitamin C is excreted from the body within three to four hours. Therefore, to receive the most benefit, spread your intake of this vitamin over the course of the day. To increase absorption, take bioflavonoids with vitamin C. These plant compounds increase its effectiveness in the body and have remarkable immune-enhancing effects of their own.

Almost everyone can benefit from increased intake of this vitamin. In the United States, it's estimated that about half the people ingest less than the recommended RDA from their food alone, and only 17 percent consume more than 150 mg. from their food. Given vitamin C's importance to proper bodily function, and its disease-fighting and immune-enhancing effects, supplementing on a regular basis may benefit your health.

If you suffer from prostatitis or would like to prevent it, consider increasing your vitamin C intake either by drinking more juices—orange juice is considered the best—or taking a C supplement. Vitamin C capsules are some of the cheapest of any supplement on the market, but be careful. Read the label carefully. Make sure you're getting real C (preferably with rose hips) and not a bunch of useless additives.

We'll talk about vitamin C again in Chapter Eight.

CHAPTER SEVEN

TAKING THE WORRY
OUT OF
AN ENLARGED PROSTATE

A scholar once asked, "Why is youth wasted on the young?"

Good question. Young men have little appreciation for life's little pleasures like:

- A deep, uninterrupted night's sleep.
- Erections you could hang a hat on.
- A wizz that rattles the windows.
- A normal sized prostate.

Oh, for the good old days, when we didn't even know we had a prostate. . . .

An enlarged prostate blocks the flow of urine from the bladder, which can produce mild to severe urinary obstruction. The inability to completely empty the bladder is especially troublesome at night. Men with prostate enlargement often complain about having to get up multiple times throughout the night to urinate. Although it doesn't cause it, "benign" prostate disease can mean a higher risk of prostate cancer in the future.

Benign Prostatic Hyperplasia, also known as Benign Prostatic Hypertrophy or BPH, is one of the most common conditions affecting men over the age of 50. It can start at about 40 to 45, with the prostate gland becoming progressively enlarged.

Maybe it's a good time to review. As you know the prostate gland is a walnut-sized gland (normally 3.5–4.0 cm and about 20 grams in weight) that surrounds the neck of the bladder and the urethra in men. As a male matures, the prostate goes through two main periods of growth. The first occurs early in puberty, when the prostate doubles in size. At approximately age 25, the gland begins to grow again, reaching around 33 grams. It is this second growth phase that often results, years later, in BPH. Now 33 grams may not seem like much (about 1 1/2 ounces,) but you have to realize that it's a 50 percent increase over normal.

Although the prostate continues to grow during most of a man's life, the enlargement doesn't usually cause problems until late in life. BPH rarely causes symptoms before age 40, but more than half of men in their sixties and as many as 90 percent in their seventies and eighties have some symptoms of BPH.

Your prostate plays a role in both sex and urination. As for its sex function, the prostate makes and secretes a thin, opalescent fluid during ejaculation that makes up part of the semen. This fluid can be thought of as the liquid in which the sperm cells "swim," as it exits you and journeys into your partner's vagina (or elsewhere, for that matter).

Prostate enlargement is as common a part of aging as gray hair. As life expectancy rises, so does the occurrence of BPH. In the United States alone, 350,000 operations take place each year for BPH. As the prostate enlarges, the surrounding capsule stops it from expanding, causing the gland to press against the urethra like a clamp. While this is normal, the danger lies when this new bulk squeezes the urethra and forces the bladder to work harder, prevents it from emptying completely or makes urination painful. Also, as the bladder pushes harder its wall becomes more muscular, thicker and smaller. It also becomes more irritable, and begins to contract even when it contains small amounts of urine, causing the urge "to go" more frequent.

As the bladder weakens, it loses the ability to empty itself, and urine remains behind. This narrowing of the urethra and partial emptying of the bladder cause many of the problems associated with BPH.

RECOGNIZING THE SYMPTOMS OF BENIGN PROSTATIC HYPERPLASIA (BPH)

Although BPH affects all men sooner or later, it can affect them differently; not everyone with BPH suffers from the same disease. It causes smooth-muscle cells to contract and glandular cells to obstruct. Some men have more muscle cells while others have more glandular ones. The effect on the prostate and urethra is different.

Also, the size of the prostate does not always determine how severe the obstruction or the symptoms will be. Some men with greatly enlarged glands have little obstruction and few symptoms while others, whose glands are less enlarged, have more blockage and greater problems.

While only half will have noticeable symptoms, only half of those one in four will end up in their doctor's office pleading for relief. Of these, very few lack symptoms; most just ignore the problem. To complicate matters further, symptoms inexplicably can come and go. So, many men assume they're fine, and assume that the next time there's a problem it will go away, again, just like the last time. Without taking appropriate steps, BPH doesn't go away. More often than not, it usually either remains the same for years or gradually gets worse.

Besides increased frequency of urination, BPH can also cause a slowing of urinary flow—think of a crimped garden hose—and symptoms such as:

- Dysuria (difficulty or pain during urination), urgency (the need to "go" now!),
- Hesitancy (trouble starting urination),
- Decreased pressure behind the stream, and
- Nocturia (the need to go often during the night).

Or, you may have "urge incontinence," meaning that your bladder is irritated by retained urine causing it to spasm. The result? You don't make it to the bathroom in time.

BPH can also cause:

- Bladder infections,
- Stones, and even
- Kidney damage.

If BPH persists or becomes severe, it can result in stasis of the urine which can lead to urinary tract infections and possibly damage to the kidneys.

Prostate problems don't always cause pain. When pain does occur due to the prostate gland, it is often felt at the anus and may occur after ejaculation. The prostate gland may also send pain to the low back but this is not usual with BPH.

Sometimes a man may not know that he has any obstruction until he suddenly finds himself unable to urinate at all. This condition, called acute urinary retention, may be triggered by taking over-the-counter cold or allergy medicines. Such medicines contain a decongestant drug, known as a sympathomimetic, which may, as a side effect, prevent the bladder opening from relaxing and allowing urine to empty. When partial obstruction is present, urinary retention also can be brought on by alcohol, cold temperatures, or a long period of immobility.

Regardless of your symptoms, BPH is a major nuisance, interfering with quality of life and disturbing normal sleep. Perhaps even more important, it can reduce your sexual desire. Face it, some of us swear we can get by with little sleep, but loss of sexual appetite? That's where many of us draw the line!

Take the case of Randy in the United Kingdom. As Randy approached his mid-50s, he noticed he had to get up and go to the toilet during the night only on occasion. Then he became aware of the trips becoming more frequent and an increase in his need "to go" during the day.

After his doctor diagnosed him as having BPH he began taking prescription drugs. They had no effect on his BPH, but did made him feel lethargic and listless. After a year he stopped taking them and his condition gradually became worse. He now had prostate pain 24 hours a day and during the night he went to the toilet 3-4 times. "The quality of my life really suffered," says Randy. "I knew I did not want invasive surgery, so I began to look at other forms of treatment."

Randy tried acupuncture, homeopathic medicine and a host of herbal remedies. Nothing worked. Then a friend gave him a supplemental formula which contained saw palmetto, bee pollen, hydrangea root, silica, Panax ginseng, the amino acids; glycine, L-alanine and glumatic acid, zinc gluconate, copper gluconate, vitamin B6, vitamins A, C and E. "I was extremely skeptical, but what did I have to lose?" says Randy. "So, I decided to give it a try."

During the first two weeks he took a total of 6 tablets a day. In the second week he noticed he had periods of up to 4 hours without pain but still had to get up at night. He was slightly encouraged.

During the third and fourth weeks he took 4 tablets a day. By week 3, he was without pain for up to 7 hours at a time and had his first uninterrupted night's sleep. During week 4, he could go entire days without pain and had several more uninterrupted nights. During week 5, he started taking only 2 tablets a day. At the end of week 5 he no longer had any prostate pain, his urine flow was normal and he slept through every night. Plus, his energy level increased dramatically. "I suddenly felt like I had gotten my life back," said Randy.

THE MAIN CAUSES OF PROSTATE ENLARGEMENT

It is not clear whether certain groups face a greater risk of getting BPH. Studies done over the years suggest that it occurs more often among married men than single men, and is more common in the United States and Europe than in other parts of the world. However, these findings have been debated, and no definite information on risk factors exists.

The cause of BPH is not well understood. For centuries it has been known that BPH occurs mainly in older men and that it doesn't develop in males whose testes were removed before puberty. For this reason, some researchers believe that factors related to aging and the testes may spur its development.

Here's one theory: throughout their lives, men produce both testosterone, an important male hormone, and small amounts of estrogen, a female hormone. As men age, the amount of active testosterone in the blood decreases, leaving a higher proportion of estrogen. Studies done with animals have suggested that BPH may occur because the higher amount of estrogen within the gland increases the activity of substances that promote cell growth.

Another theory focuses on dihydrotestosterone (DHT), a substance derived from testosterone in the prostate, which may help control its growth. DHT is produced from the male hormone testosterone by the action of the enzyme 5-alpha-reductase. We've talked about this before, remember?

Most animals lose their ability to produce DHT as they age. However, some research has indicated that even with a drop in the blood's testosterone level, older men continue to produce and accumulate high levels of DHT in the prostate which may encourage the growth of cells. Scientists have also noted that men who do not produce DHT do not develop BPH.

Some researchers suggest that BPH may develop as a result of "instructions" given to cells early in life. According to this theory, BPH occurs because cells in one section of the gland follow these instructions and "reawaken" later in life. These "reawakened" cells then deliver signals to other cells in the gland, instructing them to grow or making them more sensitive to hormones that influence growth.

The most readily accepted theory is the testosterone-DHT-enzyme 5-alpha-reductase connection.

Researchers note that the onset of BPH parallels the typical age when exercise or physical activity levels start to decrease. This sedentary behavior, they also note, causes testosterone levels in the blood to increase (even though, as a rule, older men produce less). Unless the man suddenly increases his sexual activity, there's no place for the elevated testosterone to go. His body converts the male hormone to DHT, with the help of 5-alpha-reductase, which causes prostate cells to multiply quickly and excessively, making the prostate grow and constricting the urethra.

The evidence that overproduction of DHT is the prime culprit in the development of BPH prostate enlargement comes from studies showing that men with low blood levels of DHT maintain normal muscle mass, libido and a small prostate, compared with men with average or above average DHT levels who suffer from enlarged prostates, frontal hair recession, diffuse beard growth and acne. It appears that DHT is responsible for many of life's undesirable ills affecting males!

One thing is certain; according to the government agency NIDDK, testosterone is involved in BPH development. NIDDK (The National Institute of Diabetes and Digestive and Kidney Diseases) is a division of the National Institute of Health (NIH)—the research branch of the Public Health Service under the U.S. Department of Health and Human Services.

The NIDDK conducts and supports a variety of research in diseases of the kidney and urinary tract. Much of the research targets disorders of the lower urinary tract, including BPH. The knowledge gained from these studies is advancing scientific understanding of why BPH develops and may lead to improved methods of diagnosing and treating prostate enlargement.

In one NIDDK-supported study at the Johns Hopkins University, Drs. Craig Peters and Patrick Walsh treated a small group of BPH patients with nafarelin acetate, a hormone blocker that inhibits the testes' production of testosterone by acting on the pituitary gland. While receiving the therapy, all nine patients experienced a drop in prostate size and in testosterone levels. When therapy was discontinued, however, prostate size and testosterone production returned to pretreatment levels. According to the researchers, these findings suggest that testosterone plays an important role in prostate enlargement and that continuous treatment with nafarelin acetate may help certain patients who are not candidates for surgery.

In another NIDDK-funded study, researchers at the Medical College of Wisconsin isolated prostatic growth factor, a substance found within the gland, which may contribute to the development of BPH and prostate cancer.

Additional research will further our understanding of how this newly discovered growth factor interacts with the various types of cells and hormones inside the gland to cause enlargement.

TAKE THIS QUIZ IF YOU SUSPECT BPH

The American Urological Association has developed a Symptom Index to gauge how bad your symptoms are. Here it is in summary form:

BPH QUESTIONNAIRE

1. Is your sleep interrupted 2, 3, 4 or more times after going to bed because you have to urinate?

2. After urinating, do you have a feeling of not emptying your bladder?

3. Do you have to urinate less than 2 hours after you finish urinating?

4. Do you have to urinate less than 30 minutes after you have finished urinating?

5. Do you have difficulty starting your urine stream?

6. Is your urine stream weak, with no force behind it, even if you push?

7. Do you have difficulty postponing urination? A sense of immediacy, or loss of control?

8. Is there excessive dribbling at the end of your urine stream?

If you answered Yes to more than one question, you probably have a prostate problem. You should have some valid concerns about your health. You need answers to some very important questions. Don't wait.

If you answered No to all of these questions and you're over 40 (35 for high-risk males), NOW would be a good time to start your own prostate maintenance and prevention program.

YOUR INITIAL STEPS FOR CONQUERING BPH

Of course, the diagnosis of prostate conditions is still best done by an MD who will (or should) administer:

- A digital exam (the "Up Yours" test, so to speak).
- Urine and blood tests.
- Prostate Specific Antigens (PSA) Test.

As you may recall, we covered these tests in Chapter One. Now might be a good time to review.

Once you see your doctor, it's important to tell him (or her) about urinary problems such as those described above. In 8 out of 10 cases, these symptoms suggest BPH, but they can also signal other, more serious conditions that require prompt treatment and which can be ruled out only by a doctor's exam.

Severe BPH can cause serious problems over time. Remember, urine retention and strain on the bladder can lead to urinary tract infections, bladder or kidney damage, bladder stones, and incontinence. If the bladder is permanently damaged, treatment for BPH may be ineffective. When BPH is found in its earlier stages, there is a lower risk of developing such complications.

You may first notice symptoms of BPH yourself, or your doctor may find that your prostate is enlarged during a routine checkup. When BPH is suspected, you may be referred to a urologist, a doctor who specializes in problems of the urinary tract and the male reproductive system.

In the meantime, you should do the following;

- Cut down on coffee, tea, and cola drinks which act as diuretics.
- Cut down drinking all fluids in the early evening.
- Avoid taking antihistamines which make bladder contractions less forceful.
- Try to keep bowel movements regular since constipation can aggravate the urinary tract.
- If possible have more sex. Go on, force yourself. Regular ejaculations can ease prostate fluid congestion.

SURGERY? NOT ALWAYS THE CURE

Men who have BPH with symptoms usually need some kind of treatment at some time. However, a number of recent studies have questioned the need for early treatment when the gland is just mildly enlarged. Instead of immediate treatment, they suggest regular checkups to watch for early problems. If the condition begins to pose a danger to the patient's health or causes a major inconvenience to him, treatment is usually recommended.

It used to be that surgery was the only option. Today, doctors prescribe drugs to either inhibit the growth of the prostate cells or relax the muscles surrounding the prostate. When these muscles are tight, they squeeze the urethra shut and cause difficulties urinating.

Medical drugs such as Hytrin and Cardura, which are high-blood - pressure medications are often prescribed. They are designed to relax the muscles surrounding the urethra and make urinating less difficult. These prescribed drugs, known as alpha blockers, can cost as much as $100.00 per month, and they may produce some side effects such as dizziness, lightheadedness, or fatigue. In some cases, passing out has been reported. And, as with any drug, these may not work for everyone. Even if they do work for you, noticeable results or changes in your urinary habits may take three to six weeks to appear.

To inhibit the growth of prostate cells medically, drugs such as Proscar (finasteride) are prescribed. Proscar, a 5-alpha-reductase inhibitor, is designed to work by blocking out the normal formation of the male hormone dihydrotestosterone (DHT). When DHT is removed, an enlarged prostate may shrink in size.

Proscar can cost up to $150.00 per month, as well as produce some unfavorable side effects which are more sexual in nature. Approximately 4–5 percent of men experience impotence, and approximately 4 percent complain of a reduced interest in sex. Noticeable results or changes in urinary habits with this product may take six months to a year to reveal themselves. Also, they lower PSA levels by half, which could affect testing for prostate cancer.

One problem with prostate medications is that you have to stay on them indefinitely, possibly forever. For men who would rather be done with it—at least for a while—there are surgical options. Many of them are minimally invasive, meaning less cutting and shorter hospital stays. Still, the most effective methods are the most invasive.

With BPH surgery, only the enlarged tissue that is pressing against the urethra is removed; the rest of the inside tissue and the outside capsule is left intact. Surgery usually relieves the obstruction and incomplete emptying caused by BPH. I'm not trying to scare you. Instead, I think you should know all the options, so that, should the time come, you can ask the right questions and make the correct choice for your own treatment.

The most invasive and longer-lasting procedures include:

1. TURP (Transurethral Resection of the Prostate): TURP is the commonly accepted treatment for BPH, representing 90 percent of all prostate surgeries for the condition. In fact, it is the second most common surgical procedure performed today. TURP requires anesthesia and a hospital stay.

In this procedure, the doctor uses a resectoscope, which is about 12 inches long and 1/2 inch in diameter, and contains a light, valves for controlling irrigating fluid, and an electrical loop that cuts tissue and seals blood vessels. During the 90-minute operation, the surgeon uses the resectoscope's wire loop to remove the obstructing tissue one piece at a time. The pieces of tissue are carried by the fluid into the bladder and then flushed out at the end of the operation.

While the procedure is considered safe and techniques are constantly improving, a number of complications—primarily bleeding, urinary troubles and cardiovascular disorders—can take place during and after surgery.

Many painful side effects can occur as a result of this procedure, and it also appears to increase the risk of having a heart attack later in life. According to a study conducted on 811 men who underwent this procedure between 1983 and 1992, fifty-two patients developed a first-time heart attack afterwards. The acute heart attack risk was even greater in men who had already suffered one heart attack. Whether it's because of the procedure or because the patients already had poor exercise and dietary habits, no one can say for sure.

2. TEVP (Transurethral Electrovaporization): This is similar to TURP, but an electrical current vaporizes the unwanted prostate tissue.

3. TUIP (Transurethral Incision): In this procedure, instead of removing tissue, as with TURP, the surgeon widens the urethra by making a few small cuts in the bladder neck, where the urethra joins the bladder, and in the prostate gland itself. Although some people believe that TUIP gives the same relief as TURP with less risk of side effects, its advantages and long-term side effects have not been clearly established.

4. OPEN SURGERY: In the few cases when a transurethral procedure cannot be used, open surgery, which requires an external incision, may be suggested. This is often done when the gland is greatly enlarged, when there are complicating factors, or when the bladder has been damaged and needs to be repaired. The location of the enlargement within the gland and the patient's general health help the surgeon decide which of the three open procedures to use.

As I said, TURP is often considered the "treatment of choice" by many urologists. However, prostate surgery carries its own risks including possible perforation of the bladder, infection, hemorrhage, persistent urinary incontinence, and even permanent impotency. Furthermore, the surgery is not always effective.

AVOID HOSPITALIZATION WITH THESE OPTIONS

There are some surgical treatments that don't require hospitalization. All involve treating the prostate via the penis. They can be performed on an outpatient basis.

1. BALLOON URETHROPLASTY: In this procedure, a thin tube with a balloon is inserted into the opening of the penis and guided to the narrowed portion of the urethra, where the balloon is inflated. This action widens the urethra, easing the flow of urine. Since the procedure doesn't actually remove the tissue causing the obstruction, more studies are needed to judge its long-range effectiveness.

2. TUMT (transurethral microwave thermotherapy): This is a new procedure that uses a catheter to zap excess prostate cells with hot microwaves. The Prostatron, which employs this method, was approved by the FDA in 1996.

Here's how it works. The Prostatron sends computer-regulated microwaves through a catheter to heat selected portions of the prostate to at least 111 degrees Fahrenheit. A cooling system protects the urinary tract during the procedure. TUMT takes about one hour and does not cause blood loss or lead to impotence or incontinence.

While TUMT does not cure BPH, it reduces urinary frequency, urgency, straining and intermittent flow. It does not correct the problem of incomplete emptying of the bladder. Ongoing research will determine any long-term effects of TUMT and who might benefit most from this therapy.

3. TUNA (transurethral needle ablation): Two needles attached to an endoscope destroy excess prostate cells with radio frequency energy. This procedure was also approved by the FDA in 1996.

4. VLAP (laser prostatectomy): In this procedure, a laser is inserted into the urethra to kill prostate cells. Although it can be done on an out-patient basis, it requires longer use of a catheter and general anesthesia. Although men can resume their normal lifestyle after a few days on a catheter, the long-term effectiveness of these procedures is still not known.

Compounds that inhibit the enzyme 5-alpha-reductase can be expected to have a beneficial effect on BPH. One such compound is the drug finasteride (Proscar). Unfortunately, clinical studies have found this drug to be only marginally effective. In addition, the drug has some undesirable side effects. For example, it causes impotence in about 4 percent of the men who take it. Terazosin, a blood pressure-lowering drug, has been found to relieve the symptoms of BPH in some cases. However, this drug does not slow the progression of the condition and is also not without undesirable side effects.

Fortunately, there are natural remedies that provide safe, effective, and inexpensive alternatives for men with BPH.

GAME PLAN FOR SUCCESS

The natural approach to prostate problems involves four steps:

The first is to lessen "congestion" in the lower pelvic area, that is, to improve the blood and energy flow to the prostate region. Constipation, low back problems, scar tissue and injury all affect this flow, and can be improved by the appropriate dietary changes, massage and manipulation therapies, and acupuncture.

The second is to eat a diet aimed at improving the health of the prostate. Diets containing a high amount of soy products have been recommended as preventing prostate enlargement, since soy contains natural substances (isoflavones) which help detoxify the harmful DHT.

Based upon records of dietary soy consumption in Japan, where prostate cancer rates are very low, the typical daily isoflavone intake has been estimated at 50 mg per person. By contrast, the typical Western diet has been estimated to provide only two to three mg a day of genistein. Soy phytoestrogens such as genistein may counteract some of the effects of dihydrotestosterone, and therefore may be helpful in treating benign prostate enlargement as well. This may explain why Japanese men, who eat a higher soy diet, have lower incidences of prostate problems.

Adequate fiber in the diet helps by decreasing the pressure in the lower bowel area. Finally, some foods like sunflower and pumpkin seeds seem to have a positive effect on prostate symptoms.

The third is to supplement the nutrients which seem to aid in prostate function. Zinc is required to utilize carotenes, and therefore may be cancer-protective. Zinc also, in conjunction with vitamin B6, regulates the enzyme which converts testosterone to the harmful DHT. More on zinc a little later in the chapter.

Fourth, several herbs have been studied and used extensively in prostate conditions:

1. Saw palmetto berries.

2. Pygeum Africanum.

3. Urtica dioica, or stinging nettles.

Research has shown that saw palmetto berries, pygeum, nettles, and zinc can be used safely and effectively by men with BPH. According to Alan R. Gaby, M.D., "In my experience, at least two-thirds of men with symptoms of BPH find gratifying and long-lasting relief when they follow a natural treatment program for BPH that includes some or all of these substances. Because of its low risk of side effects and high success rate, this nutritional/herbal approach should be considered the 'treatment of choice' for BPH."

For many years, the European drug Permixon has been an effective therapy for benign prostatic hypertrophy. It is a standardized extract from the saw palmetto berry. Permixon was used in Europe to treat benign prostate enlargement almost 20 years before the FDA approved an equally expensive drug called Proscar.

In lieu of the Permixon drug, Americans are able to purchase high-quality saw palmetto extracts as low-cost dietary supplements. These are identical to Permixon. Saw palmetto has been shown to significantly reduce total prostate weight and volume, even in the presence of hormones that promote prostate growth.

Studies have shown that it produces significant improvement in those with prostate enlargement, resulting in the following clinical benefits:

- Reduction of nocturnal urinary urgency.
- Increased urinary flow rate.
- Reduced residual volume in the bladder.
- Reduction in uncomfortable urination symptoms.

BULLETPROOF YOUR PROSTATE
WITH SAW PALMETTO

Saw palmetto berries, an orally-ingested herbal supplement, is the therapy most frequently prescribed by medical doctors in France for the treatment of BPH. Today it is the most reliable and frequently used extract for the treatment of an enlarged prostate. The saw palmetto bush (*Serenoa Repens*) is indigenous to the Southeast United States from the southern tip of Florida to the Carolinas.

Saw palmetto works like Proscar. In British, French, German and Italian studies, it was shown to contain substances which actively inhibit the formation of DHT from testosterone (by inhibiting the enzyme, 5-alpha-reductase, which converts it). It also prevents the DHT that is produced from acting on the prostate and enlarging it, and cools inflammation in the gland itself. Phytosterol extracts from saw palmetto are credited with interfering with the conversion of testosterone to dihydrotestosterone.

As a result of saw palmetto's effectiveness, there is currently a huge market in Europe for its use. It's also growing in popularity in the United States, and capsules are easy to find in any supermarket or pharmacy. In fact, it has been listed in the United States Pharmacopeia since 1905 and has been used safely for many decades.

A paper in *Current Therapies, Research, Clinical Experience* reports on a Belgian study involving 505 men with benign prostate disease. The results showed that saw palmetto improved urinary flow, reduced residual urinary volume and prostate size, and improved quality of life after only 45 days of treatment. After 90 days, 88 percent of the patients and treating physicians considered the treatment effective. In addition, the study showed for the first time that saw palmetto does not mask the PSA (prostate specific antigens) score as Proscar has been shown to do. The researchers concluded by stating, "The extract of saw palmetto appears to be an effective and well-tolerated pharmacologic agent in treating urinary problems accompanying benign prostatic hypertrophy." New studies are showing that saw palmetto reduces smooth-muscle contraction, thereby relaxing the bladder and sphincter muscles that cause urinary urgency.

Need more encouragement? Recent German studies of up to 2000 men with BPH confirmed the value of saw palmetto extract. General results demonstrated less residual urine after voiding, fewer nighttime visits to the bathroom, and stronger stream. In the studies, saw palmetto berry extracts were shown to inhibit 5-alpha-reductase, thus shrinking an enlarged prostate more effectively than the potent finasteride drug Proscar.

Studies show this herb to be remarkably safe, and comparisons of the saw palmetto extract with Proscar show higher effectiveness in improving prostate symptoms, with fewer side effects. Specifically, at the end of three months the Proscar group showed a 16 percent improvement (in urine flow rated) while the saw palmetto herb group improved 38 percent. It's also been shown that it does not cause any changes in standard blood chemistry measurements.

In order for saw palmetto to be effective, it must be in an extract form (usually capsules, though tinctures are also used). Since the active ingredients are fat-soluble, a tea made from the berries would not make these components usable. The dose of extracts in the studies is usually 320 mg per day, in two divided doses.

For most men, two saw palmetto extract capsules a day will shrink an enlarged prostate gland to provide relief from benign prostate disease. If this is not successful, a combination of the extract and another European prostate medication, Pygeum, will provide relief in most cases.

THE TREE BARK THAT DEFLATES ENLARGED PROSTATES

Pygeum Africanum (*Prunus Africana*) is an evergreen tree that grows in Africa. The bark of the tree has been used for years by natives of tropical Africa to treat urinary disorders; it is used extensively in France and elsewhere in Europe, and has been recently imported into the United States.

Although it is not certain what the active ingredients are, some of the compounds found in pygeum bark exert anti-inflammatory effects, while others are thought to influence testosterone metabolism. As a result, it inhibits prostate-cell proliferation shrinking enlarged prostate glands significantly.

The herb seems to work by limiting the formation of DHT and by lowering prolactin levels (a pituitary hormone related to prostate and sexual function). Pygeum also is a mild antibiotic, which may explain its good effect in prostatitis as well as with BPH.

In one double-blind study an extract of pygeum (200mg/day for 2 months) improved prostate symptoms a great deal without many side effects (of these stomach irritation was the most common). As an added bonus, in one study sexual ability was increased as well.

In the study, pygeum proved significantly more effective than placebo with respect to urinary frequency, urgency, dysuria, and urinary flow rate. There have been numerous other open and controlled studies which have confirmed its effectiveness as a treatment of BPH.

Besides reducing prostate swelling and blocking DHT binding to prostate cells, pygeum, according to new studies, also interferes with protein kinase C activity to inhibit the proliferation of prostate cells. Rapidly growing benign and malignant cells both require the protein kinase C enzyme. (FYI: Soy genistein is one of the most potent inhibitors of protein kinase C, a primary mechanism by which soy helps to prevent cancer and slows the growth of some existing cancers.)

If you'd like to try pygeum, a usual dose is 50–100 mg twice daily as an extract. It's easiest to find at health food stores.

Research has shown that pygeum is even more effective if combined with saw palmetto. So if you want to add to your protection from BPH, these two herbs work well together.

Add to this herbal arsenal against enlarged prostate the extract from stinging nettles, or urtica dioica.

NETTLES ROOT EXTRACT SHRINKS PROSTATE

Whether you call it nettle root, urtica dioica, stinging nettle, common nettle or greater nettle, this herb has a long history of use among men in Africa and Europe. Found all over the world, nettles have been used as a vegetable and folk remedy for centuries. Collected before flowering, they were thought useful as a treatment for asthma, as an expectorant, antispasmodic, diuretic, astringent and tonic.

Although more than 80 percent of men report improvement after using saw palmetto and/or pygeum extracts, some prostate enlargement often remains that continues to interfere with urinary flow and bladder evacuation. Urtica Dioica has been shown to reduce BPH symptoms by 86 percent after three months of use.

The diuretic properties of nettles are well recognized, and several pharmaceutical preparations incorporating them are marketed in Europe for this purpose. In addition, an extract of nettle root has become quite popular in recent years for the treatment of urinary retention brought on by benign prostatic hypertrophy (BPH). Some clinical studies attest to its effectiveness at blocking DHT, and German health authorities now allow it to be used for this condition as well as for irrigation (flushing) in cases of inflammation of the urinary tract.

One study showed that, after eight weeks of treatment with four capsules of urtica extract, there was an 82 percent improvement or total elimination of disorders associated with prostate enlargement. Another study showed that similar patients improved 86 percent after three months' treatment with the same extract.

After learning the results of these studies, researchers at St. Luke's/Roosevelt Hospital in New York conducted a study to discover the mechanism by which standardized urtica extract relieves the symptoms of benign prostate hyperplasia (excess cell proliferation). In their study, published in 1995, these scientists showed that urtica extract inhibits the binding of a testosterone-related protein to its receptor site on prostate cell membranes.

Prostate cells grow out of control when the DHT hormone binds to prostate cell membranes, a process that induces the prostate cells to start dividing. If cell membrane receptors are blocked, the dihydrotestosterone cannot latch onto the cell. Urtica extract appears to work by preventing the binding of testosterone metabolites to the membrane receptor sites on prostate cells.

Nettles are rich in chlorophyll and young cooked nettle shoots are not only edible but are an excellent source of beta-carotene, vitamin C, vitamin E and minerals, especially silica.

Nettle plants grow two to three feet tall, bearing dark green leaves with serrated margins and small flowers covered with tiny hairs on the leaves and stems. When brushed, nettles can inject an irritant into any skin that comes into contact with the plant. This stinging reaction is caused by the plant hairs injecting a compound containing formic acid, histamine, serotonin, acetylcholine, 5-hydroxytryptamine and other irritants. This stinging trait is lost when the plant is dried or cooked, and the tender tops of young first-growth nettles are especially delicious and nutritious.

As an aside, applying an extract of nettles to the scalp was said to stimulate hair growth (no evidence exists for the belief in its ability to treat baldness), and chronic rheumatism was treated by placing nettle leaves directly on the afflicted area. This usually led to local irritation, which could be relieved by vigorously rubbing the area. Likewise, nettles have also been used historically to treat cancer, liver disease, constipation, asthma, worms, arthritis, gout, tuberculosis and gonorrhea, with little if any effectiveness.

If you think nettles will help you, the suggested dose is 300 mg of an extract. You should be able to find it in health stores. One important note: because of its diuretic properties, be sure to drink plenty of fluids.

While saw palmetto and urtica dioica are approved drugs in Germany for the treatment of benign prostate enlargement, pygeum and saw palmetto are approved throughout Europe. Urtica may be new to Americans, but it has been safely and successfully used in Germany for more than a decade.

Be careful where you buy your prostate-shrinking herbal extracts. Some companies sell saw palmetto "berry" capsules at very low prices. They do not provide the standardized fatty acid sterols needed for therapeutic benefits. What's surprising is that there are major name-brand supplement companies that sell both the standardized extract and the berry capsules. These commercial companies know that there are no prostate benefits from taking the berry capsules, but they sell them anyway just to offer a lower-priced product.

WHAT TO DO IF HERBS DON'T WORK

For the 10 to 20 percent of men who don't reap sufficient benefit from the saw palmetto, pygeum and urtica extracts, the addition of the prescription drug Hytrin has proven beneficial. When all nutrient and drug therapies fail, the drug Casodex may provide significant prostate-gland shrinkage through testosterone blockade. Casodex is not approved by the FDA to treat benign prostatic hypertrophy, but your doctor can legally prescribe it.

The FDA-approved drug Lupron dramatically suppresses testosterone production. It is used to treat prostate cancer, but has been shown to be beneficial in shrinking enlarged prostate glands when all other nonsurgical therapies have failed. Lupron is injected at a doctor's office and will last for three months. Make sure your doctor prescribes the standard dose of Casodex or flutamide one week prior to receiving the Lupron injection in order to protect against the temporary testosterone surge that can occur immediately after Lupron is administered.

ZINC PREVENTS AND REVERSES
PROSTATE ENLARGEMENT

Zinc supplements have also been shown to improve urinary symptoms and reduce the size of the prostate both in men with BPH and in animal studies. It also, in conjunction with vitamin B6, regulates the enzyme which converts testosterone to the harmful DHT.

Zinc is required for normal testosterone and sperm production. It has been hypothesized that high levels of impotence in American males may be due to chronic zinc deficiency. This may explain why oysters, which are high in this mineral, are thought to be a potent aphrodisiac.

Zinc is also important in the production of the hormone-like substances, prostaglandins, which regulate numerous body processes including blood pressure and heart rate. We also now know that it is needed in probably more than 100 enzymes and is probably involved in more body functions than any other mineral. It is important in normal growth and development, the maintenance of body tissues, sexual function, the immune system, and detoxification of chemicals and metabolic irritants. It influences carbohydrate metabolism, and is needed in the synthesis of DNA, which aids our body's healing process.

Most diets are marginally low in zinc. Because a deficiency affects the taste buds, any shortage can compound itself as the person loses interest in eating. Although zinc is available in a wide variety of foods, marginal deficiencies are common. One reason for this may be poor soil conditions, which affect plants' ability to absorb zinc. This is passed along to the animals and humans that feed on the plants, or feed on the animals that feed on the plants.

Most animal foods contain adequate amounts of zinc. Oysters are particularly high, with more than ten times as much as other sources. (They are also high in copper and, possibly, in ocean-polluting chemicals and metals.) Zinc is added to animal feeds to increase growth rates, so meat usually contains high amounts. Red meats (beef, lamb, and pork) and liver are fairly high; herring is good, as are egg yolks and milk products (though the zinc in eggs and milk products may not be as available to the body as that found in other sources). Other fish and poultry also contain fair zinc levels.

If you cut down on meat—which you should do—you need to take supplementary zinc, since vegetables and fruits provide little. The best vegetarian sources of zinc are legumes (dried beans, garbanzos, black-eyed peas, lentils, peas, soy products) and whole grains.

Whole grains such as whole wheat, rye, and oats are rich in zinc and are good sources for vegetarians. The zinc in grains is found mainly in the germ and bran coverings, so refining them will lower its content. Approximately 80 percent is lost in making white flour from whole wheat.

Even though the mineral from these foods is utilized less well because the fiber and phytates in the grain covering bind some in the gastrointestinal tract, much of the zinc in these foods is still available to the body. Nuts are fairly good sources, with pecans and Brazil nuts the highest.

Pumpkin seeds contain zinc and are thought to be helpful to the prostate gland. Ginger root is a good source, as are mustard, chili powder, and black pepper. In general, fruits and vegetables are not good zinc sources, although peas, carrots, beets and cabbage contain some.

Since it is soluble in water, canning foods or cooking in water can cause zinc losses. Such losses have also been prevalent in agricultural soils, particularly those treated with chemical fertilizers, and it is therefore less available in foods.

If you are on a vegetarian or semi-vegetarian diet, I recommend that you take 30 milligrams of zinc a day, but do not exceed 100 milligrams a day because larger doses may have adverse effects on immunity.

When you go to the store to buy a zinc supplement, you will probably be bewildered by the variety of products offered for sale. They differ not only in dose but in composition; a well-supplied store will probably offer zinc gluconate, zinc succinate, zinc picolinate, chelated zinc, zinc in an amino acid complex, organic zinc and inorganic zinc. I'll try to explain the differences.

Zinc, as you know, is a metal, which the body cannot use in its elemental state. Your body needs it in ionic, or combined, form, as found in chemical compounds. Metals react with inorganic acids to form inorganic salts. Zinc sulfate, for example, is one type of inorganic zinc. Organic salts, those formed from organic acids, include succinates, gluconates, citrates, picolinates and fumarates. These forms may be more soluble and more easily absorbed by the body than the inorganic salts. This difference is important, because an increased need for trace minerals may be due more to failure to absorb them than to an inadequacy in the diet. Within the category of organic salts there are differences in solubility and ease of absorption. You may have to experiment to find which organic form may be the best way to ingest it.

Supplements provide zinc as zinc sulfate or zinc gluconate in dosages from 35–200 mg. Zinc gluconate is usually referred to as chelated zinc; it's more expensive, but may be less irritating to the stomach than zinc sulfate. Zinc picolinate and zinc orotate are also available and may be better absorbed by the body.

Zinc salts such as gluconate or sulfate are commonly available in 35–220 mg tablets or capsules, each providing 55 mg. of elemental zinc. Taking one of these two or three times daily may cause some gastrointestinal irritation, nausea, or diarrhea but is more likely to have positive effects. Excessive supplementation may cause some immune suppression, premature heartbeats, dizziness, drowsiness, increased sweating, loss of muscular coordination, alcohol intolerance, hallucinations and anemia, some of which is due to copper deficiency.

More than 2 grams of zinc taken in one dose will usually produce vomiting. If not, it will likely lead to other symptoms until the body clears out the excess. Luckily, only a certain amount of it will be absorbed.

Zinc may interfere with copper absorption, so taking regular zinc supplements without copper can cause copper deficiency. This will interfere with iron metabolism and possibly cause anemia, as copper and iron are important in red blood cell formation. We usually need supplemental copper and vitamin A to balance the effect of extra zinc. And don't forget the B6.

PATIENCE AND PROTEIN

Immediate results should not be expected when using the natural approach. Most research indicates that at least a two month trial is necessary before determining if the natural approach is best. A healthy diet consisting of plenty of fruits and vegetables and reducing saturated fats may also prove helpful with prostate problems. A moderate regular exercise routine such as daily walking is also beneficial.

Amino acids are the building blocks of protein. All told, there are twenty amino acids needed to build the various proteins used in the growth, repair and maintenance of body tissues.

There are three amino acids which can help us fight BPH:

- alanine
- glutamic acid
- glycine

All three are present in prostate fluid, and may play a role in supporting prostate health. One study, involving forty-five men with BPH, found that 780 mg of alanine per day for two weeks and then 390 mg for the next two and a half months, taken in combination with equal amounts of glycine and glutamic acid, reduced symptoms of BPH.

All three are produced by your body so it's important that you eat correctly. Meat, fish, poultry, eggs and dairy products are the richest dietary sources of amino acids. Vegetable sources of protein (such as beans, peas and grains) generally fall short in one or more. However, since plant foods contain the same amino acids, eating a variety of plant sources of protein easily provides the body with the entire range required. The vast majority of Americans eat more than enough protein and also more than enough of each essential amino acid for normal purposes.

Nutrition experts recommend that protein, as a source of amino acids, should account for 10 to 12 percent of the calories in a balanced diet. However, requirements for protein are affected by age, weight, state of health and other factors, so amounts vary by individual.

Most people don't need to supplement these amino acids. If you suspect BPH, or believe additional amounts of these three substances can help you, the appropriate amounts should be determined with the help of a nutritionally-oriented physician.

All three are remarkably free of side effects for the vast majority of people. However, men with kidney or liver disease should not consume high intakes of amino acids without consulting a health care professional.

MORE SEX CAN HELP

For men with mild to moderate voiding difficulties due to BPH, one solution is simply to have more sex. Many men notice that the more they ejaculate, the easier it is to urinate. That's because the ejaculation helps empty the prostate of secretions that may hamper urination.

Also, remember: the common thread between prostate diseases and sex is our old friend testosterone. Even though as we get older there's less of it, if you don't release semen you'll have an excess supply. When it's converted to DHT, that can lead to BPH and cancer. You've got to rid yourself of testosterone through exercise of sex.

So we've given you two good reasons to romance your partner, but what if the desire simply isn't there? I have some good news.

Whereas the medical approaches to prostate problems, including the drugs prescribed for prostate conditions, often interfere with sexual performance, the herbal and nutritional approach usually has the opposite effect. In other words, the natural approaches generally enhance sexual performance and enjoyment.

So what are you waiting for? Get it on!

Although some of the signs of BPH and prostate cancer are the same, having BPH does not seem to increase the chances of getting cancer. After BPH surgery, the tissue removed is routinely checked for hidden cancer cells. In about 1 out of 10 cases, some cancer tissue is found, but often it is limited to a few cells of a nonaggressive type, and no treatment is needed. So, if you treat BPH with natural methods, it's probably safe to say the 10 percent would be at the high end of the scale. Many of the things recommended for BPH to reduce DHT will help eliminate the conditions for cancer cells to grow.

Nevertheless, a man who has BPH may have undetected prostate cancer at the same time or may develop prostate cancer in the future. For this reason, the National Cancer Institute and the American Cancer Society recommend that all men over 40 have a rectal exam once a year to screen for prostate cancer.

CHAPTER EIGHT

HOW TO
DEAL WITH
PROSTATE CANCER

At the beginning of this book, I listed some well known men—men you've probably heard of—who had prostate cancer. Many like Bill Bixby, Frank Zappa and Charles DeGaulle died from this dreaded disease. Since I compiled that list, Charlton Heston revealed HE had prostate cancer. The list continues to grow. But it's not limited to public figures and celebrities, not by a long shot. . . .

MAN'S WORST FEAR

Prostate cancer is the second most common cancer in men. Only lung cancer ranks higher in terms of incidence and morbidity. The next time you're in a group, maybe on the golf course or at a meeting, look around and count four other men besides yourself. One of you will probably get it; statistics show one out of every five men is at lifetime risk for prostate cancer.

Pray it's not you. No one has discovered a cure. But even if someone did tomorrow, or the next day, or a year from now, or even five years from now, you'd have to contract it for it to be helpful. Doesn't it make sense to take steps to minimize your risk of suffering from the disease in the first place?

A recent study concluded that men who consumed more than 30 grams of saturated fat a day—mostly from meat and dairy products—had twice the risk of prostate cancer than did men who ate less than 11 grams of saturated fat a day. No other dietary factor has been shown to have such a significant correlation with prostate cancer. The authors of the study recommended that men aim for 10 grams or less of saturated fat a day as a preventative measure. Sufficient dietary intake of fiber may also be beneficial for preventing prostate cancer, as well as some other forms of cancer. More about this later.

While the disease touches the lives of millions of men and their families, myths and misunderstandings are common. It's important, then, that we get the facts straight.

Prostate cancer is an uncontrolled (malignant) growth of cells in the male prostate gland. In some patients, it is life-threatening. In many others, it can exist for years without health problems.

As you've already learned, normal prostate enlargement is not cancerous and is referred to as "BPH." Sometimes their symptoms can be confused since both BPH and cancer of the prostate can impinge upon the urethra, leading to difficulty with urination.

In the United States, nearly one quarter of a million males are diagnosed with prostate cancer annually. Nearly 3 percent of the deaths among American men are directly related to prostate cancer (second only to lung cancer and ahead of colon cancer).

Its cause is unknown, and is most likely not related to BPH. Risk factors include age, heredity, hormonal influences and environmental factors, including chemicals.

The chances of developing prostate cancer increase with age. Occurrence under age 40 is extremely rare, while it is common in men older than 80 years of age. Genetics seem to play a role in the risk. For example, African-American males are at higher risk than Japanese-American males. Prostate cancer is more common among family members of prostate cancer patients.

Testosterone, the male hormone, directly stimulates the growth of prostate cancer cells. Environmental factors, such as cigarette smoking and high saturated fat diets, seem to increase the risk. There may be additional undefined chemicals that promote its development as well.

In the early stages, prostate cancer usually has no symptoms. Frequently, cancers are first detected as a hard prostate nodule during a routine rectal examination. As the cancer enlarges, urine flow diminishes and urination becomes more difficult. Patients may also experience burning and bleeding with urination, and blood in the semen. In later stages, the enlarging prostate gland can completely block the flow of urine, resulting in a painfully obstructed and enlarged bladder. In some patients, prostate cancer can spread (metastasize), usually to the bones, causing back or pelvic pain.

There are no specific measures known to prevent this cancer. To date, the most important prevention is early detection. A yearly rectal examination after age 40 is important. Often, the earliest sign is the discovery of a lumpy or large gland during a rectal examination. The blood test Prostate Specific Antigen (PSA) is another important screening tool for early detection. The American Cancer Society recommends annual screening by both rectal examination and PSA measurement starting at 50 years of age. Initial screening is recommended at age 40 years for those men at special risk, such as those with a family history.

Even though the PSA blood screening test is more sensitive than the rectal examination, both tests are performed to improve the doctor's detection ability. There's some controversy surrounding the screening tests. For example, it is known that 40 percent of United States men in their 40s have at least evidence of tiny areas of undetected prostate cancer. Yet, prostate cancer accounts for only 3 percent of United States male deaths. This is because prostate tumors are generally slow-growing—meaning they may not harm some individuals.

But let's not kid ourselves. It's not possible at this time to identify those individuals who will go on to develop adverse effects of their prostate cancer. However, recently new criteria were developed which may help doctors predict when prostate cancer is clinically insignificant. More on this at the end of the chapter.

The diagnosis of prostate cancer is established when cancer cells are found on prostate tissue obtained by prostate biopsy. Under ultrasound guidance, a needle is inserted into abnormal areas of the prostate to obtain small tissue samples (biopsies) to be examined under the microscope by a pathologist.

After prostate cancer is confirmed by prostate biopsy, further x-ray tests may be required to determine the presence or absence of spread (metastasis) of the cancer. Since prostate cancer can spread to the bone, nuclear medicine bone scans and plain bone x-rays look for metastasis. Occasionally, lymph nodes are also sampled by biopsy to determine whether the cancer involves these areas.

Decisions regarding treatment options are based on the age and overall health of the patient, as well as on whether the cancer is localized to the prostate or widely metastatic. Treatment options for prostate cancer include:

- Observation ("Watchful Waiting").
- Surgery.
- Radiation therapy.
- Implants.
- Hormonal therapy.
- Chemotherapy.
- Cryotherapy.

Growing in popularity is essentially "no treatment." This option, commonly called "watchful waiting," consists merely of close observation of the cancer, looking for any signs of progression with blood tests, scans and physical examinations. Specific cancer treatment will be undertaken only when problems arise from the cancer growth.

While this approach may seem out of the question in most cases, withholding treatment is appropriate and justifiable in certain circumstances when the treatments might be more risky than the disease. For instance, a man in his 70s or 80s with localized cancer, and with no symptoms, might be better left alone. In the absence of symptoms, and in the presence of other medical situations which are more threatening, "watchful waiting" is probably the best course.

In some medical environments (Sweden, for example) no treatment or observation has become a fairly standard approach to early prostate cancer. Physicians there believe that in some patients, the disease will grow so slowly that radical treatment is unneeded because patients will die of other diseases. For the most part, this approach goes against the attitudes of most American cancer specialists. Still, observation has many supporters and is being considered more and more depending on the circumstances.

Watchful waiting should not be confused with "if I ignore the problem, maybe it will go away." Too often that is the approach of prostate cancer victims and could be called the "Head in the Sand" approach. No, the decision to wait should be made only after intimate counseling by the physician, with an understanding that more drastic treatments may be needed in the future.

WHAT YOU NEED TO KNOW IF YOUR DOCTOR RECOMMENDS SURGERY

Surgical removal of the prostate is the standard therapy for localized prostate cancer. Prostatectomies are more often performed on younger patients when the cancer has not spread beyond the prostate gland.

Simply, the entire prostate is removed and the bladder is reconnected to the urethra (channel through the penis). Removal of part of the prostate or just the cancer is not recommended. Too many prostate cancers have multiple areas of involvement within the gland that are undetected, making partial removal a poor choice. Also, partial prostatectomy is not technically feasible.

The major advantages of total prostate removal is the simple fact that if the cancer is localized to the prostate, then removal of the gland will cure the cancer.

The major disadvantages are:

Incontinence: 24 percent of men will have permanent problems with urinary control and will require some form of protection (diapers or pads). In those rare cases, a surgical appliance can be implanted to control incontinence if it does remain a problem.

Impotence: The nerves that stimulate erections run adjacent to the prostate on their way to the penis. If ALL of these nerves are removed during total prostatectomy, impotence (inability to achieve an adequate erection) will result. In certain circumstances, some of the nerves that create erections can be spared with a success rate between 40–70 percent.

Not every man is a good candidate for nerve sparing because of the extent of disease. Patients who develop impotence, and even those whose erections were not adequate before the surgery can be treated with a variety of modalities. Treatment of impotence in post-prostate surgery includes vacuum pumps, self injections of medications and placement of prostheses—all of which work, and work well in selected patients.

Blood Loss: Radical prostatectomy carries with it an average blood loss of greater than one unit of blood. On occasion, the blood loss can be more than three or even four units.

Surgical Complications: Pain, infection, anesthetic problems, pneumonia, blood clots, and heart problems can occur with any major operation. Unique to prostatectomy are injury to the rectum, and scarring of the new connection between the bladder and urethra. This scarring may require "stretching," in the office or in surgery.

Recovery Time: The operation lasts two to three hours and the hospitalization usually lasts 2 to 3 days. All patients go home with a catheter in place, continually draining the urine into a special leg bag. It usually can be removed after two or three weeks.

External Beam Radiation Therapy

External beam radiation therapy is a sometimes acceptable alternative to surgery. It is by far the simplest of therapies. Over a six-to-seven week period, the patient will receive a radiation treatment lasting about 15 minutes, 5 days a week. The radiation is aimed at the prostate from many different angles in an attempt to reduce damage to nearby tissues while maximizing the dosage to the prostate and the cancer.

The rapidly dividing cancer cells are more vulnerable to radiation destruction than are the surrounding normal cells.

The advantage of external radiation therapy is its ease of administration. No surgery, no anesthesia, no blood loss. The biggest disadvantage is that the cancer is left in place and one must hope that the amount of radiation delivered is enough to cure it.

During the last two to three weeks of treatment, diarrhea and urinary urgency and frequency are quite common and on occasion so severe that the treatments need to be temporarily halted. Permanent radiation injury to the bladder or rectum occurs in a small percent of patients, creating chronic pain and/or bleeding. Difficulty with erections (impotence) occurs in 35 percent of patients who were having no problems before treatment.

Implants

Implants are forms of radiation therapy with many of the same risks and benefits. Often combined with external therapy, depending on the type of implanted radiation and the extent of the cancer, they are ultrasound-guided radiation treatments done under anesthesia. The operation lasts from 1-2 hours and hospitalization lasts from 1–2 days. Some implants are permanently left in place (Iodine, Palladium, Gold) and some are temporary (Iridium). They allow for higher doses to the prostate while sparing the surrounding tissues. They must be considered experimental at this time until more is known about long term survival and cure rates.

Cryotherapy

Cryotherapy is a newer treatment which requires freezing the prostate tissue in order to kill the cancer. In this technique, needle-like probes, which freeze and kill the tissue, are inserted into the prostate gland.

MEDICATIONS THAT CAN HELP

Hormone Therapy

Hormone therapy is a drug-based approach. The prostate gland's very existence is due to the presence of male hormones, which the prostate, and most prostate cancers, require to grow. This observation led urologists to the use of hormone reduction to treat prostate cancer in the 1940s and, except for newer drugs, the principle of hormone reduction still stands today.

Therefore, treatments that suppress the production or the action of the testosterone hormone can retard cancer growth. Methods used include oral estrogen medication, injectable leuprolide (Lupron), and surgical removal of the testicles (orchiectomy). Estrogen tablets (diethylstilbestrol) inhibit the testicular production of testosterone by blocking signals coming from the brain.

Lupron, an injectable agent given monthly, also works by impairing brain signals to the testicles to produce testosterone. Flutamide (Eulexin) is an oral capsule that blocks the action of testosterone, and can be used in combination with Lupron in the treatment of metastatic prostate cancer. Pills may be added to either of these treatments to increase the reduction effectiveness.

Unfortunately, hormone therapy is effective only temporarily in most patients. Seven to nine out of 10 men will have an initial reduction in the tumor, but within 2–3 years most men that do respond will no longer and the cancer will again grow. Because hormone therapy is not curative, we usually do not recommend this for localized cancer for patients with reasonable life expectancies.

Chemotherapy

Chemotherapy is the use of medicines or drugs to stop the growth of cancers. Chemotherapy is used for the most part in patients whose disease has spread to other parts of the body (metastases) and is resistant to other forms of treatment. The drugs are very powerful and work by killing cells that tend to grow quickly. Cancers tend to grow quickly, but unfortunately, so do cells in bone marrow, gut and other areas. Anemia, weakness, nausea, vomiting, diarrhea and other side effects can occur. Unfortunately, chemotherapy rarely cures prostate cancer, but merely palliates or temporizes the cancer growth. Chemotherapy, therefore, is not used for localized prostate cancer.

To date, chemotherapy regimens which have been tried have not been shown to be beneficial. A new chemotherapy agent, suramin, is being studied in centers throughout the country.

NUTRITION TO WARD OFF PROBLEMS

A theme throughout this book has been that nutrition can help ward off prostate problems. We've given suggestions throughout on foods that can help you reduce your risk. A number of these are worth emphasizing here, as "Natural Prostate Healers."

As mentioned earlier, the National Cancer Institute's official dietary guideline, nationally promoted as the "5 a Day for Better Health" program, prescribes a minimum of 5 servings of fruits and vegetables a day. (For men eating the median 2,270 calories a day, the minimum is seven servings.) Unfortunately, only one in four people really follows this advice.

It's not consumption of one or two varieties of vegetables and fruit that confer benefit, but rather that intake of many different kinds of plant foods is higher in those at lower risk of cancer. Of all the vegetables studied, only legumes and potatoes appear to show no evidence of direct benefit. The fact that individuals who consume higher intakes of plant foods also have other healthy habits, such as a lower likelihood of smoking does not account for all of the differences seen.

There are many biologically plausible reasons why consumption of vegetables and fruit might deter the development of cancer. There are, in particular, a wide variety of chemical compounds present naturally in food that may lower the cancer risk.

It has been estimated that 75 percent of all prostate cancer could be prevented with changes in diet and lifestyle. While it may be hard to believe that some simple changes can keep prostate problems, including cancer, at bay, scientific evidence shows that they may account in large part for the variance of prostate cancer rates in different countries. For example, the rates range from 3.5 per 100,000 in Singapore to 49.8 per 100,000 in Sweden. (The rate in the United States is 32.2 per 100,000.) Among all the risk factors, only nutrition explains the differences between countries.

A Perfect Cancer Food

Scientific attention has also been focused on dietary compounds common in Asia, where soybean protein is consumed in such foods as tofu, tempeh and soy milk. Scientists believe the soy flavonoids genistein and daidzein slow the growth of tumors and may prevent recurrence.

Twenty-five years ago, the only people who knew much about soybeans in the United States were farmers who grew them to feed to their livestock. Now more and more people are discovering the disease-fighting ability of soy.

For example, the flavonoid genistein has another intriguing quality: it inhibits the formation of new blood vessels. Once we reach adulthood, there is no normal need to grow new blood vessel networks except when healing after an accident or surgery. In order for tumors to increase in size, however, they need to create networks of blood vessels to bring nutrients into their interiors. If this process is inhibited, the tumor can't grow very large. An article that appeared in the March 1995 *Journal of Nutrition* concludes that "in two-thirds of studies on the effect of genistein-containing soy materials in animal models of cancer, the risk of cancer (incidence, latency or tumor number) was significantly reduced."

I hope by now I've convinced you to add soy products to your diet. Of course, many people have no idea how to do that. One of the good things about soybeans is that they are available in so many completely different forms and textures—besides just tofu.

Low-fat soy milk is one of the best sources of soy protein. Eight ounces of low-fat soy milk contains three to four grams of soy protein, and two to three grams of fat. Although you can buy non-fat soy milk, this is one case in which fat is not necessarily to be avoided. When soybeans are defatted, they lose some of their beneficial properties. Luckily, soy milk is becoming easier to find in supermarkets around the country.

See Chapter Two for more info on the different types of soy. Also, check out the Appendix for a variety of soy-based recipes.

Lycopene Reduces Prostate Cancer Up to 45 Percent

As I told you earlier in this book, a six-year study of the dietary habits of 47,000 men found that pizza, spaghetti sauce and other foods rich in tomato substantially lowered the risk of prostate cancer. Since men who eat at least 10 servings a week of tomato-based foods are up to 45 percent less likely to develop prostate cancer, it bears repeating, don't you think?

The magic bullet is an antioxidant called lycopene. Recently, Dr. Edward Giovannucci, a researcher at the Harvard School of Public Health, said that tomato-based products and strawberries were the only foods of 46 fruits and vegetables checked that seemed to have a protective effect against prostate cancer. And the benefits of tomatoes came from several forms of the food: sauce, juice, raw and even when cooked into pizza. "We found that more was better," said Giovannucci.

He said that men who had 10 or more servings a week had a 45 percent reduction in the rate of prostate cancer, while those who ate only four to seven servings of the tomato-based food had a 20 percent reduction in the cancer. Spaghetti sauce was the most common tomato-based food eaten by the men in the study group.

The study was based on a dietary survey taken of 47,000 males in the health professions between the ages of 40 and 75. The first survey was taken in 1986 and the men were followed and periodically reexamined.

Giovannucci cautioned that the findings should not be interpreted to mean that men should load up on tomato products. Rather he believes that these findings support the idea that people should eat a variety of fruits and vegetables since nutrients in other foods may be protective against other types of cancers.

Giovannucci said that cooked tomato products seemed to be more protective than either juice or raw tomatoes. It could be, he said, that when tomatoes are heated during cooking, the cells burst and release more lycopene. So, men, break out those pots and pans and heat up those juicy Big Boys.

Essential Fatty Acids Fight Cancer

More and more men are turning to natural therapies to treat prostate cancer, either as the main treatment or to complement conventional therapy. Many of the treatments used for BPH can also be applied to a prostate cancer protocol.

One of the main goals in natural cancer treatment is to enhance overall immunity. To do this, you should start with a healthful diet full of fresh vegetables and fruits, whole grains, beans, nuts and seeds.

Knowing which fats to eat and which to minimize is important in controlling your prostate health. Some prostaglandins, a class of hormone-like compounds, are vital for proper prostate function. Unfortunately, most people's diets are low in essential fatty acids, building blocks of these necessary prostaglandins.

EFAs are found in most nuts and seeds and high-quality vegetable oils but are particularly rich in walnuts, flaxseeds and pumpkin seeds. You can also supplement your diet with capsules containing EFAs such as flaxseed oil. In addition to increasing EFAs, avoid harmful fats such as trans-fatty acids or hydrogenated fats in fried foods, vegetable shortenings, margarine and processed vegetable oils. Also, minimize your intake of fatty meats.

Other nutritional tips include reducing sugar in your diet, which improves the body's ability to heal, and eating plenty of fresh, colorful vegetables. Like other parts of the body, the prostate depends on a wide range of nutrients to function properly, and vegetables are packed with vitamins and minerals. Keeping pesticides out of your diet by eating as many organic foods as possible also benefits the prostate.

In addition, make sure you exercise and get eight hours of sleep a night, and limit the stress in your life. Numerous studies show high levels of stress increase cancer risk.

A prominent New York doctor specializing in alternative cancer therapies in New York often prescribes dietary changes, oral nutritional supplements, hormonal balancing, intravenous vitamin and mineral drips, an exercise program, fresh air and some sunlight exposure, stress management training, detoxification, possibly homeopathy, and a things to avoid list. The dietary program stresses organic whole foods with an emphasis on plants including fresh fruits and vegetables, and whole grains, some nuts and seeds, fresh organic vegetable and fruit juices and modest amounts of animal proteins, including fish, organic eggs and chicken. The vitamins he emphasizes are high doses of vitamin C, antioxidants A and E, vitamin D, the B3 vitamin niacinamide, and modest amounts of other B vitamins.

When first diagnosed with prostate cancer, H.E. was given 35 external beam radiation treatments. After one year, his PSA began to rise and a biopsy revealed residual cancer in both lobes of the prostate. A CT scan showed enlarged lymph nodes, suggesting the cancer had spread. After undergoing hormonal blockage, a year later he started the doctor's program which included vitamin C and other oral nutrients. H.E. also began IV infusions of vitamin C, minerals and amygdalin. After two years, H.E. reported he felt great and his PSA is normal.

Adding a high-potency multiple vitamin and mineral supplement, including the antioxidants beta-carotene, vitamins E and C and selenium, helps ensure that you're getting adequate nutrition.

Remember, vitamin C neutralizes cell-damaging free radicals. Also make sure that you are getting sufficient zinc each day. I can't stress enough that your prostate needs zinc, and zinc levels tend to be lower in the cancerous prostate, while cadmium, a toxic heavy metal, is markedly higher. In fact, men who work around industrial cadmium have an increased incidence of prostatic carcinoma.

Cadmium is also high in cigarette smoke, paint and contaminated drinking water. Selenium, plentiful in grains, milk, meat and onions, guards against cancer cell formation, especially when caused by cadmium.

Cut Cancer Risk with Selenium

There's lots of evidence that getting enough of this essential mineral cuts your risk of most kinds of cancer, including of the prostate. Selenium acts as an antioxidant, which means that it helps protect cells from harmful free radical reactions. Selenium acts together with vitamin E, selenium protecting within the cells and vitamin E protecting the outer cell membranes.

Researchers at the Arizona Cancer Center set out to test the effectiveness of selenium supplements on the prevention of skin cancer in over 1300 patients. Participants received a placebo or 200 mcg selenium per day over a period of 4.5 years and a total follow-up of 6.4 years. While the results did not show any reduction in skin cancer risk, the selenium group had a 37 percent reduction in cancer incidence and a 50 percent reduction in cancer mortality. The effects appeared strongest for prostate (63 percent lower risk), colo-rectal (58 percent lower risk) and lung (53 percent lower risk) cancers.

For cancer prevention, nutrition-oriented doctors recommend 50 to 200 micrograms of selenium a day (depending on what part of the country you live in and your personal and family history of cancer), taken in the form of l-selenomethionine. This is the organic form of selenium, which means it is more easily absorbed, with less possibility of adverse side effects.

Good food sources include organ meats, fish and shellfish, muscle meats, whole grains, cereals, dairy products, eggs, garlic, and vegetables such as broccoli, mushrooms, cabbage and celery. The selenium content of foods depends on the soil in which they are grown.

It's important to know that processed foods lose their selenium. Brown rice, for example, has 15 times the selenium content of white rice, and whole-wheat bread contains twice as much selenium as white bread.

Selenium toxicity can occur at doses of 600 to 750 mcg Early signs of selenium toxicity include fatigue, irritability, dry hair or hair loss, nervous system problems and bad breath.

S.R. is a 67-year-old married, vigorous, retired letter carrier. In Feb. 1995, he was diagnosed with a stage II prostate cancer and two urologists recommended a radical prostatectomy. S.R. declined.

Instead he started an intensive program including selenium, vitamin C, CoQ10, vitamin E, niacinamide and other supplements. He also received IV infusions including vitamin C and minerals. His doctor reports after a short period, his condition improved markedly.

REDUCE PROSTATE CANCER RISK BY ONE-THIRD

According to a recent study, regular doses of vitamin E may greatly reduce a man's chance of getting, and dying from, prostate cancer. In the study, published in the *Journal of the National Cancer Institute*, researchers followed 29,132 men in southwestern Finland. Of that group, half were given 50-milligram vitamin E capsules every day and the other half an identical-looking sugar pill.

Between 1985 to 1991, the vitamin-takers had a 36 percent lower risk of getting prostate cancer and a 41 percent lower mortality rate if they were diagnosed with the illness. The men taking both supplements had a 16 percent lower incidence, while those taking only beta-carotene had a 20 percent higher incidence than the placebo group.

"We feel strongly and confidently about the results," said co-author Dr. Demetrius Albanes of the National Cancer Institute in Bethesda, Md. Albanes worked with Finnish researcher Olli Heinonen of the University of Helsinki. The dosage of 50-milligrams of vitamin E used in the study is about equal to 50 I.U.

Albanes and Heinonen also admit that they were surprised by their finding, because the original goal of the study was to see if there was a link between lung cancer and vitamin E. They conducted the research in Finland because that country has a high percentage of both male smokers and lung cancer cases. Vitamin E had little effect on lung cancer, but the prostate cancer correlation was a pleasant surprise.

Multivitamins generally contain about 30 I.U. of vitamin E while single supplements most often have a minimum of 100 I.U. of vitamin E. The dose of 50 I.U. in the Finnish study is about five times the Recommended Dietary Allowance of vitamin E for men and about three times what most people get from food.

Contrary to a recent scare generated by a UC Berkeley study, vitamin E is among the safest of vitamins, according to John Hathcock Ph.D., Director of Nutritional and Regulatory Science for the Council for Responsible Nutrition. He says vitamin E, in all forms, is one of the safest of all vitamins. No adverse effects have been demonstrated with alpha-tocopherol at intakes of 1,200 I.U.'s or more.

TAKE TIME FOR TEA

Green tea contain polyphenols, or catechins, which have many wonderful properties. One is as a cancer protector. Green tea guards against cancer by scavenging for free radicals that can damage cells that block the action of carcinogens and detoxify them. Tea polyphenols may also limit cell multiplication, a cancer characteristic.

Tea makers prepare both black and green tea from leaves of the white-flowered tea plant, *Camellia sinensis*, a bush native to Asia. But to make green tea, they dry the leaves after a brief steaming, instead of crushing them, piling them in heaps and briefly "sweating" them for black tea. (During this natural fermentation process, the tea leaves darken and develop a different aroma and flavor than green tea.)

Since fermentation destroys some of the polyphenols, green tea is thought to be best for your health. It contains about 27 percent catechins; oolong is next with 23 percent; then comes black tea at about 4 percent. Unfortunately, herb tea, while it may be tasty and relaxing, doesn't deliver any polyphenols.

There is some evidence that black tea shouldn't be written off, however. As reported in the journal *Mutagenesis,* green, black and decaffeinated black tea all had equally strong abilities to neutralize cancer-causing chemicals in the test tube, leading researchers to conclude that the fermented derivatives of polyphenols may be active, too. Another study in the same journal found comparable anti-mutagenic and antioxidant activity among instant teas, a black tea and a green tea.

HONEST TALK FROM THOSE WHO HAVE BEEN THROUGH IT

A Case for Watchful Waiting

In March 1992, M. B. considered himself in perfect health. Prior to a trip to Europe he went for a physical to a general medical practitioner. The test results came back from the lab and hidden among a full page of data was this entry;

"PSA = 7.5."

This was of no special concern to him since he understood a PSA of 7.0 for someone 65 years old might be normal if not slightly on the high side, certainly not high enough to worry about. So he left for Europe.

In 1994 before M.B. headed for Southeast Asia, he had another physical exam to make sure that health would not be a problem for him in the countries he planned on visiting. This time he went to another medical group and the long printout of blood chemistry revealed;

"PSA = 8.0."

On the advice of the doctor at that center, M.B. went to a urologist. An in-office biopsy and ultrasound revealed that he had a few cancer cells in his prostate. At first, the word "cancer" struck him hard. Still, since it is not unusual for men past 60 to have a few cancer cells in the prostate, he wasn't too alarmed. The doctor suggested possible treatment with general radiation of the prostate region for about eight sessions. As time would prove, this suggested treatment would have been totally incorrect. First, eight sessions would have never been adequate to kill the cancer cells; second, the general radiation would have produced serious side effects. The negative aspects of GENERAL radiation were never mentioned by the doctor.

A second option was to do nothing and to continue "watchful waiting." Since prostate cancer is a very slow-growing malignancy in older men, M.B. chose this option.

It is important to understand the ramifications involved in "watchful waiting." There are two aspects to this decision:

1. Psychological: Some men will find it impossible to accept the fact that they have cancer cells growing inside of them and, therefore, cannot select this option.

2. Medical: Most of the time prostate cancer is a very slow-growing tumor. However, in certain cases the spread of the disease can suddenly become exponential in nature. During any period of "watchful waiting" it is imperative that the PSA be constantly monitored on a schedule set forth by the urologist or radiologist.

In August 1996 M.B. planned a trip to Africa. It was now two years after cancer cells were first identified in his biopsy specimen. During all of that time he felt fine with no adverse effect of the cancer cells which were obviously multiplying in his prostate.

M.B. eventually received treatment. During the period when he "watchfully waited," he fully educated himself about his condition. This allowed him to help choose his treatment, and continue to live his life including traveling, which he loved.

40 IS NOT TOO YOUNG

At age 42, T.M. could be found working late at the investment company he and his partner built together. On weekends he liked to ride his motorcycle in the mountains near his home in Palm Desert, California.

Today he is unable to work, more often than not, and must cope with bone pain so terrible it often keeps him up all night. "This wasn't supposed to happen to me," said T.M. "I'm just too young."

January 1997 was the month in which T.M.'s life changed forever. That's when he went to his doctor with a piercing pain in his back and chest. After a full physical, a blood test and a visit to a urologist, T. M. was given the news: he had prostate cancer. The disease had already spread outside the gland and settled in his bones.

Since he's in his early 40s, T.M. is usually the youngest patient at the cancer center near his home. After he stopped responding to hormone therapy, he enrolled in a clinical trial that has already reduced the pain. He has been undergoing a variety of therapies in an attempt to reverse the spread of cancerous cells. For one thing he has altered his eating habits for the better.

Prostate cancer is increasingly striking younger men. According to the American Cancer Society, roughly one-fifth of all prostate cancer diagnoses occur in men in their 40s and 50s. At the same time, doctors across the country report treating much more aggressive forms of the disease in younger patients. This trend has developed just as a shift in demographics—aging Baby Boomers approaching middle age—has boosted the number of men at risk for this disease.

"As this generation faces up to the facts about cancer and mobilizes to stop it, cancer is emerging as a top national priority," said Richard N. Atkins, M.D., Executive Vice President and Chief Operating Officer of CaP CURE.

Finding a cure before cancer takes its greatest toll on the Baby Boomers will save millions of lives and trillions of dollars, said Atkins. A cure in the next five years would all but eliminate the estimated $9.5 billion spent every year caring for the existing caseload of prostate cancer patients.

For T.M., the cure couldn't come too soon. "I need what's available now," he told CaP CURE. "I'm just hoping that I have enough time for something to be developed. I'm very positive that I'm going to beat it and that I'm going to be a survivor. There has to be somebody or something out there that will help me."

A Wife's Perspective

C.G. is the wife of a man diagnosed with early-stage prostate cancer. Now one of her goals is to educate other women about prostate cancer and to encourage the men in their lives to practice healthy behaviors. Here's her story:

"Most women don't like 'bugging' their men. However, if your spouse or significant other is dragging his feet about getting a prostate examination, you may need to take the initiative. Make the appointment, lasso him, and drive him in for the test.

"Women undergo mammograms, Pap smears, and endless waiting for results. While men see to it that we take care of ourselves, their health is a horse of a different color. And while I'm talking about horses, I hereby give you permission to be a nag (just about this one thing) and get him in for prostate testing. Macho men often take the view that nothing bad can happen to them, but statistics prove otherwise.

"My husband, L.G., is 63 years old. He happened to read a newspaper column where a concerned person wrote in and asked about the PSA (Prostate-Specific Antigen) blood test. L.G. was impressed by the article and went to his family doctor, who refused to give him the test, saying that the digital examination was all that he needed and that he was "fine, not to worry." My husband was persistent and contacted a new physician.

"The new doctor gave him a PSA test. Normal levels of the antigen in the prostate are under 4 nanograms per milliliter (ng/mL). L.G.'s result was 7 ng/mL. L.G. was sent to a urologist, and further tests demonstrated that he had prostate cancer. My husband and I were both called in and the doctor explained the options. Being married only six years at the time of diagnosis and still called "honeymooners," we did not want anything to change our marital relations. Therefore, we chose nerve sparing surgery. L.G. was sent to a University Medical Center where successful nerve-sparing surgery was performed.

"I have recently completed training as a certified nurse's aide and had part of my training in a urology unit. Believe me, I saw many patients undergo prostate surgery. In the annual report of the community cancer program in which I trained, 269 of the 973 new cancer cases were of the prostate gland. My work now takes me to retirement centers and care centers, and it doesn't take me long to realize that the women are outliving the men.

"Unlike the digital rectal exam, the PSA blood test is not part of a regular checkup. However, if a man has a family history of prostate cancer or simply desires to have the test done, he should be persistent until a doctor agrees to perform it. If surgery is necessary, it can be performed, as in L.G.'s case, and your life can go on together. If you hold your man's hand and get him to the doctor and through the recovery period, your relationship will be enriched and you can go on living. We love life and are active people and we're fortunate that we were persistent enough to push for a diagnosis. Together we battled cancer and won.

"So, wives, if you value your man as I do, I strongly suggest that you go ahead—be a nag. Don't let your man be a statistic.

How can we as wives help prevent cancer in our husbands?

- Help him to maintain desirable weight.
- Make sure he has a varied diet.
- Have him eat more high-fiber foods such as whole-grain cereals, breads, pasta, vegetables and fruits.
- Cut down on total fat intake. A diet high in fat may be a factor in the development of certain cancers, particularly of the breast, colon, and prostate.
- Limit consumption of salt-cured, smoked, and nitrite-cured foods (luncheon meat, bacon, hot dogs).
- Limit consumption of alcohol and tobacco.
- Encourage men 40 and over to have a digital rectal examination as part of an annual physical checkup. If the results are suspicious, further testing should be performed.

SOURCE: Zeneca Pharmaceuticals' *Innovations in Urology Nursing.*

THE FUTURE OF PROSTATE CANCER

Researchers throughout the world are ever vigilant searching for ways to eliminate, or at least minimize, one of man's greatest fears. I've mentioned many times the great work conducted by CaP CURE, the foundation Michael Milkin founded, particularly regarding dietary factors.

There is also other intriguing research being conducted elsewhere. Here are four trends that we all should follow:

1. A 1997 study by researchers at the Pacific Northwest Research Foundation in Seattle has revealed that DNA of the prostate undergoes a dramatic structural change when the tissue becomes cancerous. According

to the lead investigator, Dr. Donald C. Malins, researchers were able to distinguish the DNA of healthy men from that of men with prostate cancer by using sophisticated mathematical models based on infrared spectroscopy. "It is now clear that the development of prostate cancer results in a new type of DNA having the blueprint for generating cancer cells," said Malins.

This remarkable discovery, reported in "Proceedings of the National Academy of Sciences," allowed the researchers to classify prostate tissue as normal or cancerous with 100 percent certainty. At present, there are no tests available that can detect a precancerous condition in the prostate. This discovery holds significant promise for developing such a screening test and for predicting an occurrence of cancer long before abnormal cells can be detected.

The findings are a major advance in understanding the cause of prostate cancer, which has been unknown, as well as in providing a promising basis for predicting its occurrence. They open up the possibility for a test that could not only detect prostate cancer sooner, but at a much more treatable stage. The test could also be used to monitor a patient's response to treatment.

2. In the summer of 1998, chemists at the Sloan Kettering Institute for Cancer Research announced a novel vaccine that they hope will thwart prostate cancer. The vaccine is the first made synthetically to target abundant, but elusive, carbohydrates on the surface of tumor cells. Early human trials began soon after the announcement.

Scientists hope the vaccines will specifically attack prostate cancer cells, thereby permanently curbing cancer and reducing the side effects usually associated with chemotherapy. The new vaccine is being given to patients who have undergone prostate cancer surgery, in an attempt to ward off a recurrence. Though it is too early to know whether a series of vaccinations will provide an adequate defense, coauthor and Sloan Kettering Immunologist Philip O. Livingston, M.D. says patients are definitely producing antibodies against one of the synthetic carbohydrates dubbed "Tn."

3. According to a research study outlined in early 1998, doctors may one day use the growth protein IGF-1 to better predict which men will eventually get cancer. Dr. Michael Pollak of McGill University in Canada, who coauthored the study with Harvard University scientists, said that a

quarter of men have high levels of the growth protein which is linked to a greater likelihood of prostate cancer. If the new research is confirmed, it may point scientists toward ways to reduce the incidence of the cancer.

"This research finding was a big surprise," Pollak said. "It opens up a whole new direction of research."

The study, published in the journal *Science,* also raised a red flag for men who take growth hormone to fight the effects of aging. That still-experimental trend may raise their risk of prostate cancer because the growth hormone increases IGF-1 levels. Taking growth hormones "is, on the basis of our data, a risky business," Pollak warned.

It's too early for men to seek testing for IGF-1, Pollak said; however, he has begun animal studies to test whether drugs that lower its level could prevent men from getting the disease.

An IGF-1 link to prostate cancer makes sense, because doctors have long advised people to lose weight to lower the risk of various cancers—and overeaters have high IGF-1 levels, according to Dr. Otis Brawley, a prostate cancer expert at the National Cancer Institute.

Preliminary evidence also has found that IGF-1 spurs prostate tumors to be more aggressive, a link Brawley wants studied quickly. If confirmed, it could shed light on why black men die of prostate cancer at a higher rate than white men—because blacks typically have higher IGF-1 levels, he said.

Aging men today are often screened for high blood levels of prostate specific antigen, or PSA, which can signal cancer. But the test doesn't predict who will get cancer in the future, so doctors are seeking better "markers" that would act much as cholesterol does in predicting future heart disease.

In test tubes, IGF-1—insulin-like growth factor-1—stimulates growth of both cancer cells and normal prostate cells. So Harvard turned to its massive Physicians Health Study, which has followed men's health since 1982. Researchers checked blood samples for IGF-1 levels in 152 men who later got prostate cancer and 152 healthy "control" men. Men with the highest IGF-1 were 4.3 times more likely to have been diagnosed with prostate cancer than men with the lowest levels, said lead researcher June Chan, a Harvard graduate student.

IGF-1 was a powerful cancer predictor regardless of the men's PSA test scores, Chan said. That suggests that combining PSA and IGF testing might pinpoint the men at highest risk years before cancer strikes, so it could be caught extra early.

But detecting prostate cancer early is controversial. Because nobody knows which side effect-ridden treatment works best, many men aren't treated, and there's no proof early detection actually saves lives, Dr. Brawley said. So it's more important to follow up whether IGF-1 makes tumors more aggressive—so that doctors would know who needs more treatment—and if lowering levels could prevent cancer, Dr. Pollak said.

IGF-1 cannot be eliminated, he stressed. It's necessary for a variety of bodily functions, so he is focusing on lowering abnormally high levels. IGF-lowering drugs already are used to treat a very rare condition in which superhigh IGF spurs children to grow into giants. Pollak is giving those drugs to mice prone to prostate cancer. If they protect the mice, he would test men and check how early in life the treatment would have to start.

"No one would have thought of this 10 years ago," Dr. Pollak said. "It's a hot lead."

4. Johns Hopkins researchers, collaborating with an international team of geneticists, have pinpointed the site of the first gene for a major cancer located on the human X chromosome. The gene for prostate cancer may account for almost 20 percent of disease in families with a strong history of the cancer, the researchers say. It's the second prostate cancer susceptibility gene that this group has mapped, and the first on the X chromosome, which men inherit from their mothers.

"This is clearly a major step toward understanding the factors that lead to prostate cancer," says Hopkins urologist-in-chief Patrick C. Walsh, M.D., one of the study's authors. "We're still at the early stages in figuring out genetic involvement in prostate cancer, but this finding is real progress," says Hopkins geneticist William Isaacs, Ph.D., a co-director of the study.

The research, reported in *Nature Genetics*, describes the new gene locus, called HPCX (for human prostate cancer on the X chromosome), as responsible for 15 to 20 percent of inherited forms of the disease. Of the approximately 200,000 new cases diagnosed in the United States each year, an estimated 10 percent are inherited.

The study confirms researchers' long-held suspicion that the X chromosome might be important in prostate cancer. Since the 1960s, they have noted that a man's risk tends to be higher if his brother has prostate cancer than if his father has the disease. That inheritance pattern characterizes genetic traits carried on the X chromosome and passed from mothers to sons, such as muscular dystrophy or hemophilia. The plausible explanation is that a prostate cancer susceptibility gene lies on the X chromosome.

In studying nearly 1,000 people with earlier-than-usual onset of the disease and a strong family history of prostate cancer, the researchers found a specific area on the X chromosome that was shared more frequently than one would predict as determined by statistical analysis. That area encompasses the susceptibility gene. Isolating that precise gene is the next step for the researchers. Then, with more study, they'll know whether diagnostic tests should be done and, ultimately, how to design preventive therapies.

"Finding genes for prostate cancer is particularly difficult," says Isaacs, because it's hard to separate populations of people who get the disease due to a strong-acting mutant gene from those who have it from other causes such as, say, interactions between the environment and less influential genes. "You can have one family where four brothers have prostate cancer but only three have the HPCX gene."

In 1996, the same research team identified the location of the first specific gene that predisposes men to develop prostate cancer. The team named that gene HPCI (hereditary prostate cancer 1) and located it on a region of chromosome 1, one of 22 pairs of non-sex human chromosomes.

I've given you a great deal of information in this book, probably more than you need. I hope you've gathered that education is the key to prostate disease prevention and treatment. Francis Bacon said "Knowledge itself is power."

My hope for you is to find and use this power. That is the surest route to a long, healthy and happy life.

101

PROSTATE HEALTHY

RECIPES

You may be thinking that in order to have a healthy prostate, you can't enjoy eating any more. Before you "fall on your sword," take a look at the following prostate-friendly recipes. There are plenty of choices here to satisfy even the pickiest eater.

I've grouped them into 5 areas;

- LOTSA LYCOPENE (15 recipes)

- SIMPLY SELENIUM (12 recipes)

- THINK ZINC (12 recipes)

- PROSTATE ENDS WITH "E" (14 recipes)

- JOY OF SOY (22 recipes)

- SOUND EATING: MAIN COURSES (25 Plus Bonus recipes)

Naturally there are plenty of important nutrients in each. So, even though a recipe will be grouped under "E," for example, it may also be a good source of selenium. Likewise, you'll find good sources of "E" in the other groups as well.

LOTSA LYCOPENE

You can use the following sauce whenever you have pasta.

I. Basic Marinara Sauce

    4-1/2 lbs. canned plum tomatoes

    2 Tbs. olive oil

    1 cup onions, chopped

    1/2 cup carrots, finely grated

    4 cloves garlic, finely chopped

    1/4 cup dry red wine

    2 Tbs. tomato paste

    1/2 cup parsley, chopped

    1 Tbs. dried oregano

    2 tsp. dried basil

    1/2 tsp. ground nutmeg

    1/2 tsp. freshly ground black pepper

    salt, to taste

Drain tomatoes, reserving 1 cup juice. Crush tomatoes with the back of a spoon and set aside. Heat the oil in a saucepan over medium low heat. Add the onions, carrots and garlic. Cook stirring, until the onions and garlic have wilted, about 10 minutes. Add the tomatoes, reserved juice, wine, tomato paste, and the remaining ingredients. Cover, cook over medium heat for 15 minutes. Remove the cover and simmer another 45 minutes, stirring occasionally.

2. Middle Eastern Stuffed Tomatoes (serves 4)

    2/3 cup bulgur wheat

    1-1/3 cups chicken stock, low fat, low sodium

    1/3 cup golden raisins

    2/3 cup boiling water

    1 Tbs. plus 1 tsp. olive oil

    2/3 cup red bell pepper, diced

1/3 cup green peas, cooked

2 Tbs. plus 2 tsp. fresh parsley, minced

2 Tbs. plus 2 tsp. fresh mint, minced

2 Tbs. lemon juice

8 plum tomatoes, halved and seeded

8 fresh mint sprigs

In a heatproof bowl, add the dry bulgur wheat. Boil the chicken stock and pour over the bulgur wheat. Let stand 30 minutes to 1 hour until all liquid is absorbed. Drain off any excess liquid. Meanwhile, place raisins in boiling water and let stand 10 minutes. Drain and combine with remaining ingredients, except mint sprigs and tomatoes, in a bowl. Add the bulgur wheat and mix well. Stuff the bulgur wheat mixture into the tomatoes. Garnish each tomato with a mint sprig and serve.

3. Broiled Deviled Tomatoes (serves 4)

4 large tomatoes, cut in half crosswise and seeded

1 Tbs. olive oil

1 clove garlic, minced

1 tsp. Dijon mustard

2 cups fresh bread crumbs

2 tsp. parsley, chopped

Season inside of tomatoes with salt and pepper to taste and arrange in an oiled baking dish. Heat oil in a heavy non-stick skillet over medium high heat. Sauté garlic 1 minute, stirring constantly. Remove from heat and whisk in mustard. Stir in bread crumbs, parsley and salt and pepper to taste.

Mix well and spoon into tomatoes. Broil about 5 inches from heat source 2–3 minutes until browned.

4. Herbed Stuffed Tomatoes (serves 4)

4 large tomatoes, cut in half crosswise and seeds removed

1/4 tsp. salt

2 small shallots, minced

2 cloves garlic, minced

1 Tbs. plus 1 tsp. unsalted butter, melted

2 Tbs. parsley, chopped

1 cup seasoned bread crumbs

2 Tbs. grated Parmesan cheese

1/4 tsp. pepper

Preheat oven to 400 degrees. Sprinkle inside of tomatoes with salt. Set aside to drain on paper towels 15–20 minutes. Combine remaining ingredients, except pepper, in a bowl. Stuff each tomato half with bread crumb cheese mixture. Sprinkle with pepper and bake 10 minutes. Turn on broiler and broil tomatoes 30 seconds to 1 minute until lightly browned.

5. Tomato Pudding (serves 4)

4 slices white bread, torn into pieces

1/2 cup milk

2 Tbs. unsalted butter

6 tomatoes, peeled, seeded and chopped

1 Tbs. onion, minced

1 tsp. sugar

3 Tbs. grated Parmesan cheese

4 eggs, separated, yolks beaten, whites beaten to stiff peaks

Preheat oven to 350 degrees. Combine bread and milk in a bowl. Mash to form a paste. Melt butter in a heavy non-reactive saucepan over medium heat. Stir in bread paste and next 3 ingredients. Season with salt and pepper to taste. Remove from heat. Stir in Parmesan and beaten egg yolks. Fold in egg whites and transfer mixture into a buttered 1-1/2 quart souffle dish or straight-sided dish. Bake 35 minutes or until pudding is set.

6. Roasted Vegetable Soup (serves 4)

8 tomatoes, cut in half

1 Tbs. sugar

2 red onions, sliced

2 zucchini, sliced

2 yellow squash, sliced

3 red bell peppers, seeded and sliced

2 cloves garlic, chopped

2 Tbs. rosemary, chopped

1 lemon, juiced

Preheat oven to 425 degrees. Arrange tomatoes cut side up in the bottom of an oiled non-reactive baking pan. Sprinkle with sugar. Combine remaining vegetables, garlic and rosemary in another oiled baking pan. Season with salt and pepper to taste. Place both pans in oven and roast 25–30 minutes, stirring squash mixture every 8–10 minutes until vegetables are tender. Working in batches if necessary, combine tomatoes, lemon juice and all but 1 cup of the vegetables in a food processor or blender. Process until smooth. Chop remaining vegetables and serve soup with chopped vegetables sprinkled on top.

7. Rice with Kale and Tomatoes (serves 4)

1 cup chicken stock

1 cup water

1 cup Uncle Ben's Long Grain Rice

1-1/2 Tbs. olive oil

2 cloves garlic, minced

4 cups kale or spinach, finely chopped

3 lbs. plum tomatoes, seeded and chopped

Bring stock and water to a boil in a saucepan over high heat. Stir in rice and return to a boil. Immediately reduce heat to low. Cover saucepan and simmer 20–25 minutes or until rice is tender and liquid is absorbed. Heat oil in a heavy non-stick skillet over medium heat. Sauté garlic 3 minutes or until golden. Add kale and tomatoes. Sauté 3–5 minutes, stirring occasionally until kale is tender. Season with salt and pepper to taste. Fluff cooked rice with fork. Combine with tomato-kale mixture.

8. Zucchini Parmigiana (serves 4)

1 Tbs. olive oil

1 clove garlic, minced

1 Tbs. Italian herb seasoning

5 tomatoes, cut into wedges

1-1/2 lbs. zucchini, thinly sliced

2 cups shredded fat-free mozzarella cheese

2 Tbs. grated Parmesan cheese

Preheat oven to 400 degrees. Heat oil in a heavy non-stick skillet over medium heat. Sauté garlic and herbs 1 minute. Add tomatoes and sauté 4 minutes. Stir in zucchini. Cover skillet and simmer 3 minutes or until zucchini is almost tender. Drain excess liquid from skillet. Season with salt and pepper to taste. Stir in half the mozzarella and half the Parmesan. Transfer mixture to a lightly oiled baking dish. Sprinkle with remaining mozzarella and Parmesan. Bake 10–15 minutes or until cheese is melted.

9. Vegetarian Lasagna (serves 4)

1 Tbs. olive oil

2 onions, chopped

2 cloves garlic, crushed

2 carrots, chopped

2 large sticks celery, chopped

1 red bell pepper, seeded and chopped

7 ounces mushrooms, chopped

6 tomatoes, peeled and chopped

2 Tbs. tomato paste

1/4 cup fresh basil, chopped

1/4 cup fresh parsley, chopped

3/4 cup soft tofu

3/4 lb. lasagna noodles

1/4 cup seasoned bread crumbs

1-1/2 Tbs. grated Parmesan cheese

Preheat oven to 350 degrees. Heat oil in a heavy non-stick skillet over medium high heat. Sauté next 5 ingredients about 5 minutes until onions are soft. Stir in mushrooms and cook 1 minute. Stir in next 4 ingredients and bring to a boil over medium high heat. Reduce heat to low. Cover and simmer about 10 minutes or until vegetables are tender. Remove from heat.

Beat tofu until smooth. Stir 1/4 cup tofu into vegetable mixture. Remove from heat. Cook pasta in a large pot of boiling salted water 10 minutes or until al dente. Drain.

Spread a third of the vegetable mixture into a greased 9 × 13-inch ovenproof dish. Top with 2 sheets of pasta. Continue layering vegetable mixture and pasta, finishing with a layer of pasta. Spread remaining beaten tofu evenly over pasta. Combine bread crumbs and cheese and sprinkle over lasagna. Bake 50 minutes or until golden.

10. Ravioli with Fresh Sage Tomato Sauce (serves 4)

6 ounces fresh spinach ravioli

1 Tbs. plus 1 tsp. olive oil

3-1/2 Tbs. onion, finely chopped

1 clove garlic, minced

1-1/4 lbs. plum tomatoes, peeled and coarsely chopped

2 tsp. fresh sage, chopped

Cook ravioli in a large pan of boiling water 6–7 minutes, or until just cooked through. Drain and keep warm. Heat half the oil in a heavy non-stick skillet over medium high heat. Sauté onion and garlic 3–4 minutes, or until golden. Add tomatoes with their juice and salt and pepper to taste. Heat to boiling over high heat. Reduce heat to low, cover pan and simmer 15 minutes, stirring and mashing tomatoes with a spoon occasionally. Stir in remaining oil and sage. Serve sauce over ravioli.

11. Mayan Vegetable Stew (serves 4)

2 Tbs. vegetable oil

1 medium onion, chopped

1 large clove garlic, minced

1-1/4 cups butternut squash, peeled, seeded and cut into
  1/2-inch cubes

1 poblano pepper, seeded and finely diced

1 red bell pepper, seeded and diced

2 zucchini, diced

1/2 tsp. ground cumin

1/8 tsp. cayenne, or more to taste

1/2 tsp. orange zest, grated

1 cup corn kernels

1 lb. canned black beans, rinsed and drained

3 small tomatoes, diced

1/2 cup fresh cilantro, chopped

Heat oil in a heavy non-stick skillet over medium high heat. Stir in onion, garlic and squash. Cook about 5 minutes, stirring frequently, until squash begins to soften. Reduce heat to medium. Stir in next 6 ingredients and salt to taste. Cook 4–5 minutes, stirring occasionally, until squash and peppers are tender. Stir in corn, beans and tomatoes and cook about 3 minutes, or until heated throughout. Add cilantro and additional salt to taste just before serving.

12. Pasta with Zucchini Sauce (serves 4)

2 tsp. medium onion, chopped

2 medium zucchini, sliced

3 lbs. canned peeled tomatoes, drained and chopped

1 bay leaf

2 Tbs. packaged pesto sauce

1/2 lb. spaghetti

2 Tbs. grated Parmesan cheese

Combine first 4 ingredients in a heavy saucepan. Season with salt to taste. Cover and simmer 15 minutes. Remove cover and simmer another 10 minutes until sauce begins to thicken. Discard bay leaf. Stir in pesto and set aside. While sauce is cooking, cook pasta in boiling salted water

8–10 minutes or until al dente. Drain and serve spaghetti with zucchini sauce and Parmesan.

13. Creamy Tomato Soup (serves 3 to 4)

2 tsp. soy oil

1 medium onion, diced

1 cup soy milk

1 10.5-ounce package firm lite silken tofu

1 large tomato, diced

1/2 tsp. salt

1/2 tsp. chopped garlic

1 tsp. fresh basil, chopped

1/2 tsp. white pepper

Sauté onion in sauce pan in oil for 3 minutes or until transparent. Add tomato and garlic, continuing to sauté for 2–3 minutes. Add basil, salt and pepper. Blend in soy milk. Cook, stirring constantly, for one minute. Remove from heat and cool briefly. Add in tofu. Transfer to a food processor and puree until smooth. Serve hot or chilled.

Strawberries are also a great source of Lycopene, remember?

14. Honeyed Fruit Salad (serves 4)

1 cup pineapple chunks

2 cups strawberries, hulled and cut in half

2 bananas, cut into 1-inch slices

2 oranges, peeled, white pith cut away and thinly sliced

1 cup red seedless grapes

1/2 cup plain yogurt

2 Tbs. honey

Combine all ingredients in a mixing bowl and mix thoroughly. Let stand 15–20 minutes before serving.

15. *Strawberries and Mangoes in Snow (serves 4)*

> 2 cups vanilla lowfat yogurt
>
> 1 tsp. lemon juice
>
> 2 cups strawberries, hulled and halved
>
> 1/4 lb. mango slices, drained and chopped
>
> 4 slices angel food cake

Gently combine first 4 ingredients in a bowl. Spoon over cake and serve.

SIMPLY SELENIUM

Want to load up on selenium? Here are 12 great recipes. Obviously, seafood is your best source of this important nutrient.

16. *Grilled Orange Roughy with Lentil Salsa (serves 4)*
(897 mcg selenium)

> 2 lbs. canned lentils, rinsed and drained
>
> 2 green bell peppers, seeded and finely chopped
>
> 1 cup onion, finely chopped
>
> 4 tomatoes, chopped
>
> 1/2 cup fresh cilantro, chopped
>
> 1/4 cup plus 2 Tbs. olive oil
>
> 1/4 cup plus 2 Tbs. red wine vinegar
>
> 8 8-ounce orange roughy fillets, patted dry
>
> 1 cup all purpose flour

Combine first 7 ingredients and salt and pepper to taste in a bowl. Prepare grill or turn on broiler. Season fish with salt and pepper to taste. Place flour in a shallow dish. Dredge fillets in flour to coat, shaking off excess. Arrange fish on an oiled grill rack or broiler pan. Grill or broil 6 inches from heat source 4–5 minutes per side, or until fish flakes easily with a fork. Serve fish with a spoonful of salsa.

17. Grilled Swordfish with Tomato-Orange Salsa (serves 4)

(485 mcg selenium)

> 2 oranges, peeled, white pith removed, seeded and diced
> 1 cup tomatoes, chopped and seeded
> 2 Tbs. plus 2 tsp. red onion, minced
> 2 Tbs. plus 2 tsp. fresh parsley, chopped
> 1 Tbs. plus 1 tsp. fresh orange juice
> 1-1/4 tsp. balsamic vinegar
> 1/8 tsp. cayenne
> 2 cloves garlic, minced
> 2 tsp. fresh ginger, peeled and minced
> 1/2 cup teriyaki sauce
> 1/4 cup plus 3 Tbs. dry sherry
> 3/4 tsp. Oriental sesame oil
> 4 6-ounce swordfish steaks, 1-inch thick

Combine first 7 ingredients in a bowl. Add 2/3 of the garlic and 3/4 tsp. ginger. Season with salt and pepper to taste. Let stand at least 1 hour. (Can be prepared 4 hours ahead. Cover and refrigerate. Bring to room temperature before using.)

Combine teriyaki sauce, sherry, remaining garlic, 1-1/4 tsp. ginger and sesame oil in a saucepan. Bring to a boil. Set aside to cool. Place swordfish in a single layer in a shallow glass baking dish. Pour marinade over and turn to coat evenly. Cover and marinate in refrigerator 1-1/2 hours, turning often.

Prepare grill or turn on broiler. Remove fish from marinade, discarding marinade. Grill or broil about 4 minutes per side, until opaque in center. Serve with salsa.

18. Herbed Grilled Swordfish (serves 4)

(483 mcg selenium)

> 4-6 ounce swordfish steaks
> 1 clove garlic, crushed
> 1/2 tsp. fresh dill, chopped

1/2 tsp. oregano, or 2 tsp. fresh, chopped

1/4 cup lemon juice

1/8 tsp. paprika, or to taste

Prepare grill or broiler. Rub swordfish steaks with garlic. Place steaks on hot grill or oiled broiler pan. Sprinkle with half the dill, half the oregano and salt to taste. Grill or broil 5 minutes. Turn and brush with lemon juice. Season with remaining dill and oregano. Add salt to taste. Grill or broil another 4–5 minutes or until fish is opaque throughout. Sprinkle fish with paprika.

19. Baked Red Snapper (serves 4)

(349 mcg selenium)

1-1/2 lbs. red snapper fillets with skin, or other firm fleshed fish

2 Tbs. lemon juice

1/4 tsp. salt, or to taste

2 Tbs. parsley, chopped

4 whole wheat bagels, halved and toasted

Preheat oven to 375 degrees. Place snapper fillets skin side down in a lightly oiled baking dish. Drizzle fish with lemon juice. Season with salt and pepper to taste. Bake 10–12 minutes or until fish flakes easily. Sprinkle with parsley before serving.

20. Baked Trout with Bay Leaves (serves 4)

(343 mcg selenium)

1 clove garlic, crushed

3/4 tsp. dried thyme or 1-1/4 tsp. fresh, finely minced

4 12-ounce whole trout, pan dressed

4 bay leaves

2 Tbs. plus 2 tsp. unsalted butter, melted

1-1/4 lemons, juiced

2 Tbs. plus 2 tsp. fresh parsley, finely minced

Preheat oven to 400 degrees. Combine garlic, thyme and black pepper to taste in a bowl. Spread mixture on trout. Place 1 whole bay leaf into cavity of each fish. Arrange fish in an oiled baking dish in a single layer. Pour melted butter over and bake 10–12 minutes, basting once or twice with butter. Sprinkle with lemon juice and parsley. Remove bay leaves and serve.

21. Orange Roughy Florentine (serves 4)

(330 mcg selenium)

    1-1/2 lbs. spinach, stems discarded, thawed if frozen

    6 ounces light cream cheese

    1 egg, lightly beaten

    1/3 cup grated Parmesan cheese

    1/4 cup onion, chopped

    1/8 tsp. ground nutmeg

    1-1/2 lbs. orange roughy fillets

    1 tsp. tarragon, or 1 Tbs. fresh, chopped

Preheat oven to 375 degrees. Place spinach in a heavy non-stick skillet over medium high heat. Cover and cook 4–5 minutes, stirring occasionally, or until spinach is wilted and tender. Transfer to a colander. Press out excess liquid. Chop spinach and return to skillet over medium heat. Add next 5 ingredients and salt and pepper to taste. Simmer 10–12 minutes, stirring frequently, or until cream cheese is melted and mixture is hot. Set aside and keep warm. Arrange fish fillets in a baking dish. Season with tarragon, salt and pepper to taste. Bake 12–15 minutes or until fish flakes easily. Serve spinach sauce over fish fillets.

22. Tex-Mex Snapper (serves 4)

(329 mcg selenium)

    1 lb. canned crushed tomatoes

    4 scallions, chopped

    1/4 cup lime juice

    3 Tbs. canned green chilies, chopped (wear rubber gloves)

    1 clove garlic, peeled

4-6 ounce red snapper fillets

3 Tbs. cilantro or parsley, chopped

Combine all ingredients, except red snapper and cilantro, in a heavy non-stick skillet over medium high heat. Season with salt and pepper to taste. Mix thoroughly and bring to a boil. Reduce heat to medium low and simmer 10 minutes. Add red snapper to skillet. Cover and simmer 10 minutes or until fish flakes easily. Serve red snapper topped with tomato sauce and cilantro.

23. Grilled Halibut with Vegetables (serves 4)

(235 mcg selenium)

1 lb. small red potatoes, scrubbed

4 small zucchini

4 6-ounce skinless halibut or salmon steaks

1 large yellow bell pepper, cut in quarters and seeded

1 Tbs. olive oil

1 Tbs. plus 1 tsp. lemon pepper

1 lemon, cut into wedges

Place potatoes in a steamer basket over boiling water. Cover saucepan and steam potatoes 8–10 minutes. Remove from steamer basket and rinse under cold water. Set aside.

Prepare grill or broiler. Create zucchini fan by laying zucchini on a cutting surface. Start just beneath stem end of zucchini and cut 1/4 inch slices lengthwise. Brush fish, steamed potatoes and vegetables with oil. Season to taste with salt and lemon pepper. Place on grill. Grill fish 4–5 minutes. Turn and grill another 4–5 minutes or until fish is just cooked throughout. Turn vegetables occasionally until cooked throughout. Serve with lemon wedges.

24. Pasta with Scallops and Zucchini (serves 4)

(148 mcg selenium)

1 lb. fettuccine or other pasta

1 Tbs. unsalted butter

2 Tbs. olive oil

3/4 lb. onions, thinly sliced

4 cloves garlic, minced

3/4 lb. zucchini, cut into 1/2-inch cubes

1 tsp. dried basil

1 lb. scallops, rinsed and patted dry

1/4 cup grated Parmesan cheese

Cook fettuccine in boiling salted water until al dente. Drain pasta and return to saucepan. Toss with butter and keep warm. Heat oil in a heavy non-stick skillet over medium high heat. Sauté onions 2–3 minutes, stirring frequently. Add garlic and zucchini and continue to sauté another 4–5 minutes or until zucchini softens. Stir in basil, and salt and pepper to taste. Transfer vegetables to a platter and keep warm. Add scallops to skillet and sauté 3–4 minutes, stirring frequently, or until scallops are cooked throughout. Combine vegetables, scallops and pasta in a serving bowl. Serve with Parmesan.

25. Oven Barbecued Turkey Legs (serves 4)

(142 mcg selenium)

2 Tbs. plus 2 tsp. all purpose flour

1/4 tsp. chili powder

4 turkey legs

2 Tbs. plus 2 tsp. oil

1/2 cup barbecue sauce

1/3 cup water

3/4 tsp. chicken stock powder

Preheat oven to 325 degrees. Combine flour, chili powder and salt and pepper to taste in a heavy plastic bag. Add turkey legs one at a time and shake to coat. Heat oil in a heavy non-stick skillet over medium high heat. Sauté turkey legs 4–5 minutes, turning occasionally until browned all over. Arrange turkey in a roasting pan or baking dish. Combine remaining ingredients in a bowl. Mix thoroughly and spoon over turkey. Cover and bake 1 hour. Remove cover and bake 1 hour longer, basting often with sauce.

26. Herb Roasted Turkey (18 servings)

(136 mcg selenium)

> 1/2 cup plus 2 Tbs. unsalted butter, room temperature
>
> 2 tsp. rosemary, crumbled
>
> 2 tsp. thyme, crumbled
>
> 18 lbs. turkey(s), neck and giblets reserved for stock
>
> 1 large carrot, peeled and thinly sliced
>
> 3/4 lb. leeks, white and pale green parts only, chopped
>
> kitchen string, for trussing bird
>
> 3 cups chicken stock

Preheat oven to 325 degrees. Combine butter and half each of the rosemary and thyme in a bowl. Add a generous amount of salt and blend. Season inside of turkey cavity with salt and pepper to taste. Add carrots, leeks and remaining rosemary and thyme to inside cavity. Truss bird with string. Pat skin dry with paper towels.

Brush a portion of the herb butter mixture over turkey. Place turkey on a roasting rack inside a roasting pan. Roast turkey about 20 minutes per pound, basting with chicken stock and brushing with herbed butter every 25 minutes until a meat thermometer registers 175 degrees when inserted into thickest part of the thigh (or when thigh and leg fall easily away when pulled.) Remove turkey from oven. Let turkey stand 20 minutes before carving.

27. Spiced Grouper (serves 4)

(331 mcg selenium)

> 1 Tbs. olive oil
>
> 1/2 cup onions, chopped
>
> 1 clove garlic, minced
>
> 4 6-ounce grouper fillets
>
> 1/2 cup dry white wine or vegetable stock
>
> 1 Tbs. parsley, chopped
>
> 1/2 tsp. basil, or 2 tsp. fresh, chopped
>
> 1/2 tsp. cayenne pepper
>
> 1/8 tsp. hot red pepper sauce

1 cup tomatoes, peeled, seeded and chopped

1 lemon, cut into wedges

Heat oil in a heavy non-stick skillet over medium heat. Sauté onions and garlic 3–4 minutes or until onion softens. Add fish and sauté about 1 minute per side. Add remaining ingredients, except lemon. Season with salt and pepper to taste. Cover and simmer 7–8 minutes or until fish flakes easily. Serve fish with lemon wedges.

THINK ZINC

Zinc is extremely important for a healthy prostate. Meat—even red meat—is an important source of zinc. If you eat red meat, don't overdo it, and always trim as much fat as possible.

28. Lower Fat Oyster Artichoke Stew (serves 4)
(113.5 mg zinc)

3/4 lb. frozen artichoke hearts, thawed

2 cups chicken stock

1/2 cup scallions, trimmed and chopped

1/8 tsp. cayenne pepper

1/2 tsp. thyme

2-1/2 Tbs. all purpose flour

2 cups 2 percent milk

2 cups shucked oysters

1 Tbs. parsley, chopped

Combine first 5 ingredients and salt to taste in a heavy saucepan. Bring to a boil. Reduce heat to medium low and simmer 12 minutes, stirring occasionally.

Place flour in a bowl. Gradually stir in milk using a wire whisk or hand blender. Whisk until smooth. Stir into artichoke mixture and simmer 5–7 minutes, stirring frequently until stew begins to thicken. Add oysters and simmer 5 minutes or until oysters are just cooked throughout. Stir in parsley and serve.

29. Pressure Cooker Vegetable Beef Stew (serves 4)
(13.9 mg zinc)

> 2 Tbs. vegetable oil
> 1-1/2 lbs. beef chuck, cut into 1 inch cubes
> 2 Tbs. all purpose flour
> 1 leek, white and pale green parts cut into 1-inch pieces
> 1/2 cup beef stock
> 1/2 lb. tomato sauce
> 1 Tbs. Worcestershire sauce
> 1 tsp. dried basil
> 3 carrots, cut into 1/2-inch pieces
> 2 celery ribs, cut into 1/2-inch pieces
> 1 cup frozen tiny peas, thawed

Heat oil in a pressure cooker over medium high heat. Cook meat 6–8 minutes uncovered, turning frequently until well browned. Sprinkle with flour and stir 1 minute. Add leek and next 4 ingredients. Cover and bring to high pressure. Reduce heat and cook 10 minutes at stabilized pressure. Release pressure by running cold water over the cover. Add carrots and celery. Cover and return to high pressure. Reduce heat and cook 5 minutes. Release pressure and add peas. Cover tightly and let stand 5 minutes. Season with salt and pepper to taste.

30. Chili Con Carne (serves 4)
(13.7 mg zinc)

> 1 Tbs. vegetable oil
> 1-1/2 lbs. boneless beef for stew, cut into cubes
> 1 cup water
> 1 cup chicken stock
> 1/8 tsp. cayenne pepper
> 1 Tbs. ground cumin
> 2-1/2 Tbs. chili powder
> 1 tsp. salt
> 2 cloves garlic, minced

1-1/2 tsp. dried oregano leaves, crushed

1 Tbs. paprika

3 ounces tomato paste

1/2 tsp. sugar

Heat oil in a heavy non-reactive pot over medium high heat. Sauté cubed meat 4–5 minutes or until just browned. Add water and chicken stock and simmer over medium heat 30 minutes. Add remaining ingredients and simmer at least 2 hours over low heat, until meat is tender.

31. Herb Stuffed Chicken (serves 4)
(12.0 mg zinc)

2 Tbs. unsalted butter

1 Tbs. plus 1 tsp. olive oil, plus extra for brushing

1 onion, finely chopped

1 clove garlic, minced

1 cup fresh bread crumbs

6 slices pancetta or ham, chopped

1 cup fresh herbs, sage, parsley, rosemary, thyme

1/2 cup grated Parmesan cheese

1/4 cup pine nuts

3-1/2 lbs. whole chicken

Preheat oven 350 degrees. Heat butter and oil in a heavy saucepan over medium heat. Sauté onion and garlic 7–8 minutes or until onions are translucent. Stir in bread crumbs and pancetta, and continue to cook another 5 minutes. Remove from heat and stir in herbs, Parmesan and pine nuts. Set aside to cool. Fill cavity of bird with stuffing. Brush outside of bird with olive oil and season with salt and pepper to taste. Place in a baking pan and bake 1-1/4 to 1-1/2 hours or until chicken is cooked through.

32. Boiled Flanken (serves 4 to 6)
(11.4 mg zinc)

1 Tbs. vegetable oil

4 lbs. lean meaty flanken

2 cups onions, chopped

1 cup carrots, chopped

1/2 cup celery, chopped

4 celery leaves

4 sprigs parsley

6 whole black peppercorns

4 cups beef stock or water, or a combination of the two

Heat oil in a heavy pot over medium high heat. Brown flanken 2 minutes per side. Drain off fat. Add next 6 ingredients and salt to taste. Pour in the stock or water and bring to a boil. Reduce heat to low, cover and simmer gently 2 hours, or until the flanken is very tender and comes away from the bones. Strain broth and discard vegetables. Serve flanken with broth.

33. Slow Cooker Beef Burgundy (serves 4)

(10.7 mg zinc)

3 lbs. boneless beef for stew

11-ounce can cream of celery soup

11-ounce can cream of chicken soup

11-ounce can cream of mushroom soup

1 package dry onion soup mix

1/2 cup dry red wine

Combine all ingredients in a slow cooker on low heat. Cover and cook 8 hours. Serve over rice or noodles.

34. Chicken Dinner in a Pot (serves 4)

(10.6 mg zinc)

1 4-lb. roasting chicken, whole

2 cloves garlic, peeled

1/4 cup sun dried tomatoes (optional), chopped

3/4 lb. carrots, peeled and cut in half

1 large onion, peeled and cut into quarters

4 medium baking potatoes, scrubbed, cut in half

4 celery ribs, cut in half

Preheat oven to 375 degrees. Arrange chicken in the bottom of a large enameled covered casserole. Place garlic and sun dried tomatoes inside chicken cavity. Arrange remaining vegetables around chicken. Season with salt and pepper to taste. Cover pan and place in oven. Roast 1 hour. Remove vegetables from casserole. Set aside and keep warm. Baste chicken with juices and roast another 15 minutes, uncovered, or until chicken is brown. Remove from oven. Let chicken stand 5 minutes before carving. Serve chicken with vegetables.

35. Grilled Alaska Snow Crab with Salsa Verde (serves 4)
(9.8 mg zinc)

1 cucumber, peeled, seeded and coarsely chopped

1/4 cup green bell pepper, chopped

1 Tbs. green onions, sliced

1 Tbs. lemon juice

1-1/2 tsp. cilantro or parsley, chopped

1 clove garlic, chopped

1/2 jalapeno pepper, seeded and chopped

2 lbs. snow crab clusters, thawed if frozen

Prepare grill or broiler. Combine all ingredients, except snow crab, in a blender or food processor. Season with salt and pepper to taste and process until finely chopped. Transfer to a serving bowl. Place crab on a well-oiled grill or broiler pan 5 inches from coals or heat source. Grill or broil 5 minutes, or until cooked throughout. Serve with salsa verde as a dipping sauce.

36. Chicken with Tomatoes (serves 4)
(9.7 mg zinc)

1 Tbs. olive oil

4 lbs. chicken pieces

1/2 cup scallions, chopped

1-1/2 cups canned peeled tomatoes, chopped

1/2 cup chicken stock

1 tsp. oregano

Heat oil in a heavy non-stick skillet over medium high heat. Add chicken and sauté until browned on all sides. Transfer chicken to a platter and keep warm. Add scallions to skillet and sauté 3 minutes. Stir in tomatoes and stock and simmer 5 minutes or until tomatoes are tender. Return chicken to skillet. Add oregano, and salt and pepper to taste. Cover skillet. Reduce heat to low and simmer 20 minutes or until chicken is tender.

37. Black Bean Chili (serves 4)

(9.2 mg zinc)

2 tsp. unsalted butter

2/3 cup onion, finely chopped

1 lb. ground beef

2 lbs. black beans, drained

3/4 tsp. turmeric

1/4 tsp. cayenne pepper

1/4 tsp. pepper

4 scallions, sliced

2 cups plain low-fat yogurt

Melt butter in a heavy non-stick skillet over medium high heat. Sauté onion 5–7 minutes or until golden. Add ground round and sauté 3–4 minutes or until meat is lightly browned. Stir in black beans, turmeric, cayenne and pepper and sauté 3–4 minutes. Reduce heat to medium low. Stir in half the scallions. Sauté 2–3 minutes, stirring constantly until scallions are softened. Remove from heat, sprinkle with remaining scallions and serve with yogurt.

38. Caribbean Chicken Stew (serves 4)

(7.6 mg zinc)

> 3 Tbs. unsalted butter
>
> 3-1/2 lbs. frying chickens, cut into serving pieces
>
> 2 Tbs. fresh ginger, minced
>
> 1 fresh habanero, jalapeño or serrano pepper, seeded and minced
>
> 1 Tbs. curry powder
>
> 1 tsp. ground turmeric
>
> 1/4 tsp. ground allspice
>
> 1/4 tsp. ground cardamom
>
> 3 turnips, peeled and cut into 1/2-inch cubes
>
> 2 onions, cut into 1/2-inch wedges
>
> 3/4 cup chicken stock
>
> 2-2/3 cups water
>
> 1-1/3 cups long-grain rice

Melt half the butter in a large soup pot over medium high heat. Cook chicken 8–10 minutes, turning occasionally until browned on both sides. Sprinkle ginger and pepper over chicken. Stir in next 4 ingredients and salt to taste. Mix thoroughly. Add turnips, onions, and 1/2 cup stock. Cover and simmer gently 35–40 minutes, until chicken is cooked throughout. Add remaining stock if dish becomes too dry. Meanwhile, bring water to a boil in a saucepan over high heat.

Stir in rice and immediately reduce heat to low. Cover and simmer 20 minutes or until rice is tender and liquid is absorbed. Remove from heat and let stand 5 minutes, covered. Fluff with a fork before serving. Swirl remaining butter into sauce and serve with chicken over rice.

39. Lamb Steaks and Artichoke Hearts (serves 4)

(8.2 mg zinc)

> 2 Tbs. olive oil
>
> 1/4 cup onion, chopped
>
> 1/2 tsp. marjoram
>
> 3 cups canned crushed tomatoes

1-1/4 lbs. frozen artichoke hearts, thawed

4 6-ounce lamb shoulder steaks

2 cloves garlic, crushed

Heat oil in a heavy non-reactive saucepan over medium heat. Sauté onion 5 minutes, stirring occasionally, or until onion turns golden. Stir in next 3 ingredients. Simmer 15–20 minutes, stirring occasionally, or until sauce thickens. Remove from heat and keep warm. Turn on broiler. Rub steaks with garlic, and salt and pepper to taste. Arrange steaks on a broiler pan. Broil 4 inches from heat source 3–4 minutes per side or until well browned. Serve sauce over lamb steaks.

PROSTATE ENDS WITH "E"

Vitamin E is important for prostate health. Be careful, though; most foods containing vitamin E are also fatty. Here are some recipes that combine lots of E but are relatively low in fat.

40. Shrimp Louis Muffins (serves 4)

(34.8 mg vitamin E)

1 cup mayonnaise

1/2 cup chili sauce

1 Tbs. parsley, minced

1 tsp. lemon juice

1 tsp. prepared horseradish

1/2 tsp. onions, grated

4 English muffins, split, toasted and buttered (optional)

4 lettuce leaves

4 hard-boiled eggs, sliced

3/4 lb. cooked shrimp, thawed and drained

Combine first 6 ingredients in a bowl. Cover and chill. Top each muffin half with lettuce, egg slices, shrimp and dressing.

41. Curry Chicken Casserole (serves 4)

(34.6 mg vitamin E)

4 cups cooked chicken, chopped

1-1/4 lbs. broccoli florets or 2 bunches fresh, cooked and cut in halves

1-1/4 lbs. canned cream of chicken soup

1 cup mayonnaise

1 tsp. curry powder

1 tsp. lemon juice

1/2 cup shredded cheddar cheese

1/2 cup soft bread crumbs

1 Tbs. unsalted butter

Preheat oven to 325 degrees. Combine chicken and broccoli in a casserole. Combine next 4 ingredients and salt and pepper to taste in a bowl. Pour over chicken. Top with cheese. Combine bread crumbs with melted butter and sprinkle over top. Bake uncovered 35 minutes.

42. Tortellini Salad with Shrimp (serves 4)

(3.5 mg vitamin E)

9 ounces spinach tortellini

2 small zucchini, sliced

2 small tomatoes, cut into wedges

7 ounces marinated artichoke hearts, drained and quartered

1/4 cup sliced ripe olives, drained

1 lb. cooked shrimp, thawed and drained

1/2 cup fresh basil, chopped, or 1 Tbs. dried

2 Tbs. grated Parmesan cheese

2/3 cup Italian dressing

Cook tortellini in a large pan of boiling water 10 minutes, or until al dente. Drain and transfer to a large bowl. Combine remaining ingredients with tortellini and toss gently.

43. Chicken a la Popeye (serves 4)

(33.8 mg vitamin E)

> 10 ounces frozen chopped spinach, thawed, drained, excess moisture squeezed out
>
> 4 boneless skinless chicken breast halves
>
> 1 cup mayonnaise
>
> 11 ounces canned cream of chicken soup
>
> 1-1/2 tsp. curry powder
>
> 1/2 cup shredded cheddar cheese
>
> 1/2 cup cornflake crumbs
>
> 2 Tbs. parsley

Preheat oven to 350 degrees. Spray a casserole with non-stick cooking spray. Press spinach in bottom of casserole in an even layer. Place chicken on top. Combine next 3 ingredients in a bowl and spread evenly over chicken. Cover top with cheese. Sprinkle corn flake crumbs over top, then parsley. Bake 35–40 minutes, uncovered.

44. Lemon Herb Chicken (serves 4)

(32.7 mg vitamin E)

> 1 cup mayonnaise type salad dressing
>
> 1/4 cup lemon juice
>
> 2 Tbs. dry white wine or water
>
> 1 Tbs. dried oregano
>
> 1 Tbs. garlic powder
>
> 3-1/2 lbs. frying chickens, skin removed, cut up

Combine all ingredients, except chicken, in a bowl. Place chicken in a shallow dish. Pour salad dressing mixture over. Cover and marinate in refrigerator at least 20 minutes. Prepare grill (medium coals). Remove chicken from marinade, reserving marinade. Arrange on grill over coals. Cover and cook 20 minutes, turning after 10 minutes. Brush with marinade. Continue grilling 15–20 minutes or until cooked through, turning occasionally.

45. Chef's Salad (serves 4)

(30.4 mg vitamin E)

> 1 head iceberg lettuce, 8 outer leaves reserved, remainder torn into
>   bite-size pieces
>
> 12 radishes, trimmed and sliced
>
> 2 stalks celery, cut into thin 2-inch strips
>
> 1-1/2 cups French dressing, or Creamy French, Russian
>   or Thousand Island Salad Dressing
>
> 4 tomatoes, cut into 6 wedges each
>
> 3/4 cup Swiss cheese, cut into thin strips
>
> 1 cup cooked turkey breast, or cooked chicken, cut into thin strips
>
> 1 cup cooked ham, cut into thin strips
>
> 4 hard-boiled eggs, quartered

Arrange outer lettuce leaves around outside edges of a salad bowl.
Add remaining lettuce, radishes, celery and half the dressing. Toss.
Arrange tomato wedges around inside edges of large lettuce leaves. Com-
bine cheese, turkey and ham and add to bowl. Arrange hard boiled egg
quarters between tomato wedges. Season with salt and pepper to taste.
Top with remaining salad dressing before serving.

46. Balsamic Grilled Chicken Salad (serves 4)

(22.2 mg vitamin E)

> 2/3 cup mayonnaise
>
> 2 Tbs. balsamic vinegar
>
> 1 Tbs. plus 1 tsp. fresh lemon juice
>
> 3/4 tsp. Worcestershire sauce
>
> 1 Tbs. plus 1 tsp. extra virgin olive oil
>
> 1 clove garlic, minced
>
> 4 boneless skinless chicken breast halves
>
> 11 ounces packaged salad

Combine first 6 ingredients and salt and pepper to taste in a bowl.
Whisk until smooth. Cover and chill. Prepare grill or broiler. Season

chicken with salt and pepper to taste. Grill or broil 4–5 minutes per side, until just cooked throughout. Cut diagonally across the grain into 1/4 inch slices. Divide lettuce between individual serving plates. Pour dressing over. Top with sliced chicken breasts.

47. Simple Chicken Italiano (serves 4)

(20.4 mg vitamin E)

> 1/2 lb. spaghetti
> 3/4 lb. boneless chicken breast halves, cut into thin strips
> 3/4 cup Italian dressing
> 1 lb. frozen mixed vegetables
> 1/4 cup grated Parmesan cheese

Cook pasta in a large pan of boiling water 10 minutes, or until al dente. Drain and keep warm. Heat a heavy non-stick skillet over medium high heat. Stir-fry chicken and 1/4 cup dressing 4 minutes, or until no longer pink. Add vegetables.

Cover pan, reduce heat to low and simmer 7–9 minutes, or until vegetables are crisp-tender, stirring frequently. Stir in remaining dressing and cook 3 minutes, or until thoroughly heated. Serve over hot spaghetti and sprinkle with cheese.

48. Fruit Medley (serves 4)

(17.9 mg of vitamin E)

> 1 honeydew melon, cut into bite-size chunks
> 1 papaya, halved, cut into bite-size chunks
> 1 pear, peeled, cored, and cut into bite-size chunks
> 1 cup blueberries, picked over
> 1 avocado, peeled, pitted and mashed
> 2 Tbs. lemon juice
> 1/2 cup orange juice
> 2 Tbs. honey
> 1/2 cup mayonnaise

Combine melon, papaya, pear and blueberries in a salad bowl. Combine remaining ingredients in a blender or food processor and process until smooth. Pour dressing over fruit and toss.

49. Creamy Cauliflower Lettuce Salad (serves 4)

(17.1 mg vitamin E)

> 1/4 cup plus 2 Tbs. mayonnaise type salad dressing
>
> 1/4 cup Ranch dressing
>
> 2 Tbs. grated Parmesan cheese
>
> 2 Tbs. sugar
>
> 2 Tbs. red onion, finely chopped
>
> 1/4 cup bottled real bacon pieces
>
> 2 cups cauliflower florets
>
> 3 cups Romaine lettuce, torn

Combine first 4 ingredients in a bowl. Add remaining ingredients and mix lightly.

50. Eggplant Turkey Rolls (serves 4)

(15.3 mg vitamin E)

> 1-1/2 lbs. eggplant, cut lengthwise into 1/2-inch slices
>
> 2 cups olive oil
>
> 2 Tbs. garlic, minced
>
> 1/2 tsp. dried basil
>
> 1/2 tsp. dried oregano
>
> 3/4 lb. cooked turkey breast or smoked turkey, thinly sliced
>
> 1-1/2 cups spaghetti sauce
>
> 6 ounces Monterey Jack cheese, sliced

Arrange eggplant slices in a single layer on a lightly oiled, shallow baking pan. Brush with half the olive oil. Sprinkle with half the garlic and herbs. Broil 2 inches from heat source 2–3 minutes until golden. Turn slices, brush with remaining oil and sprinkle with remaining garlic and herbs. Broil another 2–3 minutes until tender. Preheat oven to 375 degrees. Roll eggplant slices around turkey. Arrange turkey rolls in a lightly oiled baking dish. Cover with spaghetti sauce and sprinkle with cheese. Bake uncovered 25–30 minutes or until hot and bubbly.

51. Portabella Burgers (serves 4)

(14.3 mg vitamin E)

> 1/2 cup Italian dressing
>
> 4 portabella mushrooms, stemmed, tops cleaned
>
> 1/2 cup pesto sauce
>
> 4 Kaiser rolls, sliced in half
>
> 1/2 cup bottled roasted red bell peppers, drained
>
> 4 slices provolone cheese

Combine mushrooms and Italian dressing in a bowl. Cover and marinate 2 hours. Prepare grill or turn on broiler. Season mushrooms with salt and pepper to taste. Grill or broil mushrooms about 1-1/2 minutes per side. Spread 1 Tbs. pesto over cut side of rolls. Top with mushrooms. Top with a slice of cheese, roasted peppers and remaining half roll.

52. Nut Loaf with Cheese Sauce (serves 4)

(10.9 mg vitamin E)

> 1-1/3 cups cracked wheat or brown rice
>
> 2-1/2 cups water
>
> 4 cups almonds
>
> 3/4 cup vegetable stock or water
>
> 3/4 cup onion, chopped
>
> 2 large carrots, grated
>
> 2 celery ribs, finely chopped
>
> 1/4 cup parsley, minced
>
> 3/4 cup unsalted butter
>
> 1/4 cup plus 3 Tbs. all purpose flour

2 tsp. ground coriander

2 cups 2 percent milk

2 cups half and half

1 cup Gruyere cheese, grated

Preheat oven to 350 degrees. Combine cracked wheat and water in a heavy saucepan. Bring to a boil over high heat. Reduce heat to low. Cover saucepan and simmer 30–40 minutes or until grain is tender and water is absorbed. Remove from heat and set aside.

Place almonds in a baking pan. Toast in oven 7–8 minutes, shaking pan occasionally, or until almonds just begin to turn brown. Remove from heat and let cool. Transfer almonds to a food processor or blender and chop. Set aside.

Combine stock, onion, carrots, celery and parsley in a heavy non-stick skillet over medium high heat. Sauté about 5 minutes, or until liquid is evaporated and vegetables are tender. Remove from heat and set aside.

Combine wheat, almonds and vegetable mixture in a bowl and mix thoroughly. Melt half the butter in a heavy saucepan over medium heat. Add 3 Tbs. flour and coriander and whisk constantly 1–2 minutes or until mixture just begins to turn golden. Very gradually whisk in milk. Simmer, whisking constantly 3–4 minutes or until mixture is thickened. (Do not boil.) Remove from heat and season with salt to taste.

Stir into wheat-vegetable mixture and spread evenly in a deep buttered baking dish. Bake 40–50 minutes until mixture is golden and set. Serve with mushroom gravy. Melt remaining butter in a small saucepan over medium heat. When bubbly, stir in remaining flour to combine. Gradually stir in half and half. Cook 4–5 minutes, stirring constantly until sauce thickens. Remove from heat. Stir in cheese and salt and pepper to taste until cheese is melted. At 15 minutes prior to end of baking nut loaf, pour cheese sauce over nut loaf.

JOY OF SOY

53. Soy Chili (serves 4)

Crave chili? Instead of using ground beef, use soy-based meat substitutes. They usually come already browned and crumbled and look like ground beef.

You need at least 8 essential amino acids every day from good high quality protein. This chili, along with a slice of corn bread or other bread, will supply all of these essential amino acids.

COMBINE;

1 12-oz. package of soy burgers

1 can of pinto beans

1 can of fat-free refried beans

1 can of tomatoes

1 8-oz. can of tomato sauce

1 medium onion, chopped

1 medium bell pepper, chopped

4 oz. mushrooms, chopped

Pinch of chili powder, splash of tabasco sauce, 1 Tbs. of vinegar, a tsp. lemon juice, salt and beef bouillon to taste.

Mix ingredients in a pot and cook for about 30 minutes until peppers, onions and mushrooms are cooked.

54. Pad Thai (serves 4 to 6)

This authentic Thai recipe can be made with meat or tofu. This is not something you can just throw together. You'll need a wok and adequate time for preparation.

1 pound tofu, pork, beef or chicken, sliced thin, bite sized, or shrimp, shelled and deveined

1 16-oz. package chantaboon (or jantaboon) rice sticks, medium thread

1 tablespoon vegetable oil

6 eggs beaten

1/4 cup vegetable oil

8 garlic cloves

1/4 cup white vinegar

1/4 cup sugar

1 cup sliced salted radish (chai Po) (Usually packaged in see-through containers. They are slightly orange in color)

1/4 cup fish sauce (nam pla)

1 cup coarse ground roasted peanuts

2 Tbs. chili powder or paprika

2 cups bean sprouts

1 cup sliced green onion

1 cup sliced cilantro

1 lime

NOTE: If you use tofu, press the tofu between three sheets of towel paper on the top and the bottom. Put a plate on top and a two pound weight on top of the plate. Wait 20 minutes.

Soak rice sticks in lukewarm water for 1 hour, drain and set aside. Set wok over high heat, for 1 minute. Heat wok with 1 tablespoon of oil until sizzling hot and coat sides of wok evenly. Add eggs and fry, until eggs set, turn over and fry, until light brown on both sides. Remove from wok and slice thin, bite size. Set aside.

Heat 1/4 cup of oil in wok until sizzling hot. Add garlic and cook until fragrant. Add meat, stir and cook, until meat or tofu is done, about 1 to 2 minutes. Add rice sticks and vinegar, cook until rice sticks soften. Add eggs, and the next 5 ingredients; stir to blend. Remove to serving plate. Serve bean sprouts cold on the side. Garnish with green onion and cilantro. Serve with slices of fresh lime. Squeeze lime on pad thai.

55. Scrambled Tofu (serves 4)

1 large sweet onion

1 block of tofu

1 large carrot

1 stalk of celery

Salt to taste

Sauté the finely chopped onion in a little sesame oil, until translucent. Separately, mash up the tofu, and add the shredded carrot and diced celery.

There is no need to add water, as the tofu has a watery texture.

Put the mixture in with the onions, and cook for 5–10 minutes, with sea salt to taste. If you want it to look like scrambled eggs, add a little yellow spice.

56. Japanese Tofu (Yakko-tofu; Cold poached bean curd) (serves 4)

1 lb. silky/soft tofu

2 by 4 inch piece "Kombu" (flat kelp seaweed)

1 scallion, finely chopped, both white & green

and/or 1-1/2 tsp. grated lime peel

and/or 2 Tbs. grated ginger

and/or 1 tsp. "Wasabi" (green horseradish)

and/or 4 Tbs. dried "Bonito" flakes

Soy sauce

Rinse tofu and cut each bar into quarters. Put kelp into a saucepan and add water to a depth that will cover the tofu (when added). Bring to a boil over moderate heat, removing the seaweed just before the water boils. Reduce heat to low, add the tofu and poach for 4 minutes, being careful not to let the water boil. Drain and chill the tofu quickly by putting it into a bowl of cold water for about 5 minutes. Drain and put into a bowl with water to cover and about 6 ice cubes. Surround the bowl with the garnishes in small dishes. Pour a little soy sauce into each of 4 bowls. To eat, add the garnishes to the soy sauce and dip the pieces of tofu into the sauce.

NOTE: This a traditional Japanese tofu recipe and not for those new to tofu. Still, it's easy to prepare and low-fat.

57. Two Bean Tofu Chili (serves 4 to 6)

1-1/2 cups dried black beans, rinsed and sorted.

19-oz. package of cotton tofu

5-1/2 oz.-can of tomato sauce

2 Tbs. soy sauce

2 Tbs. Dijon mustard

3 cloves garlic, chopped

2 tsp. dried oregano

1/4 cup dry red wine

2 tsp. dried basil

1/2 cup soybean oil

1 cup chopped onion

3 28-oz. cans Italian plum tomatoes, undrained

1/4 cup chili powder

1-1/2 Tbs. ground cumin

14-oz. can red kidney beans

1/2 cup chopped Italian parsley

1/4 cup chopped coriander

Salt and pepper to taste

Soak the black beans overnight. Freeze, thaw and squeeze out the tofu, then tear into pieces. In a mixing bowl, whisk together half the tomato paste, the soy sauce, mustard, garlic, oregano, red wine and basil. Add the tofu and stir to coat. In a large pot sauté the tofu mixture in half of the soybean oil until all the liquid is absorbed and the tofu has browned. Remove from the heat. In a small saucepan sauté the onion in the remaining soybean oil until transparent. Add to the tofu mixture. Also add the tomatoes, the rest of the tomato paste, the chili powder, cumin, salt and pepper and black beans. Simmer on low heat for 30 to 40 minutes until the black beans are tender. Add the red kidney beans and cook 10 more minutes. Add parsley and coriander and cook for 5 more minutes. Check seasoning. Serve with corn muffins.

(SOURCE: The Ontario Soybean Marketing board via the London Regional Cancer Center.)

(NOTE: Freezing and thawing tofu makes it chewier and sponge-like, and possible to grate or crumble.)

58. Meatless Loaf (serves 4 to 6)

1/2 cup textured vegetable protein (TVP) (buy in bulk at health food store)

1/2 cup hot broth of choice

6 oz. tofu, mashed

3 slices whole wheat bread, torn up into chunks

5 onions, 2 chopped and 3 sliced for top

2 Tbs. chopped parsley

3/4 cup tomato juice (or watered down catsup)

3 chopped garlic cloves

1/4 tsp. thyme

2 eggs (or egg substitute)

1 Tbs. Dijon mustard

Worcestershire sauce

1/2 carrot, shredded

salt and pepper

3 Tbs. catsup

1 cup diced tomatoes

2 Tbs. olive oil

Preheat oven to 350 degrees. Combine TVP with broth and tofu; add bread, chopped onions, parsley, half the tomato juice, garlic, thyme, eggs, mustard, Worcestershire sauce, carrot, and salt and pepper. Form into a soft loaf and plop in baking pan. Top with catsup, tomatoes, sliced onions, and rest of tomato juice. Drizzle with oil.

Bake 1–1.5 hours or until firm, tomato mixture is thick, and onions are caramelized and browned. Add stock or water if the onions threaten to burn.

59. Curries Tofu Scramble (serves 8)

1 pound firm-style tofu

1 cup water

2 Tbs. curry powder

2 Tbs. (or less) honey

1 tsp. ground turmeric

1/2 tsp. salt

2 Tbs. canola oil

1 tsp. cumin seeds

Garlic, 2 cloves minced

1 medium finely chopped onion

1/2 cup finely chopped red bell pepper

1/2 pound sliced mushrooms

1 tsp. dried oregano

Crumble tofu into a large dry skillet. Whisk one cup of water with curry, honey, turmeric, and salt, then stir this mixture into the skillet. Bring to a simmer over high heat. When bubbling, reduce heat to medium and cook, stirring occasionally, until liquid has evaporated and tofu consistency is as you like it (moist and soft or dry and crumbly). This will take 15–20 minutes.

While you wait, heat canola oil in a skillet over medium heat. Sauté cumin seeds, garlic, onion, and bell pepper for about 5 minutes, then stir in mushrooms and oregano and cook 5 minutes longer, until mushrooms have released their liquid and are tender. Combine mushroom mixture with tofu mixture and serve hot. Serve with toast or herbed new potatoes.

60. Special Spaghetti (serves 6 to 8)

1/2 pound spaghetti

2 Tbs. soy oil

1/3 cup parmesan cheese

2 eggs, beaten

1 10.5-oz. package firm silken tofu, crumbled

1/2 cup chopped onion

1 clove garlic, minced

1/2 cup chopped green bell pepper

1 16-oz. can spiced chopped tomatoes

1 6-oz. can tomato paste

1 tsp. dried oregano

1 tsp. dried basil

1 cup low-fat cottage cheese

1/2 cup shredded mozzarella cheese

Prepare spaghetti according to package directions and drain. Add soy oil. Combine Parmesan cheese and eggs and add to spaghetti. Lightly spray 8 1/2 × 11 1/2-inch glass baking dish with non-stick spray. Place one half of spaghetti mixture in dish. Reserve remaining spaghetti.

In large skillet, combine tofu, onion and green pepper and then sauté until vegetables are tender. Drain off excess moisture and stir in tomatoes, tomato paste and herbs. Spread cottage cheese over spaghetti. Top with tofu/tomato mixture. Place remaining spaghetti over tofu and sprinkle with shredded cheese. Bake in a 350 degree oven for 45 minutes.

61. RED AND WHITE CHILI (serves 8 to 10)

1/2 pound (3-1/2 cups) dried edible soybeans, soaked overnight

1 cup chopped carrots

1/3 cup each red, green and yellow bell peppers

1 cup chopped onions

1 cup chopped celery

3 cloves garlic, minced

2 16-oz. cans chili-style diced tomatoes

1 16-oz. can dark red kidney beans, drained

2 Tbs. chili con carne seasoning

2 Tbs. seasoned pepper

1 tsp. dried oregano

Toppings:

low-fat shredded cheese

fresh chopped cilantro

fresh chopped onions

Place soy beans in 4–6 cups water and allow to soak overnight. Remove and drain. Bring soybeans and 4 cups water to boil and simmer for 1 hour. Drain. Place soybeans and all other ingredients in crock pot. Stir to blend seasonings. Set on low and cook 8–10 hours. Add toppings. (optional).

MICROWAVE VERSION: Place water and soaked beans in large microwave dish.

Microwave on HIGH for 20 minutes. Drain. Place beans and all other ingredients in dish. Stir to mix. Microwave on HIGH for 30 minutes, medium-high for 15 minutes and medium-low for 20 minutes. Allow to stand 15 minutes.

62. Crispy Chicken Stir-Fry (makes 4 to 6 servings)

3/4 pound boned, skinless chicken breast, cut in strips

3 Tbs. low-sodium soy sauce

1 cup each: sliced onion, green and sweet red peppers, fresh mushrooms

1 clove garlic, minced

1 tsp. soy oil

1/2 cup sliced celery

1 tbs. cornstarch

1/2 cup low-sodium chicken broth

2 Tbs. dry white wine

Cooked rice

Combine chicken and soy sauce. Set aside 15 minutes to marinate. In large skillet or wok, heat oil and garlic. Add vegetables and stir-fry until tender crisp; remove from pan. Add soy sauce and chicken and stir-fry for about 2 minutes or until done. Combine cornstarch, chicken broth and wine. Return vegetables to wok or skillet and add broth mixture. Cook and stir until thickened. Serve with rice.

63. Linguine with Tofu and Pesto (serves 4)

1 pound Island Spring Traditional firm tofu—mashed

2 Tbs. pesto

2 tsp. garlic, minced

1 tsp. chili powder

2 Tbs. olive oil

Salt and pepper to taste

Cook pasta according to directions. Heat and mix all ingredients together, until smooth. Mix the tofu mixture with pasta.

64. Tofu Lasagna (serves 6)

12 lasagna noodles, uncooked

2 10-oz. pkgs frozen chopped spinach, thawed

1/2 lb. firm tofu

1 cup low-fat cottage cheese

2 tsp. olive oil

1 Tbs. pesto

4 cups spaghetti sauce

Black pepper (to taste)

1-1/2 cups mozzarella cheese, shredded

1/4 cup Parmesan cheese, grated

Cook pasta according to package direction. Drain carefully and set aside in a single layer on paper towels. Squeeze spinach as dry as possible; set aside. In a medium mixing bowl, crumble tofu and blend it with cottage cheese and pesto until smooth and creamy.

To assemble lasagna: ladle about 2 Tbs. sauce into bottom of an 11 × 8 × 3-inch baking dish. Arrange 6 noodles to cover the bottom of the dish. Top with spinach, tofu mixture, shredded mozzarella and half the remaining sauce in that order. Cover with remaining 6 noodles, then top with remaining sauce. Sprinkle with Parmesan cheese. Cover with foil. Bake in a preheated 350 degree oven 40 minutes. Remove foil. Continue baking 15–20 minutes, or until bubbling and crusty on top. Remove from oven and let cool 10 minutes before cutting into squares to serve.

65. Tofu Pot Stickers (serves 4 to 6)

Filling:

5 dried Shitaki mushrooms, soaked in warm water. Drain. Chop mushroom cap.

4 Tbs. water chestnuts, minced

1/2 pound firm tofu, crumbled

1 tsp. sesame oil

2 green onions, finely chopped

1 Tbs. garlic, finely minced

1 cup Nappa cabbage, finely chopped

1 Tbs. soy sauce

1 Tbs. dry sherry

1 tsp. arrowroot powder or cornstarch

1 tsp. ginger root, minced

1/2 tsp. honey (optional)

1/2 tsp. salt

2 dozen ready-made pot sticker wrappers

23 Tbs. oil

Dipping Sauce:

> 2 Tbs. soy sauce
> 1 Tbs. rice vinegar
> Drop chili oil (optional)
> Shredded ginger root

Mix all filling ingredients in a bowl, set aside. Place 1 Tbs. of filling in the center of each circle. Lightly moisten edges of circle with water. Fold circle in half over filling to form a semi-circle. Starting at one end, pinch curved edges together, pressing the edges to seal securely. Place filled wrapper in a platter. Heat a flat wide skillet over medium high heat until hot. Add 1 Tbs. oil, set 1/2 the pot sticker in frying pan. Cook 2–3 minutes or until golden brown. Pour in 1/4 cup of water, cover and steam cook until liquid has completely evaporated, swirling pan occasionally. Serve dipping sauce on side.

66. Tempeh, Tempeh (serves 4)

> 4 medium green red or yellow bell peppers
> 8 oz. tempeh, cubed
> 4 tsp. soy sauce
> 1-1/2 cup water
> 1 tsp. basil
> 2 cloves garlic, minced
> 2–3 Tbs. bread crumbs
> 3–4 tsp. olive oil

Preheat oven to 325 degrees F. Parboil peppers 5 minutes in gently boiling water. Remove peppers and run under cold water to stop cooking. Core peppers; toss out stems, seeds and membranes.

While peppers cook, combine tempeh, soy sauce, and water in a small pot. Bring to a boil, cover and simmer 20 minutes. Drain. Stir in basil and garlic, mashing tempeh with a fork.

Loosely fill peppers with tempeh mixture. Place upright in a lightly oiled baking dish. Sprinkle with bread crumbs and drizzle with oil. Bake 20 minutes, then broil for 5 minutes, until top is brown.

(SOURCE: Indiana Soybean Development Council.)

67. Sautéed Tempeh with Roasted Salsa (serves 4)

4 3-inch squares of tempeh

1/4 cup lemon juice

1 tsp. ground cumin

2 Tbs. chili powder

*2 chipotle chilies

1 red or orange bell pepper

1 large Poblano chili

4 large Roma tomatoes

8 cloves garlic, skins left on

1/4 cup diced red onion

1/4 cup juice of Mexican limones (or regular limes)

1 Tbs. orange juice

1 small ripe mango, diced

1/4 cup chopped fresh cilantro

Salt

Coat tempeh with lemon juice in a shallow container. Combine cumin and chili powder, rub into tempeh cutlets and return them to lemon juice. Set aside.

In a pan, quickly heat chipotles until softened and aromatic. Place in a bowl, cover with boiling water and soak for 20 minutes. Roast bell pepper and poblano over low flames in a pan on stovetop, turning as the skin blisters. Watch that the flesh doesn't burn through. When the skins are uniformly charred, enclose peppers in a plastic or paper bag to steam. This will help loosen the skins and cook peppers a bit more. When peppers are cool enough to handle, peel the skins off. Don't rinse under running water, or you'll wash away the roasted flavor. If your fingers become sticky and covered with ash, rinse them as necessary.

Stem, seed and dice peppers. Set aside in a bowl. Roast tomatoes and garlic in pan over medium heat. Turn garlic often. Remove when soft. Discard burned garlic. Peel garlic and put in a food processor or blender. The tomatoes should be allowed to char on all sides. Add them to the processor with the garlic.

When chipotles are soft, remove stems. For less heat, remove seeds and ribs as well. Blend these with garlic and tomatoes to desired consistency. Add to roasted pepper and chili with remaining ingredients.

Gently remove tempeh pieces from lemon marinade. Sauté or grill over medium heat until warmed through. Mix remaining marinade into salsa, taste and adjust seasonings. Serve tempeh topped with salsa. Salt to taste.

* If using canned chipotles, skip soaking step and use 1 Tbs. sauce in marinade.

NOTE: Instead of tempeh, you may want to substitute sea bass, shrimp or chicken breast.

68. Chicken Kyoto (serves 4)

2 Tbs. soy sauce

2 Tbs. water

1 Tbs. cornstarch

1 tsp. sugar or honey

1 tsp. instant chicken bouillon granules

1 Tbs. vegetable oil

2 whole boneless chicken breasts, skinned and cut into strips

1/2 cup onion, chopped

3 cups fresh broccoli florets

1 cup fresh mushrooms, sliced

10 oz. firm tofu, drained and cubed

1 clove garlic, minced

Hot cooked rice

Soy sauce

Combine soy sauce, water, cornstarch, sugar, and bouillon granules. Set aside. Preheat a 10-inch browning skillet in oven 5 minutes. Add oil, then add chicken strips, onion and broccoli. Stir-fry until sizzling stops, then cover and microwave 3 to 5 minutes on high power, or until chicken is no longer pink, stirring every 2 minutes. Gently fold in mushrooms, tofu and garlic. Pour soy sauce mixture over all, cover, and microwave 2 to 4 minutes longer, or until chicken is cooked and vegetables are tender, stirring every minute.

Let stand, covered, minutes before serving. Serve over hot cooked rice and pass around additional soy sauce, if desired.

69. Tofu-Mex Scramble (serves 3 to 4)

1 Tbs. butter or margarine

1/3 cup onion, chopped

10 oz. firm tofu

2 eggs or egg substitute

1/4 tsp. salt

1/8 tsp. pepper

1 cup mild cheddar cheese, shredded

4 oz. canned, chopped, drained, mild green Ortega chilies

1 Tbs. parmesan cheese, grated

Paprika

Combine butter and onion in 9-inch-round glass pie plate. Microwave, uncovered on high power for 2 to 3 minutes, stirring every minute, or until onion is translucent. In medium mixing bowl combine tofu, eggs, salt and pepper. Beat with wire whisk until well blended. Stir in shredded cheese and chopped chili peppers. Turn mixture into pie plate over sautéed onions. Microwave, uncovered, two minutes. Stir, rotate dish 1/4 turn, and microwave 3 minutes longer. Sprinkle with grated Parmesan cheese and dust lightly with paprika; rotate dish 1/4 turn. Microwave, uncovered, 3 to 5 minutes longer, or until mixture is set. Cover with plate and let stand 3 minutes before serving.

70. Chicken Fillets with Tofu Curry Stuffing (serves 4)

1-1/4 cup firm tofu, well pressed

4 breast fillets of chicken, about 7 oz.

1/3 cup parsley, minced

1/3 cup celery, minced

1/3 cup onion, minced

1 egg or egg substitute

1 tsp. salt

1 pinch of pepper

1 Tbs. curry powder

1/2 cup all-purpose flour

1 cup bread crumbs

Salad oil for deep frying

With a sharp knife cut a slit into chicken fillets to make pouches. Set aside. Crumble tofu in a bowl. Add parsley, celery, onion, 1/3 cup bread crumbs and egg. Season with salt, pepper and curry. Mix thoroughly. Fill the chicken pouches with the stuffing, leaving 1/2 inch of the edge free. Press the stuffed pouch lightly between your hands to close the edge and to distribute the stuffing evenly. Coat the stuffed chicken first with flour, then dip in beaten egg. Then roll in bread crumbs. Heat oil in a deep skillet to cover the chicken pieces and fry 10 minutes over medium heat or until golden and crisp.

71. Vegetable Chili (serves 6 to 8)

1 14-oz. can pinto beans, rinsed and drained

1 14-z. can kidney beans, rinsed and drained

1 lb. firm tofu—frozen and thawed, diced

1 12-oz. can tomato paste

1 28-oz. can crushed tomatoes

4 to 6 tomatoes, quartered or chopped

2 onions, chopped

1 large zucchini, chopped

1 yellow squash, chopped

1 green pepper, chopped

1/2 lb. mushrooms, chopped (optional)

2 Tbs. or more chili powder

1 to 2 tsp. cumin

1 tsp. oregano

1 tsp. crushed red pepper

1 tsp. garlic powder

Mix beans, tomato paste, sauce, tomatoes and spices together in a large pan. Bring to a boil and simmer. Add tofu and remaining vegetables and simmer to desired tenderness. Add water as desired.

72. Tofu Treasure Bags (serves 4)

  1 lb. firm tofu, cut in 8 pieces

  1-1/2 cup mozzarella cheese, grated

  2 tsp. garlic, minced

  2 tsp. dried sweet basil

  Oil for frying tofu

Fry tofu until crusty; slit in middle for pouch. Mix cheese and spices in bag; stuff pouches. Bake at 350 degrees for 10 minutes or until cheese melts.

73. Tofu with Peas and Mushrooms (4 servings)

  1 Tbs. butter or margarine

  1 cup fresh mushrooms, sliced

  1/3 cup onion, chopped

  1 cup frozen peas

  10 oz. firm tofu, drained and cubed

  1/8 tsp. pepper

  Soy sauce, to taste

In 1-1/2 quart microwave-safe casserole combine butter, mushrooms and onion. Cover and microwave 2 to 3 minutes, stirring halfway through cooking time, until vegetables are soft. Stir in peas, cover, and microwave 1 minute longer. Stir. Arrange cubed tofu around outside of dish, pushing vegetables toward center. Sprinkle with pepper and soy sauce to taste. Replace cover and microwave 2 to 4 minutes longer, or until peas are cooked and tofu is heated through. Let stand, covered, 2 minutes before serving.

74. Risotto Verde

  2 Cups cooked Arborio rice (substitute brown rice if you like)

  1 box frozen, chopped spinach OR 1 bunch fresh Swiss chard, rinsed and chopped; and cooked in its own water until barely cooked

Blend together:

  1/2 to 1 pound tofu (soft or firm)

  2 Tbs. oil

> 2 Tbs. juice from cooking the spinach or chard
>
> 1.5 tsp. salt
>
> 1 tsp. Tabasco

Sauté over moderately high heat:

> 1 medium onion, finely chopped
>
> 2–4 large cloves garlic, minced
>
> 2 cups coarsely sliced fresh mushrooms (optional)
>
> 1 cup red bell pepper, coarsely diced (optional)
>
> 2 Tbs. oil

Garnish:

> Small amount freshly grated Parmesan cheese

Remove from heat and fold in the rice, spinach/chard, and tofu mixture. Add a generous grinding of fresh black pepper and 1/8 tsp. nutmeg. Spray a 1.5-quart baking dish with low-fat cooking spray and bake the risotto at 325 degrees for 30 minutes without a lid.

NOTE: To cook the chard, leave a lot of the water in the chard after you rinse it. Put it in a covered pan and cook over moderately high heat for a few minutes. Watch carefully. Add a small bit of water if necessary. Don't overcook. Remove from heat while still bright green and only barely done.

75. Beef & Tofu Enchiladas (serves 8)

> 8 8-inch soft flour tortillas
>
> 1/2 cup chopped onion
>
> *1 lb. ground beef, browned and drained
>
> 1 4-oz. can chopped green chilies
>
> 1 clove garlic, minced
>
> 1 tsp. dried cilantro
>
> 1 10.5-ounce package firm tofu, mashed
>
> 1/2 tsp. cumin seed
>
> 2 cups diced tomato, drained
>
> 2 cups thick tomato salsa
>
> 1 cup shredded cheddar cheese

Preheat oven to 350 degrees. Lightly spray a 9 × 13-inch baking dish with low-fat non-stick spray. In bowl, combine all ingredients except tortillas, tomato salsa and cheese. Place 1/2 cup of mixture in center of each tortilla and roll. Place in baking dish, seam side down. Pour salsa over enchiladas. Sprinkle with shredded cheese. Cover pan with aluminum foil and bake for 25–30 minutes.

* Substitute granular vegetable beef substitute for the beef for lower red meat and lower cholesterol and fewer calories.

SOUND EATING: MAIN COURSES

76. Apple Stuffed Mushrooms (serves 6 to 8)

32 large mushrooms, fresh

Vegetable cooking spray

3 Tbs. celery, finely chopped

1/2 cup apple, minced

2 Tbs. fine, dry bread crumbs

1 Tbs. parsley, fresh, chopped

2 Tbs. walnuts, finely chopped and toasted

1 Tbs. blue cheese, crumbled

2 tsp. lemon juice

Clean mushrooms with damp paper towels. Remove stems; finely chop 1/3 cup of stems, reserving remaining stems for another use. Set mushroom caps aside.

Coat a small skillet with cooking spray; place over medium-high heat until hot. Add 1/3 cup reserved chopped mushroom stems and celery; sauté 2 minutes or until tender. Combine celery mix, apple and next 5 ingredients in a small bowl; stir well. Spoon 1-1/2 tsp. apple mix into each reserved mushroom cap. Place mushrooms in a 15 × 10-inch jelly roll pan; bake at 350 degrees for 15 minutes. Serve hot.

77. Baked Eggplant (serves 4)

1 large eggplant

Olive oil

1 large onion, peeled and quartered

3 garlic cloves, unpeeled

1 red bell pepper, halved and seeded

1 tsp. oregano, chopped

2 tsp. lemon juice

1 Tbs. olive oil

1/8 tsp. each salt and pepper

4 oz. feta cheese, crumbled

2 Tbs. parsley, chopped

Pita bread or crackers

Preheat oven to 350 degrees. Halve eggplant lengthwise. Brush all sides with olive oil. Place halves cut-side down on a baking sheet. Bake 25 minutes. Brush onion, garlic and red pepper with oil; add to eggplant. Bake 25–30 minutes longer or until vegetables are tender. Cool eggplant; scoop out flesh and place in a food processor or wood bowl. Squeeze garlic pulp from skins, peel red pepper, and add to eggplant along with onion, oregano, lemon juice, olive oil and salt and pepper. Process or finely chop by hand. Do not puree.

Mix in 3 oz. of the feta cheese. Spoon mixture into a serving bowl. Sprinkle remaining feta cheese around the edge of the mixture; place parsley in the center. Serve with fresh bread, pita bread or crackers.

78. Oriental Ginger Shrimp (serves 4)

8 unshelled raw jumbo shrimp, thawed if frozen

1/2 cup all-purpose flour

1/4 tsp. salt

1 tsp. corn oil

1/4 cup water

1 piece ginger root, peeled and grated

1 garlic clove, crushed

1 tsp. chili sauce

1 egg white

Vegetable oil

1 green onion daisy

Red bell pepper strips

Shell shrimp, leaving tail shells on. De-vein the shrimp. In a bowl, combine flour, salt, corn oil and water. Stir in ginger, garlic and chili sauce and mix well. Stiffly whisk egg white, then gently fold into batter until evenly combined.

Half-fill a deep-fat fryer or saucepan with oil; heat to 375 degrees. Hold each shrimp by its tail and dip into batter, then lower into hot oil. Fry for 3 minutes, or until golden. Drain on paper towels. Garnish with chopped scallions and bell pepper strips. Serve hot.

79. Fresh Walleye (serves 4)

1 pound Walleye fillets

Make a paste of:

2 Tbs. lemon juice

2 cloves fresh minced garlic

3 Tbs. soy oil

2 Tbs. white wine

Pinch fresh chopped sweet basil

Place fillet flat side down on broiler. Brush fillet with paste. Dust with paprika. Broil one side 10 minutes per each inch of thickness. If sauce is desired, use marinade of fresh garlic, Dijon mustard, lemon juice, mayonnaise and soy oil. Garnish with lemon wedges, chopped parsley or chopped green onion.

Salads and Fixings

80. Italian Mixed Greens Salad (serves 6-portions of size 2 cups)

5 cups Mesclun salad mix or assorted salad greens

3 cups spinach leaves, stems removed

2 cups red Radicchio

1/2 cup thinly sliced fresh fennel

81. Creamy Herb Miso Dressing (serves 10)

Serve with your favorite salad greens.

    1/2 cup low-fat soy milk

    1/4 cup white miso

    1/4 cup brown rice vinegar

    1/4 cup onions, chopped

    1 Tbs. fresh basil, chopped

    1 Tbs. fresh tarragon, chopped

    1 Tbs. fresh parsley, chopped

    1 tsp. honey

    1/2 tsp. Dijon mustard

    1/8 tsp. coriander powder

In a blender or food processor, combine all the dressing ingredients until smooth. Cover and refrigerate at least 4 hours to allow flavors to develop.

82. Apple Salad with Sweet Tofu Dressing (serves 8)

    2 Granny Smith apples, sliced

    2 Gala apples, sliced

    1/4 cup fresh lemon juice

    1 cup water (or more if necessary)

    3 stalks celery, sliced diagonally

    1 8-ounce can pineapple tidbits, drained

    1/3 cup walnuts, coarsely chopped mint sprigs

Dressing:

    1 cup plain low-fat yogurt

    1/2 cup soft silken tofu

    1 tablespoon honey

    1 tsp. ground cinnamon

Place sliced apples in mixture of lemon juice and enough water to cover apples. At serving time, drain liquid from apples. Combine apples, celery, pineapple and nuts.

For the dressing: Combine yogurt, tofu, honey and cinnamon in a food processor and blend until smooth. Chill. Combine apple mixture with dressing and toss gently. Serve on a bed of fresh greens. Garnish with mint sprigs.

83. Herbed Vinaigrette (yields 18 tablespoon servings)

3/4 cup soy oil

1/4 cup tarragon white wine vinegar

1/4 cup chopped fresh parsley

1/4 cup chopped fresh basil

1 tablespoon finely chopped green onions

Combine all ingredients in a jar. Shake well. Refrigerate. May be used as a marinade or salad dressing.

84. Chicken Romaine Vinaigrette (serves 4 to 6)

4 chicken breast halves, boned & skinned

1 recipe Herbed Vinaigrette (see above)

1-1/2 pounds Romaine lettuce

1/2 cup sliced water chestnuts

1/3 cup fresh Parmesan cheese

3/4 cup seasoned croutons

Score chicken breasts and top with 1 tablespoon Herbed Vinaigrette per breast. Marinate in the refrigerator for at least one hour. Grill chicken 15 minutes and slice diagonally. Wash and tear lettuce leaves into large bowl. Top with 1/2 cup dressing, cheese, water chestnuts and croutons. Toss together. Divide lettuce onto plates and top with sliced chicken.

Breads

Man doesn't live by bread alone, but that doesn't mean we don't crave it. Here are a few nutritionally-packed bread recipes. Note that soy often makes its presence known.

85. Soybean Bread (Makes 4 loaves)

1 cup raw soybeans

4 cups water

2 Tbs. dry yeast

2-1/2 cups warm water and remaining liquid from soaking beans

1 cup skim milk powder

1/2 cup sugar

9–10 cup white bread flour

1 Tbs. salt

1/4 cup vegetable oil

1/2 cup soy flour

Soak the soybeans overnight in 4 cups of water. In the morning, drain but reserve liquid. Chop beans with at least one cup of soaking liquid, in food processor or blender until coarse.

Make a sponge with yeast, enough warm water and remaining liquid from soaking beans to make 2-1/2 cups, skim milk powder (if desired), sugar and 3 cups of the bread flour. Once blended, stir one hundred times in same direction, to develop the gluten, and cover with plastic wrap (or plastic bag) for at least half an hour.

Sprinkle salt on sponge and drizzle on oil. Stirring gently, add bean mixture and soy flour. Fold in bread flour, one cup at a time, until kneading is necessary to add remaining flour. Turn onto floured board and knead at least ten minutes, until smooth and elastic.

Place in greased bowl, turning once, cover with plastic and let rise half an hour. Punch down, turn over and let rise until double (at least one hour). Turn onto floured board; knead a few minutes, then shape into four loaves and place in greased loaf pans. Cover loaves with damp cloth or plastic and let rise until doubled, and well above sides of pan.

Bake at 350 degrees for 30–35 minutes.

86. Better Bran Muffins (yield: 12 muffins)

1-1/4 cups flour

1/2 cup soy flour

1 cup bran flake cereal

1/2 cup brown sugar

1 tsp. baking powder

1 tsp. baking soda

3/4 tsp. ground cinnamon

1/8 tsp. ground cloves

2 slightly beaten eggs

2/3 cup soy milk

1/2 cup raisins

1/4 cup soy oil

Spray muffin pan with vegetable cooking spray or line with paper baking cups. Stir together all dry ingredients. Combine eggs, soy milk and soy oil. Add egg mixture to flour mixture; stir until moistened. Fold in raisins. Fill muffin pan 2/3 full. Bake in a 400 degree oven for 15–20 minutes.

(SOURCE: The Indiana Soybean Development Council.)

87. Oatmeal Bread (yields one 1-1/2 pound loaf)

If you have a bread-making machine, try this: (1-1/2 pound bread-machine recipe)

3 cups bread flour

1/3 cup soy flour

3 Tbs. sugar

1-1/2 tsp. salt

1-1/2 Tbs. margarine

1/3 cup oatmeal

3/4 cup soy milk

3/4 cup water

1-1/2 tsp. dry yeast

Add ingredients to bread machine according to manufacturer's directions. Bread machine tips: all ingredients should be at room temperature, unless otherwise noted in the recipe. Always use powdered milk when using the timer on your machine.

(SOURCE: Indiana Soybean Development Council.)

88. Crusty Corn Muffins (makes 12 muffins)

3/4 cup flour

1/4 cup soy flour

1 cup yellow cornmeal

2 Tbs. sugar

4 tsp. baking powder

1 tsp. salt

1 cup buttermilk 1/4 cup soy oil

2 eggs, slightly beaten

1/2 cup shredded cheddar cheese

1/4 cup chopped green chilies

Preheat oven to 425 degrees. Spray muffin pans with non-stick spray. In medium bowl, combine first 5 ingredients. Stir together buttermilk, soy oil and eggs, and add to dry ingredients. Gently stir in cheese and green chilies. Pour into muffin pan. Bake for 22 to 25 minutes.

Desserts and Snacks

89. Berry Berry Shortcake (serves 8)

Shortcakes

1/2 cup sifted defatted soy flour

1-1/4 cups all-purpose flour

1 Tbs. sugar

3 tsp. baking powder

1/4 cup margarine, regular (not diet) or butter, cut up

1 cup low-fat or non-fat soy milk vegetable spray

Berry Filling

3 cups fresh sliced strawberries

3 Tbs. sugar

1-1/2 cups fresh blueberries, or frozen, thawed, drained

1/4 cup powdered sugar

Heat oven to 450 degrees. Lightly spray cookie sheet with vegetable spray. Combine flours, sugar and baking powder; mix well. Using a pastry blender, cut in margarine until crumbly. Add milk and stir just until ingredients are moist. Do not overmix. Drop dough by 1/4 cupful (or use a 2-ounce scoop) onto baking sheet. Bake 9–12 minutes or until light golden brown.

While shortcakes are baking, blend 2 cups of the strawberries with the sugar. Fold in the blueberries and remaining 1 cup sliced strawberries. When baking is complete, immediately remove shortcakes from sheet. Split cakes and fill with fruit. Sift powdered sugar over shortcakes. Shortcakes are best when served shortly after they are baked.

90. Roasted Soybeans

An excellent way to cook fresh soybeans is to toss them in olive oil and salt, and then slow-roast them at 350 degrees. Taste after 20 minutes or so; they should be golden-brown and nutty.

Like tofu, soybeans have a mild flavor of their own, and tend to pick up the flavors of whatever they are added to. They have a firm-mealy texture. You can use them from a can or can buy them fresh at any good produce market. (Think of them as exotic lima beans.)

The fresh ones are delicious but require work; you have to peel the thick green skin off each bean. The skin comes off in one or two pieces, but there are lots of beans. The canned ones can be tossed into just about anything you are cooking—a stew, a sauce, a salad—or added to any vegetable dish. The fresh ones have a more distinctive taste and are quite delicious. Again, like a lima, they should be cooked but not overcooked. A few minutes in the microwave, and then toss them into a stir fry or stew. Eating a baked potato? Coarsely chop a handful of cooked fresh soybeans and serve them over the potato. You can even add them to turkey stuffing.

91. Chocolate Chip Soybean Cookies
(makes approximately 10 dozen soft cookies)

3 cups light brown sugar

1 cup soy margarine

4 large eggs

3 cups cake or all-purpose flour

1 cup soy flour

1 tsp. salt

2 tsp. baking soda

2 Tbs. milk

1 tsp. vanilla

2 cups crushed roasted unsalted soybean nuts

4 cups semi-sweet chocolate morsels

Preheat oven to 350 degrees. In large mixing bowl, cream brown sugar and margarine with electric mixer. Beat for 2 minutes. Add eggs one at a time and cream until smooth consistency. Combine dry ingredients and add to mixture. Add milk and vanilla. Stir in soybeans and chocolate chips. Chill batter, if desired.

Spray baking sheets with nonstick vegetable coating. Drop cookie batter onto sheets. Bake for 8–10 minutes.

(SOURCE: Indiana Soyfood Development Council.)

92. Fancy Pumpkin Pie (yields approximately 2-1/2 cups of filling)

3/4 pound firm tofu

2 cups cooked or baked pureed pumpkin

2/3 cup honey or maple syrup

1/4 cup oil

2 Tbs molasses

1 tsp. ground cinnamon

3/4 tsp. grated nutmeg

3/4 tsp. powdered ginger

1/2 tsp. mace

1/4 tsp. salt

1 unbaked pie crust

Preheat oven to 350 degrees. Blend ingredients for filling until smooth and creamy in a blender or food processor. Pour into pie shell and bake for 1 hour. Chill and top with Cashew Cream.

Cashew Cream

1 cup raw cashews or cashew pieces

1 cup water

1 to 1-1/2 cups soy oil, approximately

4 Tbs. maple syrup

1/2 tsp. vanilla extract (optional)

Pinch of salt

Grind cashews in a blender. Add water and blend to form a thick cream. Slowly add the oil in a fine stream until cream thickens. Blend in maple syrup, vanilla and salt. Chill and serve.

NOTE: Cream will thicken substantially when chilled.

Here's a simpler pumpkin pie recipe.

93. Simple Pumpkin Pie

3/4 pound firm silken tofu

2 cups cooked pumpkin pulp

1-1/2 tsp. cinnamon

1/2 tsp. nutmeg

1/4 tsp. ground ginger

1/4 cup maple syrup

1/4 cup oil

1/4 cup brown sugar

Preheat oven to 350 degrees. Crumble tofu into food processor. Add remaining ingredients and blend completely. Pour into prepared unbaked pie shell. Bake for 50 minutes until set in center.

94. Chocolate Swirl Cheesecake (serves 10)

Crust:

1 9-ounce package Famous Chocolate Wafers (2-1/2 cups)

6 Tbs. soy margarine, melted

1/4 cup sliced almonds

Filling:

2 8-ounce packages light cream cheese

1 10.5-ounce package firm silken tofu

4 eggs

3 Tbs. lemon juice

1-1/4 cups sugar

Topping:

1 16-ounce carton light sour cream

1/3 cup sugar

1 tsp. vanilla

1/8 cup chilled chocolate syrup

Preheat oven to 350 degrees. In food processor bowl, process crumbs. Add almonds and margarine and process. Spread evenly across bottom and up sides of a 10-inch springform pan. Press onto bottom and up sides of pan. In clean processor bowl, combine cream cheese and tofu with sugar until smooth. Add four eggs and lemon juice. Process until smooth. Pour the filling over the crust and bake for 50 minutes. Remove cheesecake from oven. Reduce heat to 300 degrees. Mix sour cream, remaining sugar and vanilla. Spread over cheesecake. Drizzle chocolate syrup over top of sour cream and gently marble. Bake for 20–25 minutes. Cool for one hour, then refrigerate overnight. Serve plain or top with fresh fruit.

95. Cranfu Cookies (makes 60 cookies)

1 cup tofu, mashed

1/4 cup orange juice

1 tsp. baking soda

1-1/2 cup sugar or artificial sweetener

1 Tbs. grated orange rind

1/4 cup salad oil

2 cup flour

1 cup cranberries, coarsely chopped

1/2 cup pecans, almonds, or other nuts (optional)

Mix orange juice and baking soda. Add sugar/sweetener, orange rind, oil and flour. Add tofu, cranberries, and nuts; mix until just moistened and well distributed. Drop by tsp. on greased cookie sheet. Bake at 400 degrees for 14 minutes or until lightly browned.

96. Chocolate Tofu

1-1/4 pounds firm tofu pressed in a linen towel

1-1/2 cup of sugar

6 oz. semi-sweet melted chocolate

1 tsp. vanilla

1/2 tsp. almond extract

Crumble tofu and its liquid into food processor. Slowly add sugar. When completely creamed together add melted chocolate, vanilla and almond extract. Bake in 9-inch pie pan that has been oiled and floured at 350 degrees for 1 hour or until top of cake puffs.

97. Devil Drops (makes 3 dozen 2-inch cookies)

1 cup corn oil

2/3 cup mashed Island Spring Traditional firm tofu

1 cup sugar

1/2 cup brown sugar

1/2 tsp. salt (optional)

1/2 cup cocoa

1 tsp. baking soda

Combine ingredients in blender and mix. Pour mixture into a bowl and add:

2-1/2 cups flour

1 cup chocolate chips

Mix; and then drop by tsp. on a greased cookie sheet. Flatten. Bake at 350 degrees for 10–12 minutes or until cookie is set and slightly brown around the edges.

98. Tofu Gingerbread

Preheat oven to 350 degrees.

1-1/2 cup brown sugar

1 cup Island Spring Traditional firm tofu, mashed

1/2 cup salad oil

1/2 cup light molasses

3 tsp. ginger

2 tsp. cinnamon

2 tsp. baking soda

1 tsp. salt

1/4 tsp. clove

1/4 tsp. nutmeg

5 cups all-purpose flour

Mix first 10 ingredients in a blender until smooth. Set aside. Pour flour into a large bowl. Add tofu mixture to flour and mix until combined. Toward the end of mixing, dough becomes stiff, so you may want to use your hand. Chill dough for 3 hours or overnight. Place dough between 2 sheets of waxed paper and roll out 1/4 to 1/8 inch thick. Cut dough into desired shapes with cookie cutter. Bake at 350 degrees on greased cookie sheet for about 8 minutes or until slightly brown around the edges.

99. Tofu Peanut Butter Cookies *(makes 48 cookies)*

Preheat oven to 350 degrees.

3 cups unbleached white flour

1 tsp. baking soda

1/2 tsp. salt

1/2 cup oil

1/2 cup Island Spring Traditional firm tofu

1/2 cup honey

1 cup peanut butter

1 cup brown sugar

1 tsp. vanilla

In a bowl combine flour, baking soda, and salt. Mix all other ingredients together in a blender until smooth. Set aside. Mix dry ingredients into wet ones. Form the dough into 1-inch balls on a cookie sheet about 3 inches apart. Press with fork (dipped into cold water) in a crisscross design. Bake for 10–12 minutes.

100. Tofu Carob Parfait (serves 3)

> 10-1/2 ounces silken tofu (or 9-1/2 ounces regular tofu
>   and 1 Tbs. water)
> 2 Tbs. honey
> 2 Tbs. maple syrup
> 1 Tbs. carob powder
> 1 Tbs. (soy) margarine
> 1 Tbs. oil
> 1/4 tsp. vanilla extract
> Dash salt

Combine all ingredients in a blender and puree until smooth. Serve chilled as a dessert.

(SOURCE: Indiana Soybean Development Council.)

101. Quick Cookie Bars (makes 24 to 36 bars, depending on size)

> 2 16-ounce packages refrigerated slice-and-bake cookie dough
>   (chocolate chip or oatmeal chocolate chip)
> 1 10.5-ounce package firm silken tofu
> 2 eggs
> 1 cup sugar
> 1 tsp. vanilla

Preheat oven to 350 degrees. Soften one roll of cookie dough. Spray the bottom of a 9 × 13-inch baking pan with non-stick spray. Line the bottom with the softened cookie dough, spreading to all sides. In food processor bowl, combine tofu and remaining ingredients until smooth. Spread over cookie dough. Drop second roll of cookie dough by the tsp. on top of filling. Bake for 40 to 45 minutes.

GOOD BEHAVIOR BONUSES!

Cranapple Snack Bars (makes 24 to 36 bars, depending on size)

    1 cup honey
    3 Tbs. orange juice
    1 tsp. salt
    1/3 cup soy oil
    1 10.5-ounce package firm silken tofu
    1 egg
    1 tsp. vanilla
    2 cups flour
    1 tsp. baking soda
    1 tsp. cinnamon
    2 cups peeled apple slices
    *2-1/2 cups cranberries (fresh or frozen)
    1/2 cup chopped walnuts

Preheat oven to 350 degrees. Spray a 10 × 15 × 1-inch pan with non-stick spray. Whip honey, orange juice and salt together; then blend with oil. Add tofu, vanilla, egg, and beat well. Sift together flour, baking soda and cinnamon. Add to the honey/oil mixture and stir well. Fold in apples, cranberries and nuts.

Pour batter into prepared pan. Bake for 30 to 35 minutes or until a toothpick inserted near the center comes out clean. Sprinkle with powdered sugar.

* If you prefer, you may substitute 2-1/2 cups fresh blueberries for the cranberries.

Harvest Pumpkin Bars (yields 24 to 36 bars, depending on size)

    1-2/3 cups sugar
    1 cup soy oil
    4 eggs
    1 16-ounce can solid pumpkin
    1-1/2 cups flour
    1/2 cup soy flour

1 tsp. cinnamon

1 tsp. salt

1 tsp. soda

2 tsp. baking powder

Preheat oven to 350 degrees. Spray 10 × 15 × 1-inch pan with non-stick spray. In large bowl, combine sugar, eggs and oil. Add pumpkin and mix thoroughly. Combine flours and spices and stir into pumpkin mixture. Pour batter into prepared pan. Bake for 25–30 minutes, or until tester comes out clean from middle of pan.

Cream Cheese Frosting

1 3-ounce package light cream cheese, softened

1/2 cup soy margarine

1 tsp. vanilla

2 cups sifted powdered sugar

1/2 cup chopped pecans

Combine all ingredients except nuts, and mix until smooth. Frost when bars are cool. Sprinkle with nuts.

Dr. Israel Barken's Israeli Salad (serves 4)

2 large tomatoes

2 medium bell peppers

1 medium onion

2 large cucumbers or 6 pickling cucumbers

1 tsp. extra virgin olive oil

salt, pepper to taste

juice from 1/2 lemon (optional)

1 Tbs. chopped Italian parsley

1 Tbs. reduced fat feta cheese (optional)

2–3 sliced Greek olives to garnish (optional)

Dice all vegetables into very small cubes. Put in bowl, mix in rest of ingredients. Serve chilled. Excellent with warm pita bread.

INDEX